PIONEER OF TROPICAL LANDSCAPE ARCHITECTURE

University Press of Florida

GAINESVILLE   TALLAHASSEE
TAMPA   BOCA RATON
PENSACOLA   ORLANDO
MIAMI   JACKSONVILLE

Pioneer of

TROPICAL LANDSCAPE ARCHITECTURE

William Lyman Phillips in Florida

Faith Reyher Jackson

Copyright 1997 by Faith Reyher Jackson
Printed in the United States of America on acid-free paper
All rights reserved

02 01 00 99 98 97   6 5 4 3 2 1

LIBRARY OF CONGRESS CATALOGING-IN-PUBLICATION DATA
Jackson, Faith Reyher, 1919–
Pioneer of tropical landscape architecture: William Lyman Phillips in Florida /
Faith Reyher Jackson
p. cm.
Includes bibliographical references (p.) and index.
ISBN 0-8130-1516-2 (cloth: alk. paper)
1. Phillips, William Lyman, 1885–1966. 2. Landscape architects—Florida—
Biography. 3. Landscape architecture—Florida. I. Title.
SB470.P48J33   1997
712'.092—dc21   96-37166

Frontispiece: William Lyman Phillips, landscape architect in the tropics.
(Courtesy Fairchild Tropical Garden Archives)

The University Press of Florida is the scholarly publishing agency for the State
University System of Florida, comprised of Florida A&M University, Florida
Atlantic University, Florida International University, Florida State University,
University of Central Florida, University of Florida, University of North
Florida, University of South Florida, and University of West Florida.

University Press of Florida
15 Northwest 15th Street
Gainesville, FL 32611

For Melvin Hoffman Jackson, 1914–1983

vestigia nulla retrorsum

CONTENTS

ILLUSTRATIONS

Unless otherwise noted, all photographs were taken by William Lyman Phillips.

William Lyman Phillips, architect, engineer, landscape architect, was born in New England in 1885, into a world that ceased to exist before he was thirty. It was a golden age for landscape architects to whom wealthy clients gave carte blanche to make their "cottage" grounds grand. Phillips was in the thick of it during his apprentice years. Frederick Law Olmsted Jr., of the great firm in Brookline, Massachusetts, wrote that Phillips was his best student at Harvard. Olmsted hired him after Phillips graduated in 1910 and later offered him a partnership. Phillips's peers referred to him without rancor as a genius. He was an active practitioner for fifty-six years. In the first fourteen, he laid out the towns of Balboa and Pedro Miguel in Panama; built the cantonment Camp Jackson in Columbia, South Carolina, during World War I; was superintendent of graves for the American cemeteries in France; and designed suburban developments, roads, and numerous residences in Montreal, Florida, California, Texas, New York, Massachusetts, and Washington State. Agents for Sun Yat-sen asked him to rebuild the town of Canton; only revolution kept him from it, and there were other such major disappointments, which he accepted with remarkable stoicism.

Fame, as we think of it, appeared to elude him early on, possibly because for years instead of signing his name, he put "Olmsted Brothers" on his plans and ghosted the work of other colleagues. Perhaps, it has been suggested, he did not push himself forward because for the most part he had what he wanted and needed. Perhaps it was because the many years of his wife's terminal illness prevented him from accepting the new challenges that came his way and would have brought him more immediate public notice. Likely, too, it was because from 1924 until his death in 1966, he remained and worked in Florida, away from major contacts and greater professional activity in his field.

Few people elsewhere were aware of the amount of remarkable work Phillips was doing in tropical botany, until his pioneer use of tropical plants in landscape design with spectacular results was extensively copied. Known as the "dean of Florida landscape architecture" once fame began to catch up with him—had he lived ten years longer, he would have been widely known—Phillips was increasingly sought after. Ironically, being brought so low by the Great Depression proved to be more fortuitous than calamitous. In his mature years, as project superintendent in the Civilian Conservation Corps and later as consultant to the national and Dade County park systems, he was able to design all of south Florida's public parks and was in position to design his master work, the Fairchild Tropical Garden in Miami. At the same time, his output was prodigious; he covered the state, designing landscapes and acting as collaborating architect for private residences, public housing, industrial buildings, hospitals, hotels, cemeteries, airports, and campuses. The work was stunning and much has been preserved or restored; Greynolds and Matheson Hammock parks and the Lake Wales residence El Retiro, now Pinewood, are on the National Historic Register, and his plans are still sought after and studied. Phillips's story is an integral part of Florida's history and development, from boom and bust to postwar rebuilding.

Phillips often referred to himself as an "exile" in an "alien" land, where few knew what he was talking about; Florida "landscapers" in the early days, without technical schooling or wide experience, could not appreciate his expertise. This was a key factor in his bouts of depression and loneliness. He claimed that he never missed Florida whenever he left for Maine, that he only returned in order to eat and buy groceries and for the simpler climate in which to raise his girls. Then, in honesty, he confessed in a letter to Olmsted in 1950 that he had become "strangely drawn to the place. . . . All of my earth knowledge and bag of tricks is here."

He was a veritable magician with that "bag of tricks," an understated way to describe his sensitivity, perception of harmony of form and space, and ability to weave the elements of light, water, sound, and character into his designs on the Florida landscape. Everything he learned before he came to the state, all of his experience elsewhere, enabled him to transform arid palmetto scrub barrens into magnificent gardens and to enhance natural settings of tropical and subtropical plants.

IN 1957, my husband and I built a house on Schoolhouse Road in South Miami, and William Lyman Phillips came to design the grounds. In the process we became friends. We shared enthusiasm for sailing, France, the state of Maine, where he and I had lived and summered all our lives, history, music, crossword puzzles, and jazz. I can see him now, slightly rumpled, sitting on our screened patio, a tall man in a low chair. He wore khakis and a short-sleeved shirt, and a duck-billed hat for keeping the sun off his bald head was beside him. His long legs seemed folded, the knees almost to his chin. A pad rested on his lap. He was seventy-two years old then, and he had not lost his curiosity for learning; he was making a telescope, setting up a homemade stereo system, studying mineralogy, and playing the stock market.

Our two-story contemporary set in a pine glade was not Phillips's favorite architecture, but once he put his mind to any matter of whatever size, he always paid close attention to detail and planned the garden to fit the

The Jackson house, South Miami, Florida. Between the large trees in the foreground—red-flowered *Bombax ceiba*, sapodilla, and the golden *Cassia fistula*—and the foundation planting of red *Ixora* bushes are colorful red, pink, and white smaller ornamental trees and shrubs. Drawing by Phillips. (Courtesy of the author)

client's pocket and special interests. In the year that followed, I had the unique opportunity of watching and learning from him as he quietly went about directing me in the process of transforming an ordinary piece of ground into a handsome design in keeping with the natural woodland surrounding us.

He sent me to nurseries for the plants he wanted, and he took me to the Fairchild Tropical Garden—we brought home a wealth of tropical seedlings and planted them immediately (he carried his tools in the back of his car). On rainy days when the ground was soft I could count on seeing him. I could hardly wait. I came to know him as extraordinarily literate, urbane, spare with words, amusing, depressed, beset, stubborn, oversensitive, thrifty, and hopelessly romantic.

After Phillips died, Juliette Phillips Coyle authorized me to write her father's biography. Some of his personal and business papers, plans, and drawings had been taken from his home office right after his death and deposited at the University of Miami, Fairchild Tropical Garden, and Harvard's Special Collections, Francis Loeb Library. All of the rest—photos, memorabilia, letters received, onionskin carbon responses, and several unpublished articles, a whole life in boxes—came to me. I have designated them for clarity the "Author's Collection." In 1993 some material from this collection was presented to the Historical Association of South Florida, Miami-Dade Cultural Center, in Juliette Phillips Coyle's name. The remainder is still in my possession in Washington, D.C., pending distribution to an institution satisfactory to Phillips's heirs. This material should be collated and available for research by the year 2000. The greater part of this book was written from these documents.

For most of Phillips's professional life, he was without a secretary or assistant draftsman, yet his records were meticulous. He wrote five to ten letters a day—writing, he said, helped him to solve problems. It also insulated him from the business of living: Phillips, to his detriment, often communicated far better on paper than in person. Fortunate it was for the Phillips story that he was such a saver. Some gaps had to be filled in elsewhere.

Thanks to Juliette, I spent a month in 1991 in Phillips's East Boothbay cottage, which he built himself. The paneled living space is small and perfectly proportioned, with plenty of cupboards and shelves, a great stone fireplace, and wide windows; the sleeping porch was a delight. I worked there and watched the sunset, and when the sporting raccoons filled the night with clamor, I thought of Phillips, listening to them and the ticking black clock he brought from his Somerville home. Perhaps he was reading one of Simone's French books, still on the window shelf, or lighting up the Tilley stove and writing to Prentiss French and Nixon Smiley: "It is October, and everyone is gone. There is nobody to talk to, or visit."

When I began to work in Florida, in 1988, Dr. John Popenoe, then director of the Fairchild Tropical Garden, gave me a desk in the research center. Bertram Zuckerman, Garden historian, made me welcome and has helped me immeasurably. James Watson, herbarium assistant working on the Garden newsletter, published my first article on Phillips in 1989, in the Garden's fifty-year gala book. Dr. Jack B. Fisher, director of research, answered many questions, and Don Evans, director of horticulture, drove me over the grounds in a golf cart, pointing out trouble spots and describing future planting plans, and he tried to teach me the difference between a red and a black mangrove.

The late Nixon Smiley was director of the garden when Phillips was there. Smiley and I met at facing desks in the *Miami Herald* city room. He was generous to me with his time and with the notes for a book he intended. To my sorrow, he will not see mine. Neither will Nell Montgomery Jennings, with whom I spent hours discussing Phillips, old friends, and the garden's beginnings. Succeeding directors, Dr. William McKinley Klein, Jr., and Dr. Brinsley Burbidge, have been extraordinarily kind.

I spoke often with relatives and with people who knew Phillips professionally: Grady Clay, former editor of *Landscape Architecture*, had corresponded with him; Joseph Hudak, American Society of Landscape Architects fellow, author, Harvard professor in the Graduate School of Design, and a vice-president of Olmsted Brothers, worked with Phillips at Lake Wales; Stanley Kiem, who walked and drove the garden with me, spoke perceptively and warmly of Phillips's design goals and methods, observed when they worked together at Fairchild Tropical Garden in the 1950s; Jonathan Seymour, landscape architect, well-known throughout Florida and the Bahamas, was part of a group who met regularly when Phillips was head of the Florida ASLA chapter; Phillips's niece Nancy Kimball Dunlap and her husband Chesley found photographs and told me family stories when I visited them on a foggy weekend in Stonington, Maine. I am indebted to Charles E. Beveridge for giving me "The Master List of Design Projects of the Olmsted Firm, 1857–1950," compiled for the National Association for Olmsted Parks, and for putting me in touch with Charlotte Olmsted Kursh; I am indebted to her for her subsequent letters to me. I was happy to find Pamela Prentiss French, daughter of Phillips's oldest friend, thanks to Sarah C. La Cour, historic landscape coordinator at Chesterwood, Massachusetts, the late Daniel Chester French property.

Joyce Connolly, Lee Farrow, and Linda Genovese at the Frederick Law Olmsted National Historic Site in Brookline, Massachusetts, gave me invaluable assistance, as did Mary Daniels, head of Special Collections at the Loeb Library in the Graduate School of Design at Harvard. Barbara A. Fuller, assistant to the secretary for Panama Canal Commission affairs in Washington, D.C., and M. Jeanne Hinek, chief, Records Management Branch, Panama Canal Commission, in Balboa, C.Z., found Phillips material after others had given up. S. J. Boldrick, Miami-Dade Public Library, and Joan Morria and Joanna Norman, Florida State Archives, made available important historic photographs. Archivists Brett Davis and Jodi A. Nolde, in Alexandria, Virginia, searched early issues in their stored *Parks and Recreation* files, and Anne Lewis, reference librarian at the Library of Congress, went out of her way for me when I was ill. The late Helen Purdy, head of Archives and Special Collections in the Otto G. Richter Library at the University of Miami, made available to me all of the Phillips material that she had; her successor, Dr. William E. Brown Jr., continued to work with me. Martin A. Washington, director of the Dade-Metro Park Service, allowed me to quote from the unpublished A. D. Barnes memoir, an invaluable and fascinating document of the history and development of Dade County parks. At the County Planning and Research Division, Landscape Architecture Section, in Kendall, I found many Phillips park plans with help from Kevin Asher, Roger Bridewell, Paul Carey, and Robert McLane.

At Lake Wales I met with Helena Caldwell, Bok Tower Garden librarian, and her husband, John Caldwell, author of *Mountain Lake: A History*; Terence McKinney, new librarian and assistant carillonneur; Director of Horticultural Services and Grounds David M. Price; Susan Wallis, in charge of restoration of Pinewood gardens; and Charlene W. Johnston, administrative/public relations director for Bok Tower gardens. Jonathan Shaw, president of the Bok Tower Gardens Foundation, Inc., and director of Bok Tower Gardens, arranged for me to stay in Pinewood; in the early morning I could sit at breakfast and watch the light play down the lawn to the pond. Robert E. Martin, vice president and general manager of Mountain Lake Colony, permitted me to use photographs of the Colony grounds. Long-time friends helped me: Barbara Bitter put me up for three winters; Madelene Charles photographed Phillips parks for me; and author Helen Muir smoothed my progress through Florida archives; author-columnist Marguerite Kelly's unfailing advice and encouragement kept me from foundering; and I have depended upon Nina Graybill, my agent and lawyer, for her good humor and sound advice.

To all the other people in Washington, D.C., Maine, Massachusetts, Panama, France, and Florida who gave me time, encouragement when I needed it most, and considerable expertise in their field, who reintroduced me to the tropics and moonlit walkabouts, my deepest thanks: Claire Barger, Joan Blank, Helen B. Correll, Nan Dennison, Anita Dickuth-Tsakiris, Rudy Favretti, Anthony J. Fedele, Mme. Jean Fenestre, Andrea Hammer, Elsa Voorhees Hauschka, Rebecca Hirsh, Susan Klaus, Fairfax Lomonosoff, Charles Capen McLaughlin, Patricia Matuzewski, E. Lynn Miller, Judith Grummon Nelson, James T. Parker II, Suzan Phillips, Nettie Belle Robinson, John Ruggiero, Lisa Gaye Ryavec, Rebecca Spain Schwarz, Barbara Smith, Nancy Stephenson, Regina M. Travers, Lelia Washburn, Karen Van Westering, Ray Vernon, James West, Nina Woessner, and the Washington Biography Group, to which I am proud to belong.

My three sons drove me over Phillips's roads in Balboa and showed me Panama and its islands, introduced me to Olmsted parks in Seattle, helped me to reasonable compatibility with the computer, showed me how a plane table works, and vetted my technical descriptions. They and their families' staunch support kept me on course and made the distance a little shorter.

PART I

The Early Years

WHEN WILLIAM LYMAN PHILLIPS was a young boy, he began to draw pictures of towns, complete plans or plats which improved in accuracy and detail. At first he drew to rough scale, from memory, what he knew intimately: West Somerville, Massachusetts, where he was born and raised, and Murray Hill, East Boothbay, Maine, where he spent every summer in the family compound. He knew the owners in both places and named each house on the plat. He drew the main streets and buildings: school, library, church, depot, drugstore, and post office.

It was as if he were making an inventory of the town he loved as part of his own being, the larger perimeter of his life, wherein he walked and studied and played. In Somerville, he was observing the best: by the 1890s the suburban community had become a national showcase of Victorian middle-class progress.

Somerville houses were of stone or brick or clapboard, with gardens, parks, or plots surrounding them: large houses behind tall hedges or small frame cottages with a short path from the front porch to the sidewalk. William noticed their similarities, design, or differences. The differences interested him most—a special gate, a double swing, a gazebo, a handsome front door and steps. William's own front door was at the corner of 211 Holland Street, in a large three-story, square-towered Queen Anne house, newly built for his father. The youngest of three children, he was born there, on June 11, 1885, after the family settled in Massachusetts.

Franklin Folsom Phillips, William's father, was born in North Searsmont, Maine, in 1852. A graduate of Bates College, he settled in Lewiston with his new wife, Julia Agnes Lyman, and taught chemistry until he became the high school principal. A vigorous and ambitious man, he moved to Somerville because it was by then a "commuter-streetcar suburb" of Boston, with

The house where William Phillips was born, 211 Holland Street, Somerville, Massachusetts. Photograph by Patricia Conley. (Courtesy of City of Somerville Community Development)

low taxes and good housing and business opportunities. The town was run by entrepreneurs whose broad mandate of civic duty put high priority on volunteerism and public education. Franklin, now a chemist in the paper mill business, fit right in. He served two years on the common council and two as alderman. However, he never let go of his Maine roots and the family continued to share long vacations there.

Steadfast, hardworking, and civic-minded, "Pa" was an unusual man, at once a scientist, agriculturist, scholar, historian, and author. Although his book of poetry, *Idylls of the Strand*, was excessively florid and full of classical allusions in the meter of "Hiawatha" and John Masefield, his Maine novel, *The White Isles*, while suffering from the same effusive language and silly plot, contains delightful bits of seacoast and logging in his beloved state, plus a serious message. He believed passionately in the "science of the coming time [agriculture, chemistry] . . . the key that unlocks the door . . . to a newer world."[1]

Left: Julia Agnes Lyman Phillips, 1856–1943. Photographer unknown. (Author's Collection) *Right:* Franklin Folsum Phillips, 1852–1921. Photographer unknown. (Author's Collection)

Franklin's hobbies were the history of his home state of Maine and genealogy; he brought forth an impressive family tree, traced back to Henry II of England. He was never wealthy but always free of debt, and managed to travel, maintain two houses, and send three children to college and two to graduate school. He believed in education for women as well as for men.

William's mother, "Mamsie," adored him to excess, perhaps because she and Franklin seemed to live a tandem life. She considered it her natural prerogative to monitor all of the domesticity of her sons' lives; when, in his mid-twenties, William took his first job in Canada, she was writing regular directives about his laundry. She was very sociable—"She had such a wide acquaintance," said her granddaughter, "it took her forever to come home from church." She loved to play bridge and to travel and belonged to the Harvard Dames and other clubs. Julia outlived Franklin by twenty-two years; her daughter and son-in-law rearranged their lives to care for her until her death.[2]

When he was a teenager, William's hero was his older brother Frank, who together with sister Florence, their friends and sweethearts, made every summer memorable. Family pictures show the whole tribe on the beach

Left: The Phillips children: Florence May, 1879–1969, William Lyman, 1885–1966, and Franklin, Jr., 1880–1932. Photograph by Chickering Photographic Studio c. 1888. (Author's Collection) *Right:* Billy and Frank Phillips, Somerville, Massachusetts, c. 1890s. Photographer unknown. (Author's Collection)

or perched comfortably on the rocks, the women in hats, shoes, and long dresses; men in long trousers, coats, and "boaters"; boys in knickers and caps. For the brave, it was "taking a deep breath and diving" into Maine polar water.

Day sailing and cruising was the family passion. Frank took his younger brother along in the Phillipses' *Drumlin*, even after William acquired his own boat, the very pride of his life. In all of the months of picnics, midnight hay rides, songs and dances, summer jobs, and later, Peggy, a special girl who was Julia Phillips's first choice, William never learned how to instigate social activity for himself. All he ever had to do was be there; his brother and sister did the rest. The lack of this skill hampered him as an adult in both personal and professional life.

William was handsome and intelligent, with a fine sense of fun; he was an excellent listener, a voracious reader. He was also inclined to be unusually quiet and thoughtful for long periods and slow to move forward until sure of his goal. He was always a perfectionist. Although he was perfectly capable of working quickly when he chose or needed to, his seeming lack of hurry and failure to push himself forward—Olmsted's running complaint—would prove maddening to clients and colleagues in the future; Wil-

Maine summer picnic—a clambake on the rocks at Murray Hill, Linekin Bay, East Boothbay, Maine, c. 1902–3. Phillips, second from right, tending the fire. Photograph by Florence Phillips Kimball. (Author's Collection)

Eating watermelon at Murray Hill. Phillips and sister Florence Phillips Kimball, center. Photographer unknown. (Author's Collection)

The Phillips family summer home, Murray Hill, Linekin Bay, East Boothbay, Maine. Photographer unknown. (Author's Collection)

A special gathering in front of the Franklin Phillips house on Murray Hill, undated (Fourth of July? A wedding?). Photographer unknown. (Author's Collection)

liam was unperturbed. He was inclined to be didactic: after thoroughly examining a problem to his satisfaction, he rarely changed his mind, and he could never be persuaded to make a hasty decision.

WILLIAM WAS FORTUNATE in the schooling he received at Somerville Latin High School, a mind-opening classical education. The Massachusetts Latin schools were justly famous for their curricula and high standards. In contrast to the "English schools," attended for the most part by students who would not go further, Latin high schools were free for students from every economic or social background who could meet the difficult requirements of a classical college preparation: four years of Latin, mathematics, rhetoric, and composition; Greek, German, French; science, history; drawing, music, and art, as well as extracurricular electives (sports and clubs) that counted heavily for college admission.[3]

In 1900, the year William entered high school, the American Education exhibit at the Paris World's Fair showcased the English and Latin schools of Somerville, Massachusetts, as exemplars of the American public high school's "consequential role in social change and the formation of the industrial social order." In 1904, when William graduated, the same schools were selected for the St. Louis World's Fair, so it is not surprising that the ambitious young students in this group felt themselves chosen to be the leaders of the new century.[4]

Left: Rowing team, Harvard, c. 1907. Phillips standing, left. Photographer unknown. (Author's Collection)

Below: Harvard team practicing on the Charles River, Phillips third from right. Photographer unknown. (Author's Collection)

William brought to his schooling a family tradition of excellence in academic achievement. For the Harvard-bound senior it was thrilling to look down from Somerville High's math classroom window at the tower of Harvard's Memorial Hall, and the red roof of Sever, where entrance exams were held—"a view of the promised land . . . which kept us keyed up." Music was also important to him. He sang in the chorus and played cello. He became a member of Sigma Delta fraternity, organized in his sophomore year for "athletic and social purposes," and in his senior year, he was an editor of the June issue of *The Radiator,* the school magazine that served as yearbook. "Perhaps here, [at Latin High]," wrote the graduating Phillips, "the pupil caught the first glimpse of his power, his work in life; possibly here he first realized what he could do."[5]

Harvard graduation, magna cum laude, 1908. (Author's Collection)

In 1904, William began study at Harvard University. He took a basic fine arts program, heavy on history, philosophy, music, and art. It must have seemed to him like more of the same, a continuation of high school, in depth. He took more languages: "I could manage the technical literature in French, German, Spanish and Italian."[6] He was on the rowing team, raced "second class crew," and ran "through the [Cambridge] streets at night for exercise, splashing through the winter slush."[7]

He received his bachelor of arts degree magna cum laude in 1908 and went on to two years of graduate school in landscape architecture, intending to become an architect. He had been hearing of the exciting and controversial new curriculum developing in the graduate design department, wide ranging in allied subject matter and broad in scope, and he wanted to be part of it.

Graduate Study

"Mr. Phillips studied Landscape Architecture under my general direction at Harvard, 1907–1910 . . . [and] was among the very best of the students under my observation [there]."

FREDERICK LAW OLMSTED JR.[8]

However he may have affected other students or his employees in the landscape architecture profession, Frederick Law Olmsted Jr. became the pivotal influence in William Phillips's career in ways Phillips could scarcely imagine—first as teacher to student, then as employer to designer, as associate, as independent colleague, and finally with an offer of a partnership. Theirs was a fifty-year relationship founded on mutual admiration and need, respect, and even affection, although sometimes complicated by ambivalence and irritation.

In 1900, at Harvard President Charles W. Eliot's request, Olmsted developed and taught the first course of study offered at any university in preparation for professional activity in the field of landscape architecture. "More than any man," wrote Phillips and his colleague Edward Clark Whiting half a century later, "Frederic Law Olmsted Jr. is responsible for the establishment of formal training for the standards and strength of the profession today."[9] Olmsted continued to teach at Harvard and conduct his business in Brookline until he resigned from the college in 1915 to devote more time to his work with the National Commission of Fine Arts, and the War Board, in Washington.

By 1908 the chairman of the design department, James Sturgis Pray, was teaching the first course ever to be given in city planning and was conducting the courses Olmsted initiated; the catalog recorded "occasional instruction by Professor Olmsted." In addition to Olmsted and Pray, Henry Vincent Hubbard and Bremer Pond gave "special instruction in Landscape Architecture," and some forty other instructors were listed in the department. The goal was explicit: to provide students with sufficient technical knowledge and principles of design for the "professional practice of Landscape Architecture," a field considered by the department to be closely akin to the other fine arts.

Phillips's work for the Master of Landscape Architecture degree included studies in landscape architecture, architecture, and civil engineering. The

Graduate school. Harvard Engineering Camp, Squam Lake, New Hampshire. Phillips second from right. Photographer unknown. (Author's Collection)

curriculum combined these with fine arts, drawing, principles of design; languages—usually French, Italian, and German; horticulture, forestry, and dendrology—the study of trees; geology, physiography, and physics; and there was even a course in law. Wherever applicable, courses were "illustrated by stereopticon," a projector which used transparent slides, usually double, to produce a single view with greater depth than the one-dimensional photograph.[10]

Olmsted's two special core courses (eventually taught by Pray and Hubbard) were: "Practice in Design: Private Estates and Related Problems," and "Practice in Design: Park and City Planning." This last was Phillips's favorite; his thesis was on the town of Chelsea, Massachusetts, addressing "The Effect of Successive Improvements in the Means of Transportation upon the Street Plans of Cities."[11]

Phillips earned high honors as an academic scholarship student. He had the distinction of being made an Austin scholar in 1909–10.[12] They were hardworking, happy years. As part of his required studies, he attended the engineering camp at Squam Lake, New Hampshire, and worked on assignments at Harvard's Peabody Museum, in the Arnold Arboretum, and in the Harvard Forest at Petersham. As an advanced student he made topographical maps of areas of the Boston Metropolitan Park System and visited nearby estates to study residential design. His expertise in mathematics was recognized early and made him invaluable in the layout of roads, parks, and large projects. Initially he was not deeply interested in horticulture. He came to appreciate its unique design potential only later, after intensive study of botany and art history, and after further development of his own painting and photography. His ambition to express his latent artistic desires was aroused when he sensed that he had found his niche in landscape architecture, a medium in which he would combine his strong practical and technical knowledge with his creative ability.

The innovative program at Harvard was not without problems. Years later, in December 1949, Phillips wrote to Dr. David Fairchild in Miami of the diversity of his training:

> The Olmsted and Harvard group expected to mark out a special field by combining parts of several existing fields, that is to say, parts of architecture, of engineering, of forestry, of horticulture, town planning, etc. . . . a good idea but hard for a single individual to cultivate all these fields effectively; it requires an organization. Result: On the Isthmus, architects thought I was undoubtedly a fine engineer, engineers thought I was surely a good horticulturist, horticulturists thought I could be an architect but didn't know botany. Each of these groups was right enough. Like Montaigne I have always been ready to admit that I speak more from ignorance than from knowledge. Yet I had something which they did not have, either individually or collectively, which fitted me for the kind of thing I was trying to do.

Throughout his career Phillips tended to be sensitive about his "guinea pig" training, especially after World War II, when the field underwent a dramatic international design revolution led by bright young men who produced a whole new set of aims and values in architecture and urban planning. Phillips shared some of the excitement but was afraid of being left out at the height of his powers, and he hated to think that the components of the Harvard experiment might break apart and return to the traditional separation of fields. Nevertheless, he would not align himself with two other Harvard design graduates and colleagues who wrote to him, evaluating the program in hindsight.

A. Burton Tripp was specifically bitter about the "smattering training" which he said hampered him professionally. After years of working in the Olmsted office and around the country, he went into Washington public housing, using his engineering skills. He called the Harvard program an "exaggerated notion," which turned out what proved in his judgment to be incompetents (Tripp included himself)—not architects, not engineers, and many lacking artistry.[13]

Phillips's former classmate, Jack Wister, head of the department of landscape architecture at Swarthmore, when he wrote, was inclined to agree with Tripp. He reminded Phillips how badly Olmsted and their "dear impractical Pray" had taught—badly prepared, generally incomprehensible lectures.[14]

Phillips defended his teachers, Pray, Olmsted, and Hubbard, "though I know that many of the boys felt as you do, that they were ineffectual. Doubtless they were no better prepared for teaching than were the boys they attempted to teach. Prexy Eliot put it up to them; they were all there was to draw on. And they were attempting to work up a new line of instruction in a rather arbitrarily defined new profession. They were all young men, though they seemed old to us, and had no great amount of practical experience."

All right, Phillips admitted, they were terrible speakers, but "in spite of their bum execution there was a fire of conviction and enthusiasm in Olmsted and Pray that ignited a similar fire in me. And Pray, for example . . . treated me like a son. God knows how many evenings he welcomed me into his book lined study at home, where we smoked and talked till far into the night, surveying and speculating on the wonderful possibilities in landscape architecture and city planning. I cherish a letter he gave me to take to some professional man in England and never got to deliver. His firm, full and fluent handwriting, his buoyant and gallant words were so different from his hesitant, clumsy and involved speech."[15]

First Jobs

Immediately after Phillips's graduation in 1910, Olmsted offered him a position with Olmsted Brothers, but the independent spirit so strong at the end of Phillips's life was already evident. He wanted to separate from his teachers and family and go on his own for a while, even though he must have known that to join the firm of the brothers John Charles and Frederick Law Olmsted Jr. was to be at the heart and center of the landscape profession.

Montreal, 1911, working for Rickson Outhet. Written on back of photo: "This is the first job I ever tackled. It sits on the ridge of the mountain; Preble Macintosh's house, after 'treatment' by the landscape architects." (Author's Collection)

He went to Professor Pray for suggestions about other work, and Pray, who had been helpful to him all through the college years, gave him a number of leads. After much inquiry and lengthy correspondence with several firms throughout the country, Phillips was offered an associate position with Rickson Outhet, who had apprenticed at the Olmsted firm and was now running a lucrative landscape architectural practice in Montreal, Canada.

During the eight months he was there, Phillips gained "experience in design and construction of smallish home grounds, land sub-divisions, small parks, small city and suburban places, and in small office practice."[16] Knowing Phillips's special interests, Outhet encouraged him to give lectures to civic organizations on city planning and made time available to Phillips to make a study of traffic conditions and facilities for the Montreal Metropolitan Parks Commission.

Outhet dangled a near-future partnership as an inducement to stay with him, but Phillips was dissatisfied with what he considered the banality and unimaginative sameness of the work without hope of change. Fresh from school with the highest standards of excellence, still inexperienced and impatient, he wanted a brighter challenge.

Boston Common. Notes by Phillips, c. 1912–13. (Author's Collection)

Boston Common. Crown 3I/2" between gutter lines. Gutter 2'
wide, 3" deep. Brick I6'.

In 1911, he returned to Massachusetts and was hired by Olmsted Brothers. "We should be glad to take you in the office . . . [for] forty cents an hour—higher than we have heretofore given at first—till [next] June, then a raise [to sixty cents]," Olmsted wrote, and permitted himself a dry question: "Perhaps you will tell me why you left Montreal?"[17]

Phillips worked at the famous office on 99 Warren Street in Brookline, Massachusetts, from 1911 to 1913, from 1915 to 1917, and from 1920 to 1922. In between those years he worked independently, and thereafter whenever he worked for Olmsted it was as his representative in the field. "I became familiar with large office practice in [the] design of estates subdivisions, and public grounds . . . specs and contracts," he wrote of his early days in the firm, "and I was outdoors a lot, [with] considerable supervisory responsibility for work in the field—e.g. Boston Common, and Franklin Park, for the Dept. of Public Grounds. . . . I worked much with F.L. then in the prime of his rare analytical powers at a moment when good opportunities abounded and there was much work to be done."[18]

All of Phillips's dealings at the firm appear to have been with his mentor, "F.L.," and he had little if any interaction with John Charles Olmsted before John's death in 1920. Born in 1852 and eighteen years older than his half brother Frederick, John had spent his boyhood "in the midst of designing and construction of works of landscape architecture."[19] John already had more than twenty years' experience working for his stepfather/ uncle when Phillips came to work in Brookline. John was widely acknowledged to be the firm's major designer (after the tragic early death of Charles Eliot, son of the Harvard president, in 1897). He was a superb administrator who continued the Olmsted tradition in park design into the twentieth century, making changes and developing new principles to meet the recreational needs of increasing population and urban growth. His excellence in art, engineering, and photography were a great asset to the business (and sound like a precursor to the other Olmsted's curriculum requirements at Harvard). John worked ceaselessly, and in the last twenty-two years of his life "presided over a practice that grew from 600 to more than 3500 commissions."[20]

In forty-five years as a landscape architect and a businessman with an eye for the least and all-important details, John developed an efficient office procedure and filing system, widely copied elsewhere, and established the professional practice of the firm on a sound basis. Every job was now assigned a number, as was every designer—Phillips's was 383–1—and into each individual's file went firm correspondence, jobs worked on, salary, and so forth.[21]

Before the senior Frederick Olmsted retired, the younger Olmsted, only recently out of college, was made an "equal" partner with John in Olmsted Brothers. John and Frederick cofounded with others the American Society of Landscape Architects (John was first president) and cooperated on other matters, but they concentrated primarily on individual projects and were rarely in the same place for long, although John kept a close eye on all phases of the business. Perhaps it was the only way that half brothers a generation apart and with the intricacies of their family history could work together.

A good deal has been written about Frederick Law Olmsted's irrational behavior toward his children shortly before his death. In one account he claimed that his stepson John was undermining the firm with intent to destroy it and cajoled his "true son" Frederick to give up selfhood to become the continuing embodiment of his father and his father's goals. To their credit, the sons accommodated themselves to a difficult and emotionally charged situation and between them provided a large volume of commissions for the firm.[22]

When Phillips came in 1911, Frederick Olmsted Jr. had just married and brought his bride to live at Warren Street with his mother, Mary Olmsted. In residence, he was at the center of the office work in Brookline, teaching at Harvard, and deep in committee work, but for most of the pre-war and early war years, he was in Washington and working on planning reports for several major cities. John and family lived down the street, where Mrs. John Olmsted kept close watch on the other family and wrote to her husband when he was away to keep him informed.

In contrast to John, the compulsive worker, the younger Olmsted enjoyed life. He spent a lot of time sociably, with friends and his widowed mother. He had intellect and verve and enthusiasm. And he was a talker. "I wish," Phillips noted more than once, "that F.L. would draw more and talk less."[23] Olmsted needed to express his ideas on-site and receive honest opinions, not simple acquiescence, Phillips wrote. Olmsted throve on long and thorough discussion of fact, philosophy, and aesthetics on-site and in committee—many committees; he enjoyed problem solving by consensus, then he would write his summation reports on lengthy train rides. As a young bachelor, Phillips was free to undertake the constant travel his position required, with or for Olmsted.

The Grand Tour

In 1913, William Phillips was twenty-eight years old. He had been working hard and well in an environment known since childhood, surrounded by family. His brother and sister, both now married, and college friends provided the social activity, his colleagues and former professor-turned-boss regulated his life. Perhaps Olmsted sensed that Phillips was growing impatient and feeling understimulated, that he wanted to break away from the stifling predictability of his days, for he encouraged him to take leave without pay to study town planning and the great gardens of Europe.

At about the same time, three of Phillips's equally promising peers made the same trip: Fletcher Steele was sent abroad by Warren Manning; Charles

Phillips, contemplating the next step. Photographer unknown. (Author's Collection)

A. Gillette was sent by his patron, Mrs. Elon Huntington Hooker; and Beatrix Farrand accompanied her aunt, Edith Wharton. Such a tour was an absolute requirement for a successful professional career. Professor Pray sent Phillips a "sort of University passport," on department letterhead, to some of Europe's leading planners and landscape architects. Pray supplied three short notes written on his card with personal greetings, "to introduce Mr. Wm. L. Phillips, MLA from our department who is studying City Planning on your side, and will be glad of any suggestions of both men and things to see—" to Professor Raymond Unwin of Hampstead Garden Suburb, London; Ewart G. Culpin, Esq., of the Garden City and Town Planning Association at Gray's Inn, London; and to Dr. Adolph Otto, secretary of the Deutschen Gartenstaat Gesellschaft in Berlin.

Phillips was away for four months. If he kept a diary while he traveled, it has vanished; only a few letters to his family remain. He covered a lot of ground, walking, drawing, photographing, absorbing as much as possible. He developed a high degree of excellence in photography and was thereafter called upon by Olmsted Brothers for more of his "fine photos" wherever he worked. Italy, Switzerland, Austria, Germany, Holland, England, Belgium, and France were among the countries he visited.

He acquired maps, postcards, and guidebooks for every city and country. He walked through central plazas and parks and followed roads to business and industrial areas, outlying suburbs, and farms until he had them memorized: small linear towns on the route to somewhere else, or more important places with roads fanning out like spokes on a wheel. Roads were an important part of Phillips's business; he checked them here for function and design. He photographed old streets, gateways, outdoor stairs, fountains, monuments, and architectural solutions to highly irregular terrain in the hill towns (and referred to numerous sketches he made, which have been lost). He was intrigued with the many different bridge designs he saw, from ponderous stone arches to airier spans. He recorded details new and interesting to him of window grilles, massive doors and ornamental doorways, street lights, intricate paving, and cobblestone designs.

Munich, Germany. One of a dozen or more road critiques on Phillips's study abroad, 1913. The odd construction, a reverse uphill turnaround, appealed to him. (Author's Collection)

Massive retaining wall in Avignon, with long flight of steps to an observation point above the sheer drop to the right. (Author's Collection)

Like a traveler of old, he would follow a road with a feeling of expectation and promise as it wound before him. He was aware of changes of mood caused, he thought, by the different trees planted on either side along the way—limes, hornbeams, or cypress—as well as by alternative treatment in different countries, when he walked between the plane trees of Arles, along the Appian Way, or Unter den Linden. It is safe to say that he had never seen in the landscape so many kinds of trees that unmistakably showed a controlling human hand in their selection, placement, and shaping.

What moved him the most, beyond all expectation, although he had thought he was well prepared, were the French and Italian Renaissance palaces, villas, and their gardens: their conception, their grand design, their scale. As an Olmstedian, he had been thoroughly schooled in the English garden tradition, but these villas took his heart. A partial list of those he visited in Italy and Sicily includes the villas Aldobrandini, Borghese, d'Este, Farnesi, Giulia, Lante, Madama; the Medici (in Rome) and Medici di Castello, Petraia, Scaasi, and Tasco. He saw the Boboli Gardens in Florence and the Botanical Garden at Palermo. In France, it was on to villa Noailles; Versailles and Fontainebleau; and the châteaux d'Anet, Chantilly, de Courance, de Hautefort, and Vaux-le-Vicomte.

At Harvard Phillips had pored over slides and illustrations; now he was going to see for himself. It made him eager to see the Italian "pleasure" villas built high in the hills above Rome and Florence to escape the lowland fevers. He was enraptured. Of the villa Aldobrandini he wrote: "At Frascati in springtime, the misty effulgence of the sun-drenched Campagna beats impotently on the gloom of the ilexes, the silence of distant plain and surrounding grove is broken only by the faint rustling of lizards in the last year's leaves and the slow dripping of water into the lichenous pool against the terrace wall."[24]

Here in this accommodating climate was the ultimate blend of cultivated and natural indoor-outdoor rooms and garden spaces, connected by colonnaded loggias, allées, and vine-covered pergolas. As he walked through one after the other, he noted the way one garden flowed into another and another through unusually tall hedges and stone walls, detouring around half-hidden or dramatic fountains in man-made pools; great open stairways ascending to some vistas; others so narrow and artfully enclosed that when you climbed up you saw only the plants growing in the wall beside you and an expanse of sky above. On the way down you caught a glimpse of the sea far below or the great plains stretching to the horizon, still punctuated by the feudal boundary planting that makes this section of Europe, seen from a distance, a glorious patchwork.

In his later gardens for Florida residences it is clear how well he absorbed the look and shape of garden ornaments, urns, great terra-cotta pots of orange trees set out in orderly rows on a terrace, tubs of different sizes filled with blooms. He copied benches carved in a wall and stone tables. He photographed the statues in niches or freestanding and in the fountains. Now that he had seen firsthand how vistas and other effects were achieved through mathematical perspective and attention to the strict rules of classical proportion in the formal garden, he understood exactly how he could choose portions of what he admired in the French, German, or Italian styles and adapt them to any scale as inspiration for designs on his native ground. He remarked the function and beauty of the allées and bosques (a planted wooded grove), was captivated by grottoes and labyrinths; he delighted to

Villa Aldobrandini, Frascati. Architecturally the villa was considered inferior to its neighbors, clumsy and heavy in design. But Phillips was enchanted by the conception of the famous water theater that once cascaded down from the hills, soaking the unwary. (Photograph courtesy of Alinari/Art Resource, N.Y.)

The free-form pool, level with the lawn, and the unmatching terra-cotta pots caught his eye. Italy, 1913. (Author's Collection)

see how given spaces were made to seem much larger, and what natural or created materials made intimate gardens.

It could have been here, at this time in his life, that he firmed up his personal philosophy of design, of how he would deal with the elements common to every garden: Air. Rain or drought. Sound. Light. All had to be taken into account before the first spadeful was dug, before the plan was drawn, the structure planned. Heretofore his talents had been subordinated to interpretation rather than creativity. Now he wanted to make his own gardens that would present a scope and range of beauty. Like his peers who had made similar tours, Phillips exulted in the European experience.

He stored memories of the colors and the special quality of the Mediterranean light, which he would never forget. But for him the real miracle in the gardens on this journey was *water*: in streams, cascades, sprays, lakes, ponds, and reflecting pools. Fountain jets directed up in the air to sparkle in sunlight; water flowing down from the hills over rocks and steps; water that could be heard before it was seen.

CHOSEN TO PLAN TOWN OF BALBOA

SELECTED TO LAY OUT NEW ISTHMIAN TOWN

Phillips, Harvard '08, Named by Goethals as Landscape Architect.

William Lyman Phillips, Somerville Latin high school '04, and Harvard College '08, has been appointed by Col. Goethals to the position of landscape architect and first assistant in a municipal department for the Panama Canal zone, for the purpose of laying out and building the permanent town of Balboa at the Pacific end of the canal, and for rebuilding and extending existing towns in the zone.

Mr. Phillips took his landscape degree at Harvard, having won two distinctions in course of his studies there. He has since done landscape work with the Olmsteds of Brookline, Mass. He is on a four months' leave of absence in Europe, studying outdoor art there, and it is from Munich, Germany, that he is called to his important work on the Panama Canal zone. Mr. Phillips was born in Somerville, of Maine and New Hampshire parents, his father, Franklin F. Phillips, being a Maine born and college bred man, and his mother being a descendant from the Connecticut river valley Lyman family. He has a brother, also a Harvard man, Franklin F. Phillips, Jr., a Boston lawyer, and a sister living in Waban, the wife of Herbert S. Kimball, chemical and mill engineer of Boston.

WILLIAM LYMAN PHILLIPS
Harvard Man Who Has Been Named Landscape Architect by Col. Goethals. He Is a Resident of Somerville.

"Somerville man" chosen for an exciting commission in the Canal Zone of Panama. Photographer unknown. (Author's Collection)

IN MAY 1913, when he headed for Paris, there was an exchange of family letters in which Phillips showed remarkable calm, considering his mounting anticipation about a job he had been offered, recommended by Olmsted: "In the American Express reading room, I read in the *Boston Herald*, a paragraph concerning myself, with my picture, reprinted in the *Paris Herald*: Somerville man has been appointed by Col. Goethals to position of landscape architect and first assistant in a municipal department for the Panama Canal Zone, for the purpose of laying out and building the permanent town of Balboa on the Pacific end of the Canal, and for rebuilding and extending existing towns in the Zone."

"Everyone," wrote Phillips, "knows more about it than I."[25]

PART II

The Wide Palette, 1913–1924

"I did an extraordinary amount of work in the relatively brief time of less than 16 months, when I was less than 30 years old, and perfectly competent work in the lights of that period and the materials I had to work with. I was as good then, and as productive, as I ever was afterwards. The sort of thing I did there was actually my forte."

PHILLIPS TO PRENTISS FRENCH[1]

THE RACKET WAS INCONCEIVABLE. The heat, intolerable. In season, the rains came in torrents, followed by hundreds of thousands of cubic yards of mud slide, tumbling back into the Cucaracha and Culebra cuts, from the walls, or forced upward from the bottom.

When nurse Sister Marie, enamored of the luxury of tropical growth— "a hillside blazing with hibiscus, feather palms and plantains"—first set out royal palms and flowers around the grounds of the Ancon Hill hospital and left standing water in all the pots and tubs, perfect breeding places for the stegomyia mosquito, she had no idea that she was contributing to the high mortality rate in the Zone.[2] Thanks to the persistent colonel Dr. William C. Gorgas, the incidence of fevers and disease was in due course dramatically reduced, but they were still there, waiting for the least want of vigilance in mosquito control and sanitation.

For Phillips, who went to Panama a year before the canal opened, this assignment was the ultimate challenge and adventure, in spite of all the difficulties he encountered. It was in Balboa that he fell in love with the tropics and began his study of tropical vegetation. He would devote much of his professional life to this interest, becoming a pioneer in the use of tropical plants in landscape design and for a considerable time a leading authority in tropical botany for horticultural purposes.

The Panama Canal Zone is a ten-mile-wide strip of land in the heart of the Republic of Panama; through its center the Panama Canal was hacked and dug through jungle, hills, marshes, and river from the Atlantic Ocean to the Pacific. The canal is a fifty-one-mile-long cut, a minimum of thirty-eight feet deep, from which 225 million cubic yards of rock and dirt were removed and dumped in strategic places for landfill. Begun in 1881 by the French, the canal was completed by the United States and opened for navigation in 1914, at a cost of millions of dollars, scandals and controversy, and the loss of thousands of lives in fearful accidents and illness. Despite constant fear of recurring slides, workmen searched through the extravagant colors of earth in the cuts, where they found and sold beryl, moss agate, bloodstone, and moonstone—but no gold.

One more hazard for life and sanity was the pervasive smell of rotting vegetation from dying jungle and farmland when the waters swept through the depopulated villages of the Zone to drown them in the artificial lakes and canal. Stubborn patches of land remained, "floating islands" of dying trees and vines, covered with brilliant terrestrial plants, a constant threat to navigation. It was cheaper to try to wait until the islands submerged, but finally many had to be towed out to sea.[3]

Soon after Colonel George Washington Goethals took charge of operations in 1907, as the chairman and chief engineer (often referred to in Panama as the "Zone Czar" or "His Brahmin Highness"), the sculptor Daniel Chester French and Frederick Olmsted Jr. came to Panama at the request of the National Commission of Fine Arts, to suggest how the locks and surroundings "might be dressed up or improved upon." But their report found, in sum, that

> the canal itself and all the structures connected with it impress one with a sense of their having been built with a view strictly to their utility. There is an entire absence of ornament and no evidence that the aesthetic has been considered except in a few instances. . . . Because of this . . . there is little to find fault with from the artist's point of view. The Canal, like the Pyramids or some imposing object in natural scenery is impressive from its scale and simplicity and directness. One feels that anything done merely for the purpose of beautifying it would not only fail to accomplish its purpose, but would be an impertinence.[4]

There the matter ended for the time being, until the commission was consulted again. This time "in regard to the general disposition of streets and buildings, the architectural forces of the Canal made extended studies, and a landscape architect was employed in the final preparation of the lay-out and construction."[5]

After Austin Lord, a noted landscape architect from New York, had come but had resigned in anger and frustration, Olmsted recommended hiring Phillips to take Lord's place: "When in the spring of 1913 Col. Goethals asked my advice as to a landscape architect to undertake certain work on the Isthmus in connection with the new towns," Olmsted wrote, "Mr. Phillips, who was then travelling abroad studying examples of landscape architecture in Europe, was my first recommendation."[6]

IN JUNE 1913, Phillips arrived to build a permanent town at La Boca, which would be renamed Balboa, at the Pacific end of the canal, on top of 22 million cubic yards of fill. The projected site consisted of 676 acres, of which the new town site amounted to 150 acres, 5,600 feet long by 2,100 feet wide. It was to be the administration center for the entire Canal Zone.

"Mr. W. L. Phillips, landscape architect, will lay out and construct the streets, sewer and water systems and grounds for Balboa townsite," wrote Col. Goethals, who was determined "to build a town that shall be a credit to the nation and a place of comfort for those who inhabit it."[7] At the same time, Phillips was assigned "duties . . . in connection with the planning of the permanent settlement at Pedro Miguel, the permanent silver settle-ment at La Boca, and for other work requiring the services of a landscape architect."[8]

Phillips's salary for this undertaking, to start with, was $250 per month; during his time in Panama he oversaw a budget of $350,000. He recorded in his Balboa memoir:

> I was in responsible charge of a work unit composed of 18 "gold force," and a labor force up to [finally] about 300 men; [I was] engaged in town site design and construction. My work covered 150 acres and 130 build-ings. . . . The problem presented to the landscape architect, was that of locating, on the given site, as fixed by the engineers and with given con-ditions as regards the disposition of the various terminal works to be

moved in from other towns, about one hundred buildings to be used as quarters for officials and employees and about fourteen departmental buildings, together with the necessary roads, paths, water and sewer system. The site of the Administration building, which is the largest building-mass and the most important single structure in the whole group, had been already chosen previous to the employment of a landscape architect, and work on the building had been started.

As Phillips began to design the town plan, he sited the old frame buildings then in other parts of the Zone, which were to be moved and rebuilt for the U.S. draftsmen, engineers, and foremen known as the "Gold Force." West Indian and other laborers were housed at La Boca, one-third of a mile south of town; their presence in Balboa was limited to post office and commissary privileges.

Next, he determined the location of standard government housing units, which differed according to rates of pay, and the commissary, post office, railroad station, quartermaster's office, store house, dispensary and dental office, sanitary office, police and fire stations, schoolhouse, churches and parsonage, and an employee YMCA club house. "I believe in the clubhouse principle," Goethal said, when Congress questioned a $52,000 expenditure for the Balboa YMCA. It was to be a social center where everything

Panama, 1913. The challenge begins. Phillips is standing at right, with white shirt, black hat, and a rolled plan in hand. Photographer unknown. (Author's Collection)

possible was done to keep canal workers happy and willing to stay in the Zone. Wages were higher than in the United States, food and commissary prices lower.[9]

In addition, Phillips made site provision for a pump station, an electric substation, and a motorcar house for railway motorcars (self-propelled rolling stock). At his suggestion, a few private interests were included: a bank, newsstand, and steamship offices for canal business. Balboa as a government town offered no private land ownership. Phillips thought this would make it much easier and more economical for him to design a group of buildings in any way and wherever he thought best, without having to worry about personal boundary and property lines or where to place all subsurface structures.

The area selected for the town site was divided into twenty-nine acres on the north and northwesterly slopes of Sosa Hill, 79.5 acres on the southwesterly slope of Ancon Hill, known as Balboa Heights, and about fifty-eight acres of the level filled ground between the hills, the Balboa Plain.

As Sosa Hill was nearest the railroad shops and terminals, housing would be provided there for employees working in this area. The administration building was on Ancon Hill, as were twenty-eight acres of the Ancon hospital grounds, a site chosen by Goethals for his residence, and an area allocated for gold force worker residences. There was no way the town could expand to the northwest as it was permanently bounded by the tracks of the Panama railroad, and a sizable portion of the central northeast section was held by the navy for a future marine reservation.

Phillips's plan focused on the Balboa Plain, the core area between the two hills. He cut a long straight line—a wide avenue, or *prado*, with double roadways on either side and central parking—from the administration building on Ancon directly across to the large elliptical Balboa Plaza below it at the foot of Sosa Hill, ending at the clubhouse square, which he designed, on the old La Boca road. He designated the prado the "formal part of our town," outlined with royal palms, with a long driveway entrance, also palm-lined, "a setting for the important, if not architecturally charming, existing Administration building. . . . I am not fond of this feather duster tree [the royal palm], but the chairman is; he thinks it is the finest tree that grows . . . [so] I intend to use it [freely]."[10] The Balboa roads Phillips planned would curve away from the prado up into the hills, to the residential and business sections, and to the docks and waterfront.

BALBOA PUBLIC BUILDINGS.

Sites for Most of Them have been Selected and are now Available.

The committee, consisting of Civil Engineer H. H. Rousseau, chairman; Capt. R. E. Wood, Lieut. Frederick Mears, and Mr. W. L. Phillips, appointed to consider sites for the proposed permanent public buildings at the new town of Balboa, has submitted its report and recommendations. As a basis, the committee took the layout of the streets and roads that has received general approval, with the main axis of the town passing through the center of the administration building site on the north, and the location tentatively recommended for the new clubhouse on the old Balboa road, on the south. The following

(g) Passengers arriving and departing from the railroad station at the foot of the administration building.

(h) Silver employs, living at La Boca, to be served by the commissary and post-office.

Clubhouse Plaza was considered the central point most convenient to serve the foregoing, and the adoption of a central axis along Balboa Prado was recommended. The grouping of the public or semipublic buildings along this axis will, it was believed, result in economy of operation by reducing foot and team travel to a minimum.

Certain locations are not available as building sites at the present time. In general, these are in the area filled in hydraulically, the material in which has not yet hardened sufficient-

The recommended site for the Balboa railroad station is at the foot of Administration Hill, situated so that the passenger platform will not be on the curve. The main line tracks with reference to the roundhouse and the roundhouse tracks are fixed, so that work on this building can be started at any time.

The site for the permanent fire station is in Block A. This brings it near the quarters on Ancon Hill, which will consist largely of frame buildings reerected from along the line. Work on the new station may be begun at any time.

The site of the courthouse for the combined use of the magistrate's court and police station is in Block D, and erection of the building can be proceeded with.

The schoolhouse for children of gold em-

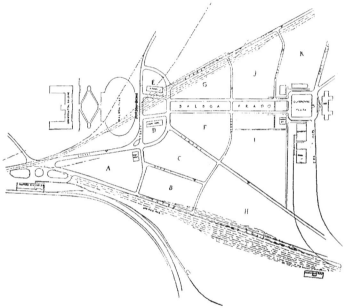

PLAN OF BALBOA TOWNSITE, SHOWING LOCATION OF PUBLIC AND SEMIPUBLIC BUILDINGS.

groups, or classes of groups, will be served by the buildings considered by the committee:

(a) Employes quartered on Ancon Hill in the rear of the administration building.

(b) Employes in the administration building.

(c) Employes in the present Commission settlement, east of Balboa.

(d) Employes to be quartered on the slopes of Ancon Hill.

(e) Employes connected with Balboa shops and piers.

(f) Employes that may be quartered on the flat between Ancon and Sosa Hills.

ly, and certain areas at present occupied by yard or construction tracks, which cannot be moved for several months to come. Blocks B, H, and I all under this head, and for the above reason, these blocks were tentatively recommended by the committee for assignment as general athletic and recreation grounds, as it was considered that this was the best use that could be made of them.

The following building sites were considered by the committee, all of them being free of tracks, with the exception of the site for the proposed schoolhouse in Block E:

ployes is to be situated in Block E. If desired, ground may be had in the rear of the schoolhouse for recreation purposes. Work on this building cannot be started until the yard and construction tracks at present on the site are removed, which will be, probably, within a few weeks.

The Sanitary Department recommended that the building for use of the sanitary inspector be located in Block I, adjoining Clubhouse Plaza, and that the building to be used as a dispensary and as an office for the district physician be located in Block K, also adjoin-

Phillips's plan for Balboa, C.Z., as published in the *Canal Record*. South is to the right, north to the left. Note large areas marked A, B, H, I, unusable until hydraulic fill in that area hardened sufficiently and old railroad tracks were moved. (Copy courtesy of Records Management Branch, Panama Canal Commission, C.Z.)

Along the Sosa Hill end of the prado he sited the post office, commissary, and community buildings like the dispensary, around the clubhouse plaza and the Hotel Tivoli; at the Ancon end would be the school, police station, courthouse, and other buildings needed for administration. The intervening space of the plain would be "lined with quarters, which will also be built on lateral streets branching out from either side of the prado, but irregular and picturesque in character."[11]

Soon after his arrival in the Zone, Phillips was introduced to the little island of Táboga and was utterly charmed by the "tropical island [with] volcanic hills, hollow-curved, grandly ascending, darkly wooded; rocky headlands where the seas boomed and grumbled . . . palm-fringed beaches, in crescent coves, cultivated fields . . . stonewalled, wherein grew a particular kind of pineapple . . . a mass . . . of aroma and succulence." What particularly interested him about the "diminutive village of tiny sun bleached houses skirting the least precipitous flank of the mountain," and influenced his thinking when he worked on the plan of Balboa, was the way it contained—small but in perfect scale—all the requisites for a tropical urban center: a section of prosperous-looking red-roofed villas high on the hill; a dense

THE OLD LA BOCA ROAD LOOKING TOWARDS CLUBHOUSE PLAZA.

Balboa (formerly La Boca). This straight road, the *prado*, was originally designated "the mall." It was to be a long covered arcade with shops on both sides. Although the arcade was not built, commercial through traffic was prohibited. The prado is the central axis of the plan. (Author's Collection)

Right: The island of Taboga, 1913. Photographer unknown. (Author's Collection)

Below: Balboa. Road work. Main roads followed busy traffic lines and discouraged heavy traffic on residential streets. Width of roadways: 16, 18, and 24 feet "minimum width," a disaster for present-day traffic. (Author's Collection)

LOOKING UP THE PATH FROM THE STATION TO THE ADMINISTRATION BUILDING AND THE OFFICIAL QUARTERS.

community and shops on the way down to the central plaza; the Rampa de la Independencia with its hotel (formerly the Panama convalescent hospice), the town hall, and the dominating cathedral. He was, as always, captivated by the quality of the light, "saturated," he said, "with a cool green reflection of the mass of 'jungle trees' on the hills." He was not at all bothered by the primitive conditions, the rough paths that were hardly roads; it was the simplicity of the village, the orderly flow pattern for the necessities of life, that he admired.[12]

From Taboga, Phillips understood the importance of "a plaza, where people may enjoy social diversion of walking about and looking at one another to the accompaniment of a band." He wanted Balboa's prado to be such a place, grander, and with much peripheral planting. Phillips had ridden the Panama railroad many times, from Panama to Colón, and had explored the towns in between; he knew the charming plazas, parks, and squares built by the Spanish and French, who also considered it a necessity to provide open-air street life with cafés and shops on the perimeter. Balboa, Phillips wanted to make sure, would become the best of them. He may have been the only man on the isthmus who understood the importance of making a visually harmonious tropical town, which would reflect the rhythm and style of life in Central America.

He explored much of the Canal Zone and the rest of Panama hunting for plants, away from the sounds of the Bucyrus steam shovels, the disagreeable odors, and the hordes of tourists who came by train and ship and private yacht throughout the time of canal building. He found the countryside to be the most beautiful he had ever seen—mountains and savannas, jungle, white sands and blue sea—the surroundings by turns luminous and brilliant with flowers and thick tropical foliage of many shades of green and varying texture.

Panama waterfront, market day. Native *cayucas* made of a single log, to 35 feet and schooner-rigged, sail in from the San Blas, Taboga, Chorrera, Bayano River, and the bay of San Miguel with fish and fresh produce. Phillips tastes for the first time the mango, *Mammea*, and sapodilla.

The coconut palms pleased Phillips the most, in groves or in lines along the seafront, for the natural curve of their trunks and for fronds that caught the breeze in constant movement. These, rather than the royal palms, he told Olmsted, seemed to Phillips "the very symbol and mark of the land. A grove of these trees would make a good screen, and, besides, each tree brings in to the Commission a revenue of $5.00 [for the coconuts on it]."[13]

Phillips collected seeds and created plant lists. "Mangoes and many other broad leaved trees," he noted, could "be got without special [care in] propagation . . . [because] the depopulation of the Zone has resulted in the abandoning of many small plantations from which plants can be taken." He set up a nursery at the Corozal farm "for the Sanitary Department to propagate and raise the necessary plants, under the direction of N. E. Coffey, the farm superintendent. It is estimated (by Mr. W. L. Phillips) that 15,500 trees and shrubs will be needed." From the infinite range to hand for his landscape design, Phillips chose indigenous tropical plants and some "which it has been found by experimentation, will thrive on the Isthmus."

The list he drew up was prodigious. The palms alone included Puerto Rico royal, coconut, fan (*Pritchardii pacifica*), Panama hat (*Carludovica palmate*), fern (*Caryota urens*), and sago palms (*Cycus revolututa* and *C. circinalis*), screw pines (*Pandanus utilis* and *P. regalis*), and date palm (*Phoenix dactylifera*). Other trees on the list were royal and dwarf poinciana, frangipani *(Plumeria)*,

Balboa. New planting of coconut palms. The best residential sites (on Road #5) were as far as possible from canal shops, railroad, and commercial docks. (Author's Collection)

THE JUNCTION OF ROADS #7 AND #4 FROM ROAD #5. IN THE MIDDLE DISTANCE, BALBOA SHOPS, ON THE UPPER RIGHT HAND SOSA HILL.

mahogany (*Swietonia mahogani*), *Ficus*, Jamaican cedar (*Cedrela odorata*), many kinds of eucalyptus, bamboos, tamarinds (*Tamarinda indica*), avocados, mangos, guavas, citrus, and breadfruit (*Artocarpus altilis*). The shrubs, flowers, and vines to be used included hibiscus, gardenias, moonflowers, jessamines, yuccas, morning glories, and bougainvillea. Phillips noted that shoots from most of these trees, planted originally by the French, "were to be found on the grounds of the Ancon hospital, and would be ready to transplant and set out in July."[14]

"THE GREATEST LIBERTY MAN HAS EVER TAKEN AGAINST NATURE"[15]

Others may have been better engineers, made better decisions, fewer mistakes, but the chief engineer had the two qualities that ensured success for the project: charisma and iron nerve. When yet another severe mud slide dumped 15 million cubic yards of dirt back into Culebra Cut, Goethals, with a fine sense of drama, lit a cigarette and said, "Hell, we dig it out again." Goethals's undeniable gifts and stature were a combination of his experience and his position atop a pyramid of equally talented men and an enormous labor force. He was the object of world admiration, even hero worship, and was mentioned more than once for the presidency. "Goethals was not sufficiently human for everyone, but then, others did not have the responsibilities he had."

Unfortunately, Admiral Harry Harwood Rousseau—one of Goethals's assistants and a member of the seven-man Canal Commission appointed by President Theodore Roosevelt after he had placed Goethals in supreme command with the last word on any decision—was charged with designing and building the terminals, wharves, dry docks, warehouses, coaling stations, and machine shops. Phillips and Rousseau should have made a great team, for their work was contiguous, but Rousseau was a company man who safeguarded his authority. He saw no reason why a subordinate should tell him where to place his shops, even though it was part of Phillips's job list. "I don't want to hear of any conflicts," President Roosevelt had declared at the outset; "any disagreement with Colonel Goethals will result in your departure from the Canal."[16] Rousseau heard, but Phillips, making his first acquaintance with government methods of operation and unfamiliar with military procedure, did not thoroughly appreciate or pay sufficient attention to the protocol and hierarchy under which he was to work. "A capacity for persuasion by some means or other was often in requisition," wrote Phillips; it never worked with Rousseau. Before he knew it, Phillips was enmeshed in petty bureaucratic chicanery with a man who lost no opportunity to criticize Phillips's performance in written reports to the colonel.

Phillips had initially been excited by "the opportunity [to be] a part of one of the world's most efficient engineering organizations. . . . The first principle [there] was cooperation and coordination of effort," he wrote. "I . . . [had] frequent contact with . . . a great variety of technical workers. The atmosphere . . . encouraged self assurance and accomplishment rather than nice discrimination. . . . I saw bold and difficult problems expeditiously executed. We were confronted by novel problems, found workable solutions."[17]

One of the most novel of Phillips's tasks was trying to keep the constantly moving ground on which he had to build his roads and water lines

Balboa. Work speeding up in the clubhouse plaza and Balboa prado. Administration building in background. Photograph taken by Phillips from the YMCA building. (Author's Collection)

Looking across the plain at the developing Balboa prado. From this vantage point one can begin to see the layout of the road system and the emerging town. Sosa Hill in background at right. Photograph taken by Phillips from the administration building. (Author's Collection)

from sinking or sliding out from under him. In 1913, at the Culebra Cut and Cucaracha, the slides were still active, digging was constant, and "the end was not in sight. . . . The proportions of the slide were terrifying and the chief geologist declared they would not cease until the angle of the Canal bank became so gentle that gravity would not pull the crest down." This required raising grade for suitable drainage throughout the plain, formerly a tidal marsh. The quality and depth of the fill was questionable; the soil was predominantly tufa, soft sandy stone, volcanic detritus, and sterile, which might make planting difficult. However, in some areas of the Isthmus covered with volcanic ash, many plants flourished.[18]

Further constraining Phillips's designs were imposing existing buildings—the hotel and administration buildings—which had to remain in the area he was developing. He had managed to build his roads without too much bureaucratic interference, but even here the "smooth flowing lines which some consider inseparable from good landscape practice [were] at

Balboa. YMCA. "I believe in the clubhouse principle," Goethal said. Congress thought $52,000 for the Balboa YMCA was too much. Goethals won. (Author's Collection)

times deliberately set aside." In all, he said, "it is difficult to overcome one's training, and give over to the banal."[19]

Alterations to his plan and subsequent misplacement of houses by his superiors further frustrated Phillips—he had planned to site houses to get the benefit of prevailing breezes in the relentless heat, and he knew that those placed too far down the hills would suffer runoff problems as well. Some of what Phillips said on this subject penetrated, for when Goethals selected the location of his own house, necessitating the removal of the filled fever and tuberculosis wards on Ancon (popularly known as Cemetery Hill, for the graves there), he sent word to Phillips to disregard his architect's original plans and set the house farther back up the hill and turned to the "prevailing direction of the wind."[20]

Phillips had been given to understand that he would have two years to complete his work, but then in the final maniacal push for the grand opening of the canal in 1914, he lost a year. All too soon the directives changed. Paranoia had set in. *Every* matter had to be presented for Goethals's approval, in writing. To Olmsted, Phillips wrote: "Indeed I am beginning to think that this town, while a useful exercise for myself in the matter of design, will soon be warped out of all semblance to itself by settlement. . . . [And] it now looks as though the sites will have to be abandoned, as Mr. Holmes, the engineer of building construction has been digging test-pits and claims that the heavy buildings will have to be placed somewhere off of filled ground."[21]

Now, in the August rainy season, work was slowed and required a contingency budget for the extra time needed. Goethals hated spending money, and at that moment he was particularly annoyed with Phillips for corre-

THE NORTHERLY SIDE OF THE ADMINISTRATION BUILDING
FROM ROAD #3.

Above: Balboa. Administration building. Arguments and political maneuvering over completion of road and grounds here forced landscape architect Phillips and engineer Holmes to resign. (Author's Collection)

Left: Balboa. Road #7 looking up past official quarters. Although this area has been heavily rebuilt, it still retains vestiges of Phillips's work. (Author's Collection)

Balboa. The first house built on Road # 5. There are no gutters on any of the public buildings or residences because they clog up with leaves, hold water, and breed mosquitos. (Author's Collection)

Balboa. The governor's (Goethals's) residence is on a summit to make best use of any prevailing breeze. Much planting was already in place; a better plan was in progress. (Author's Collection)

sponding with the Boston Society of Landscape Architects without consulting him first: Phillips had been asked to speak and exhibit his landscape plans and photographs of Balboa town site at the upcoming Boston ASLA Panama-Pacific Exposition. From that time on, Goethals dogged Phillips's every move with the help of Rousseau, who put his hand squarely on Phillips's business.

Phillips had men working on the entrance and steps of the Hotel Tivoli, steps which would be very prominent in the front of the hotel facing the plaza. When consulted on the preliminary drawings, Phillips had called the steps "unsightly, ungainly . . . [adding] nothing to the appearance of the grounds."[22] He prepared an alternative design, which he felt would be handsomer and more functional: moving the steps, making a better vehicle turnaround, calling for a group of palms between the curb and a low retaining wall, and joining the two sides of the large open oval space before the hotel to make a more symmetrical appearance.[23]

Rousseau began to interfere to such an extent that everybody's nerves grew raw. One can only conjecture as to why he decided to be a world-class meddler like his chief and to harass Phillips off the isthmus. Perhaps Phillips, popular and evidently gifted, threatened him in some way. A small group was being formed to remain. Perhaps Rousseau wanted to stay on after the canal opened, as administrator of the terminal facilities, but Phillips, who loved the area and still had a lot of horticultural work to supervise, would undoubtedly stay, too. The Zone became too small to hold them both. Rousseau made sure Goethals knew when Phillips was obliged to spend money. Perhaps Goethals too was annoyed by Phillips's independent air, not sufficiently subservient—who can tell? Goethals was not above pettiness. His overweening ego and power hunger could not permit a subordinate to act independently.[24]

Foremen did not know whose orders to obey when Rousseau countermanded Phillips. Memos and complaints flew back and forth. Phillips protested but he was no match for a polished infighter. Goethals became so angry with Phillips and Holmes, Phillips's work partner, the engineer who had refused to put heavy buildings on filled ground, that he sent both of them off to another job and brought in new men to complete Phillips's work on the stairs. Phillips and Holmes resigned, "a method of getting separated from the Isthmian service which is quite the thing."[25]

On October 31, 1914, there was a farewell banquet at the Hotel Tivoli and another at the Hotel Aspinwall on Taboga, for Landscape Architect Phillips, Resident Engineer John Holmes, three superintendents, and one junior engineer, all "tendered by the Friends and Associates in the Canal Zone." By December Phillips was at home in Massachusetts. He had resigned with the same frustration and anger as had his predecessor, Lord, who wrote to him: "I presume you found that there were certain exactions that were unreasonable and uncalled for . . . [which made it] impossible [for you] to arrive at satisfactory results."[26] On February 26, 1915, at his request, the Panama Canal Commission Washington office sent Phillips a transcript of his service record: Appointed as L.A. in the Canal Zone at $250 per month, effective June 13, 1913; resigned effective November 10, 1914. General workmanship "excellent for design"; general conduct "excellent."

In 1965, Phillips summarized his Panama experience in a letter to Prentiss French: "To take the most charitable view possible it is evident that foresight, judgement and interest were not strongly displayed, and that the Isthmian Canal Commission failed to avail itself to the fullest of its unique opportunity to put into practice modern ideas of town planning. That failure is the most lamentable in that the town is located in a rather conspicuous part of the globe." He never forgave himself for quitting the fight and

Balboa. The landscape architect's "yellow shack," often known as the "beauty shop." Phillips is seated at back right, wearing a cap. Everyone was in suit and tie in hundred-degree heat. Photographer unknown. (Author's Collection)

Balboa. Cartoon by G. New-
bold presented to Phillips at
farewell banquet, October
1914. (Author's Collection)

the work he loved: "I have never ceased to regret that circumstances did
not favor a continuation of that line."

All of Phillips's plans, he was told, were carried out after he departed:
"The 'beauty department' has been greatly missed since it folded its wings
and flew away; we are constantly reminded of them however, when we see
Balboa grow more beautiful each day."[27]

In presenting the Thomas Barbour medal to Phillips at the Fairchild
Tropical Garden on January 30, 1950, David Fairchild spoke of Phillips's
days in Panama. He quoted one of the landscape architects who worked
there later: "The only good landscaping we found when we came there,"
the successor said, "is the road system laid out by a fellow named Phillips. I
don't know who he was, but he was a master."[28]

[Phillips] has always seemed to me to have a particularly level head and good all round grasp in matters of design, particularly in the field of City Planning. Moreover, his practical bent makes him much more than ordinarily dependable in matters of construction drawings. I should think he would be very useful with you as your force [U.S. Army Quartermaster Corps] expands. Of course he is a mighty good fellow and would want to do his part.

JAMES STURGES PRAY[1]

HOMECOMING FROM Panama in the winter of 1914 was dreary, a bad letdown. Phillips could close his eyes and remember the sunlit land he had left so precipitately, open them to Cambridge's monochromatic slush. In February, he was invited to show his Balboa plans and photographs at the Boston Society of Landscape Architects Exhibition at the Boston City Club.[2] He gave talks and wrote newspaper articles about the canal and its ongoing problems.[3]

Although he longed to return to the isthmus and put out feelers about this until the end of World War I, he in the meantime also wrote to his colleagues across the country throughout all of the next year about possible other work. He followed every suggestion given him by James Pray and met with firms that contacted him, but the situation was not encouraging. He was in touch with Stephen Child in Santa Barbara, California, in January 1915; with the Alaska Engineering Commission office in Washington, D.C., in February; the New Orleans Chamber of Commerce in May; Ernest Walker, "Landscape Architect and Civil Designer" in Portland, Oregon, in August; and Austin Lord in New York in October. With the Massachusetts Agricultural College he had a protracted series of interviews from October 1915 to January 1916. He was further in contact with civil engineer and landscape architect Charles Leavitt in November 1915 and with landscape gardener Harry Franklin Baker of Minneapolis in October–November that year.

He took the Civil Service Examination for the position of "Expert Landscape Architectural Designer" in April. Olmsted wrote a strong recommendation: "[Mr. Phillips] was a Landscape Architecture designer in my office from January 1911 to February 1913, and I have taken pains to see . . . his work at other times and places. . . . I have no doubt that [his] experience in government work . . . [and] his qualifications are far above average of those who will apply."[4] His drawings drew a score of 90; education and preliminary training, 92; experience and fitness, 89. But Phillips was turned down, on May 11, 1915, because he failed "to show the required architectural training and experience."

During the summer of 1915, Phillips built a small summer house for himself in East Boothbay, Maine, upon the ledge overlooking Linekin Bay and next to his parents' summer home; he built it largely, he said in a resumé, with his own hands. "[Father] told me he pirated [the plan] from a very contemporary design of the time," his daughter said.[5] Building the house gave him much pleasure; sailing on Linekin Bay lifted his spirits while he tried to decide what to do next. War shadows hung over all of them, in what Phillips called a period of stagnation in professional work. Then, in 1916, Ferruccio Vitale, whose nationally known firm specialized in large estates, contacted Phillips: "Before you engage yourself permanently I should appreciate a personal interview."[6]

Olmsted's "CONFIDENTIAL" reference for Phillips was remarkably double-edged, considering his recent praise of Phillips elsewhere. Was he angry at Phillips for wanting to leave the firm again so soon when Olmsted looked forward to working closely with him? "As far as we know," Olmsted wrote, "Mr. Phillips would be quite capable to [do your] work. . . . [He] has had considerable experience in outside construction—even thought of [going into] the contracting business. He is bright and capable, although inclined to be slow. He has a somewhat peculiar personality, which, although not displeasing to most people, might occasionally prove disturbing."[7]

What did he mean? Olmsted's fulsome praise coupled with remarks about Phillips's "peculiar character" came up constantly in their ambivalent relationship. Olmsted explained himself only years later, in a letter of recom-

The house Phillips built "largely with my own hands" next door to his parents' summer home on the rocks at Murray Hill, 1915. (Author's Collection)

mendation to the Civil Service Commission. To the CSC question "Desirable traits?" Olmsted wrote, "Notable skill and versatility as a designer, both in analyzing and solving problems functionally and in obtaining beauty in the result." And to the question "Undesirable qualities—dishonesty, poor personality, immorality, etc. etc.?" Olmsted answered: "Mr. Phillips has a trait *which under some circumstances* can have the effect of a 'poor personality'. It is a lively and penetrating sense of humor which I have often found very clarifying and usefully 'debunking'; but which not infrequently finds inopportune expression in a way that produces a false impression of nonchalant cynicism, seriously irritating to some people. A related reason for his not having attained a degree of national prominence in his profession and a degree of wordly [sic!] success commensurate with his technical ability is that he has too little of the commercial instincts and self-pushing qualities of successful salesmen." It was the lack of salesmanship that galled Olmsted.[8]

Phillips's interview went well; Vitale offered him the job. He accepted and moved to New York in 1916, to work at 527 Fifth Avenue for sixteen months. He conceded that it was an experience of sorts, in the office and in

New York. Men and mule team at work on a large estate designed by Ferruccio Vitale, c. 1916–17. (Author's Collection)

New York. Completed excavations and forms, used and discarded, lower right, for the curved terraces and sunken garden by Ferruccio Vitale. (Author's Collection)

the field, but he "had no sympathy with Vitale's practices." He explained this later in a letter to John Wister at Swarthmore. Wister was deploring poorly trained landscape architects who gave the profession a bad name; and worse, what he had been hearing about the practices of well-known, established men, such as Vitale, who would order his draftsmen to double all quantities of plants on the plan so that he could charge more for the work.[9]

Brookline, Massachusetts. Olmsted Brothers staff on a September 1917 outing, Phillips third from left. (Courtesy of the National Park Service, Frederick Law Olmsted National Historic Site)

From his own years in the firm, Phillips wrote, he could back up that story:

Whenever Vitale got a new job, he would dash out to a nursery where he could find big trees and expensive specimens, order $15–20,000 worth of whatever caught his eye, and present the invoice to his client—they were almost always copper magnates—along with a bill for his commission; he always charged on a commission basis. Then he would hand the list over to a fellow named Page, who made the planting plans, and tell him to work it up. Poor Page would sit there all day staring wildly at the plan . . . a picture of a man fast slipping into lunacy, until he couldn't take any more, slipped his office key under the door and took off, never more to be seen by Vitale.

I suppose Vitale thought he was doing the right thing, or perhaps he merely thought his ethics were as good as those of his clients. He was, however, pretty much of an ass, though I ought not to be ungrateful as he gave me a job in time of need and treated me well in some ways. When he was president of the ASLA—and imagine having such an old scoundrel as president of a professional society—Hubbard used to get very sore at him.[10]

Phillips left New York in May 1917. Olmsted coaxed him back to Brookline for a higher position than the one he had previously held with Olmsted Brothers, "with more responsibility for design, specs, and oversight of work."[11] The new job came because Olmsted was in Washington working with the National Council of Defense and needed Phillips in the office. The firm's business was suffering; landscape work was drying up everywhere as the United States entered the war. As soon as he could extricate himself from supervising a public athletic field job at Fitchburg, Massachusetts, including steel concrete bleachers and locker buildings—typical of the kinds of jobs coming to the office—Phillips turned as usual to Pray for advice to find a war opening in which he could best serve.

PHILLIPS JOINED THE Quartermaster's Corps Construction Division, U.S. Army, in February 1918; his rich experience in Panama and now considerable engineering skills would be in great demand. In his first post at Camp Las Casas, San Juan, Puerto Rico, from February to August 1918, Phillips found himself back in the tropics he loved, "a sort of place in which I thought then, and still, that I could live."[12] There he learned to draw carefully, but more importantly for his future work in Florida, he expanded his knowledge of tropical vegetation and of "the scenic value of tropical scenery." He traveled about the island, spoke Spanish fluently, and seems to have had a

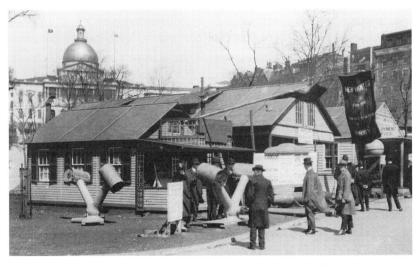

"Men Wanted." World War I recruitment, 1918. (Author's Collection)

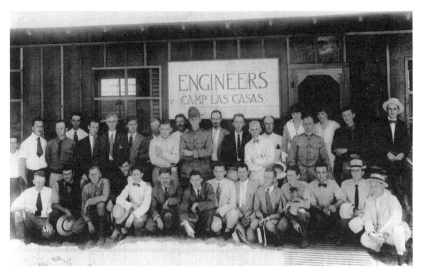

Camp Las Casas, Puerto Rico, 1918. Phillips, with beard, is standing in the back row, center, under the "Las" on the sign. Photographer unknown. (Author's Collection)

torrid romance with a local woman, which caused a friend to ask, "Are you planning to take the little lady home to meet mother?" Throughout his travels, Phillips thought of himself as a confirmed bachelor, enjoying exotic companions who would never be accepted at home.

By the end of his army career in September 1919, Phillips had worked at seven camps: six months at Las Casas, San Juan, Puerto Rico, in 1918; another six in Washington, D.C., and at Camp Jackson in Columbia, South Carolina; at Camp Bragg, South Carolina, for two months in 1919; at Camp Benning, Georgia, for "a few days! Got wind of something better"; at Camp Normoyle and other posts based out of San Antonio, Texas, for three months; a month at Camp Knox, Kentucky; and three months at Watertown, Massachusetts.[13]

The largest was Camp Jackson, where he was directly responsible for the entire layout. It was, he said, "a kind of city planning requiring comprehension of large-group problems, an understanding of how to work in an organization, and powers of bold and quick decision." Phillips was in his element. It was very much the same kind of responsibility he had had in

Balboa. In San Antonio for three months in 1919, he was asked to recommend mosquito control measures at the Mexican border posts and a soil control plan for the fort at Laredo;[14] he studied local flora and made planting plans for Camp Normoyle. Phillips's duties included mapmaking, yet another skill that would serve him well on later projects.

Brookline

After the war, Phillips returned to work for the Olmsteds. "It was a period of generally lean practice, vaguely recollected," he wrote, three long years during which "rich people continued to die—there were refined burial plots to be designed. There were studies of great estates that came to naught. I went to Florida with F. L. Olmsted one winter and worked there on a prosy layout for Kelsey City, which was carried out but never prospered. During all this time there was a restlessness in the office which I shared."[15]

Restlessness gave way to crisis. In February 1920, one of the country's most eminent landscape architect practitioners, John Olmsted, was dead at sixty-seven. There was a widespread sense of loss in the profession and an appreciation by one of his colleagues serves to illustrate the tenor of others: "an artist foremost and always . . . with . . . a scientific training that made his work . . . conspicuously successful in aesthetic merit . . . [and] feasibility . . . John Charles Olmsted—a master artist . . . his works are a priceless national heritage."[16]

F. L. Olmsted, at fifty, was now the only surviving family member in the firm. Questions uppermost there and in his own mind were: in which direction would he lead and was he qualified to do so? The consensus was admiration and respect for his vision, his imagination and ability to see every aspect of a large problem, for his stimulating ideas and knack of being in the right place at the right time; but not as a practical landscape designer. Mundane details bored him, and he was color-blind.[17]

Burton Tripp was more often than not disparaging. He wrote to Phillips that he had been to the Corcoran Gallery in Washington to see the exhibit of the Greater Washington Plan and had seen the 1901 Mall Development plans by Olmsted and his committee. He found them an appalling example of what not to do. There was an accompanying notice, Tripp reported, saying the plan had had to be abandoned because it was so impractical. Had his own name been on it, Tripp wrote to Phillips in 1945, he would burn it and hide; but then, possibly, all Olmsted had contributed was a selection of trees for the Mall.

Olmsted assistants made his drawings and plans while he went hunting for more projects. He did not care for residential work, never had, and was not very good at it; he disliked the subservient role. Although he was adept at dealing with them, "clients," he once told Phillips, "are the only thing wrong with this business."

Olmsted's special ability, according to Phillips, was engineering; his passion, as had been his father's and John Charles's, was land preservation and encouraging the development of public and private parks for future generations. "[FLO] turned more and more away from residential and urban problems . . . to conserving natural scenery . . . from the beginning [of his life] the sociological values of public parks had special appeal."[18] The Olmsted-Phillips Florida correspondence contains much about Olmsted's active interest in the Everglades, Highland Hammock in Sebring, and Texel, Florida, and attempts to get Edward Bok and other wealthy clients to buy land for public parks.

But it was John who had brought more commissions to completion, who had designed park systems and landscape for public buildings throughout the United States and Canada, had made further developments of Frederick Olmsted Sr.'s parks, and had followed through on some of Olmsted Jr.'s work, notably Rock Creek Park in Washington, D.C., the area the younger Olmsted had carved out for himself.[19]

Now there were no more shoulders for him to lean on; he was the shoulder, with a payroll to meet. The men who knew him best were rightfully concerned. However, Olmsted had his own talents. He was always a survivor and he had created for himself one enormous asset for the future: nearly twenty years' worth of his Harvard students, office apprentices, and students of Olmsted students. He was convinced that, properly directed, those former students now working in his office might, in the aggregate, take John Olmsted's place, freeing him for the work that best suited him. He would give them every opportunity; several became partners.

One of his first moves was to persuade Henry Vincent Hubbard that he owed it to the continuity of the great Olmsted firm to leave Pray, Hubbard and White, and return to Olmsted as a partner. Hubbard had graduated from M.I.T. in architecture and apprenticed with Olmsted Brothers, from

1901 to 1906. He continued to teach at Harvard from 1906 to 1941, and his work there and expertise in city and regional planning added strength to the Olmsted firm.[20]

With each new commission, Olmsted usually developed good rapport with his client right away. Whenever the office was approached for a big job, he went out personally as often as necessary and engaged in lengthy correspondence until a tacit agreement was reached:

> F.L. was never content to work out any problem solely from a map. A map he would have at any cost, but also, at any cost, he would see for himself what the ground looked like, what circumstances surrounded it, what grew, what did not grow, what soil was there, what rock, etc. In the inspection of sites, he was again indefatigable, and without thought to the capacities, tastes, or interests of those who accompanied him. Through swamps and thickets he would go, over flooded marshes or up crumbling hillsides, determined to see all, to miss nothing. He liked to get up high, for a comprehensive view, and so was a great climber of trees and abandoned water towers and decrepit house roofs, where few cared to join him.[21]

Following procedures that had been established before Olmsted took over the firm, contracts—except for government or industrial work—often consisted of a letter of intent between the client and the firm. At that point, Olmsted wrote a long preliminary report, part or all of which went to the client. The rest was for office record and for the benefit of his assistant, who might well have been with him all along, and who was now called upon to make the sketches, to take over and complete the job as the "Representative in Complete Charge for Olmsted Brothers, with Full Responsibility for Dealing with Clients." Olmsted's report was the controlling factor that put the Olmstedian stamp on every project.

As he began to generate new activity, he needed men of proven ability whom he could trust to complete the jobs he began, while he went on to the next project. Representatives—Olmsted's best designers out in the field—were instructed to sign all of their plans "Olmsted Brothers," to send daily progress reports directly back to him, and to route all material bills and other costs directly to the firm. Olmsted Brothers would settle the bills, pay representatives a flat hourly fee, and charge the client two and a half times for overhead. The staff anonymity of "Olmsted Brothers" was in practice from the beginning when all documents were signed by F. L. Olmsted, Sr., and his first partner, Calvert Vaux.

Phillips interpreted Olmsted's ideas for years and did not hesitate to add his own; this was Olmsted's "ungrudging cooperation without regard to personal authorship," which had so impressed him when he observed his father working with David Burnham and others in Chicago, years before. Yet Olmsted was often driven, perhaps for reasons of office policy, to appear to be doing it all himself. Men who were not altruistic enough to subordinate themselves for the common good of the office went elsewhere or out on their own; those who preferred to remain with Olmsted, without the worry of seeking individual commissions, were rewarded for good work and loyalty with bonuses and eventual partnership. In its best years, Olmsted Brothers was a very lucrative concern.

In the 1920s, Olmsted men made up the office staff. They took meals together, worked and socialized together, and occasionally dined under the benevolent eyes of Mr. and Mrs. F. L. Olmsted Jr. and Mary Olmsted, F.L. Sr.'s widow. Olmsted assumed a patriarchal manner to the men who worked at Warren Street. He went to great lengths to preserve a congenial and familial atmosphere. During the Depression, he and his partners made every effort not to fire anyone.[22]

They were a select group, a fraternal order of landscape architecture gypsies, who through the years met one another coming and going across the country or back in Brookline, sometimes on the same job, sometimes replacing or recommending one another. Phillips was part of a group that included, beside Hubbard, Richard Bassett, William Cook, James F. Dawson, Prentiss French, Percival Gallagher, George Gibbs, Hans Koehler, William Marquis, N. Saigh, A. Burton Tripp, Edward C. Whiting, Jack Wister, and Leon Zach, all with short-term or permanent connections to Olmsted Brothers. Wister went to Swarthmore. Cook, horticulture specialist, was briefly at Lake Wales after Phillips left, then at Reasoner's Florida nursery, and at Dade County Parks, before he became National Park Service inspector in the Virgin Islands. Bassett also came to Lake Wales and went to Europe with Phillips but left the profession to become an artist. Tripp was in Panama briefly, concentrated on engineering in Washington, painted and had a greeting card business; Gibbs was Olmsted Brothers' chief designer and settled in Palos Verdes after World War I. Saigh directed an engineering firm in Texas, and Zach became head of the Site Planning Section of the U.S. Army Corps of Engineers.

French and Phillips became lifelong friends. "I first met him [Phillips] in 1921 at the Olmsted office in Brookline where he was known mostly as Doc, sometimes as Bill. Over the years, working with him from time to time and corresponding and seeing his works, I concluded that he knew more about the many facets of landscape architecture than anyone I have ever known. Design, engineering, planting, execution of work—he was excellent at all phases of any project or size. He had a fine analytical mind and a wonderful memory. He could quote at length from authors in English and French, even Spanish. . . . FLO Jr. once said to me that he wished he could write as well as Phillips."[23]

French's father, William Merchant Richardson French, was the founding director of the Chicago Art Museum. His uncle was the sculptor Daniel Chester French, whose father had been the first president of the Massachusetts Agricultural College. Prentiss graduated from "Mass Ag" in landscape architecture and was an instructor there for a while. On occasion, the family's achievements weighed heavily on his spirit. He was prone to a feeling of inadequacy, which he often confided to his mentor, Phillips, his senior by nine years. As a well-connected young man, French was comfortable in society and had all of the manners and push Olmsted admired but missed in Phillips.

It was an even friendship; French often sent good clients to Phillips. Through French, Phillips designed the Venetian Causeway at Miami Beach; French and Zach recommended him for work at Jackson Memorial Hospital; he worked with French for William Vanderbilt and several other clients. French was the promoter—"well, we lost that one" or "I've written Honore Palmer you would contact him"; "Bill, we should get on that street planting article we promised L.A." (on the Hillsborough Road in Tampa)— or French called him in as a partner, scolding him constantly for not charging enough when Phillips went out on his own. French had family in Florida and spent considerable time there, as chief landscape architect and planner for the city of Venice, besides freelancing in Sarasota, Tampa, St. Augustine, and Boca Raton, often with Phillips. The two men worked and spent time together with their wives and children until the Frenches left for New

England and his ultimate office in San Francisco. On several occasions, he called Phillips to help him with work he felt uncertain about, the most important example being the job of laying out Camp Shelby, which Phillips ghosted from Miami, and for which help French paid—"I couldn't have done it without you, doc." Phillips's answer was generous: "The fact is, I think we both like to do and are better at different things."[24]

It was French who, with Leon Zach, nominated Phillips to become a fellow of the ASLA and worked on Olmsted to second him, and it was French who wrote to him weekly when Phillips was terminally ill. They shared humor and love of their work.

PHILLIPS WOULD BECOME uneasy when he stayed in Brookline too long. In 1922 he was happy to be engaged by Sun Yat-sen's commissioner to be the city planner for Canton, but a revolution in that part of the country prevented him from taking the job. It was a blow to his spirit of adventure and romance.

However, in April, George Gibbs wrote to Olmsted Brothers from Washington requesting Phillips for work in France at the American cemeteries.[25] To Phillips he wrote that "a job may come up in a few days. I should be glad to get a man of your training on the 'work'."[26] Whiting answered for the firm two weeks later: "We would release Phillips . . . not anxious to do so but wouldn't stand in [the] way. Having worked with him in the army you know him as well as we. He has not perhaps as much push as might be desirable but has good (valuable) ability."[27] Gibbs was pleased to engage Phillips as civilian resident engineer, superintendent of graves, for the American military cemeteries in France. Phillips left for Paris in July 1922.

POSTWAR FRANCE

I am doing some effective designing here . . . ornamental gates, balustraded walls, enclosures and grilles in the style of Louis XIV, planting schemes.
WILLIAM PHILLIPS[28]

The Graves Registration office was in the Hotel d'Iena in Paris, which enabled Phillips to explore the city he grew to love. His job required frequent trips to the cemeteries in Flanders; one could not fail to be affected. "On our trip last week," Phillips wrote home on September 25, "we went as far as Bony, our last station to the north in France. (There is one beyond

Paris, 1923. Office of Graves Registration based in the Hotel d'Iena. Photographer unknown. (Author's Collection)

in Belgium.) It is near St. Quentin and Cambrai, where the British fought for four years, a wide and windy country of wheat fields, and beet fields where the wind blows incessantly and the rain falls about the same. . . . [We] came back through Cambrai and Senlis, one of the deepest devastated zones of all. . . . The magnitude of the war . . . in the shattered towns [was] most graphically revealed."[29]

Phillips reported the difficulties Majors Gibbs and Green were encountering, constructing the American cemeteries in impoverished postwar France, dealing with local customs, giving orders in two languages, and the shortage of skilled labor and materials. "It is slow work," he wrote, "[but] I am pleased to see the first planting I have done in years. It looked pretty good . . . [and] I feel I am contributing more to it than I usually did at Olmsted's."[30] He had to experiment with many plants unfamiliar to him and needed to adjust to climate and planting schedules different from his experience in North America or the tropics: "It was startling to think of them doing the work in mid winter when with us the ground would be hard as stone."[31]

Most valuable, by Phillips's own account, was the opportunity for "leisurely observation of some of the world's most notable works of landscape architecture and city building, the opportunity to revive and enlarge my knowledge of French, till then merely academic."[32] He traveled extensively in France, by official car on business, by train and foot when he was on his own. A big man, over six feet and three inches tall, Phillips was at his physical best when daily walking miles from place to place or on the job, outdoors *en plein air*. The weekly letters home describing trips in the countryside were enthusiastic in spite of recurring bouts of ennui and depression. "Paris isn't the place it was in fairer months but I . . . am still contented, or reasonably so."[33]

During the first Christmas week abroad, Phillips left Paris, spent the night in Lyons, and went on to Avignon, where he spent Christmas day prowling about, and then traveled to Arles, "the next town below where that wind [the tramontane] blew cold and clear out of the north, in a faultless sky," a memorable trip. "It was bully coming down the Rhone," he wrote, "a wonderful valley better than the Loire, far better than the Rhine. The mountains close in on it in places—snowcapped outlying masses of the *Alpes* and *Pyrannes*, and each constriction seems like a gate letting you in to a warmer region, till you come to pines and olives. At Lyons, the sun breaks through the last of the northern mists . . . [and you] come to clear skies."[34]

Hyères, in comparison to the Loire valley, was the region of winter resorts and "omnipresent English . . . [and] dull." The only good reason he could see for being there was that it was an important center for market gardening, where the climate put things at least two weeks ahead of any other part of France. The square was full of palms, eucalyptus, and "suchlike subtropical stuff." He seemed dissatisfied, with a sense of disorder— the villas "all mixed up with the market gardens," a field of artichokes in front of the hotel. He was unhappy the town was set so far back from the sea. He was lonely.

WHEN HE CAME back to Paris, Major Gibbs informed the graves office their jobs would terminate at the end of the fiscal year, June 1, 1923. Phillips was unhappy at the news. "I really hate to think of going back to the States," he wrote to his mother, "not so much because I am set on this here, as because it means taking up again the old problems of what to do, where to live. Gibbs feels more keenly than I do, with a wife and his children. We both regard the Olmsted office as a fatal whirlpool into which we may be drawn back again in spite of everything. It seems so tragic that the place should be so deadening, whereas if Olmsted were a little different type of man it would have made a fine career for all of us."[35]

Perhaps, at the back of his mind, he was still hoping to return to Panama. At some time before he left Brookline, Phillips had made an overlay to the central part of his original plan for Balboa, which Olmsted sent down to the isthmus. Now, in February 1923, Phillips received a copy of a letter written to Olmsted from the acting governor, M. L. Walker in Balboa Heights, in response to Olmsted's letter of December 14, 1922, "containing report of yourself and Mr. Phillips, on proposed additional plantings at Balboa." Walker had delayed pending the return of the governor, but as he had been delayed "beyond my expectations, I wish to express to you and to Mr. Phillips, sincere thanks for the care and attention you have given the above matter, and to say I feel sure your plan will meet with the Governor's approval." He pointed out that all government expenditures were being rigidly held down and there was at present no money "in sight" for the work. But he noted "your suggestion about Mr. Phillips, and hope when plantings are undertaken we will be in financial position to avail ourselves of Mr. Phillips's services." But nothing more transpired.

COURTSHIP AND MARRIAGE

There is always risk [in marriage]. I thought it best to take a few risks in preference to drying up and blowing away. You will regret that I did not prefer to take them with one of our friends back home. Too bad, but it was impossible, impossible.

WILLIAM PHILLIPS[36]

Phillips met his future wife on November 25, 1922, on St. Catherine's Eve: "this was undoubtedly the work of St. Catherine. It was the merest chance." He was in a Paris restaurant and just about to leave when his friend spotted the Guillots, a family he knew. They were invited to join the table.

Simone Guillot was petite, bright, lively, and musical. Barely into her twenties—Phillips was thirty-seven—she had achieved her *diplôme normale*, to teach, but had been raised primarily to be a model French wife. She had lived in Paris and Vichy, with only a short time outside France in Morocco, as *au pair* to the children of a French writer. Simone knew how to gain attention; she was "the life of the party, very gay, very youthful, who loved to dress up and sing Algerian songs." She fell in love with Phillips almost at once, and he was enchanted.

After work he would go to Pigalle, second station on the Metro east of Clichy, where the boulevard Clichy changes to de Rochechouart, to meet Simone, who lived on the rue de la Fontaine, and they would go to the Lapin Agile, run by "old Freddy in his sheepskin coat and Robinson Crusoe hat." Simone combined the exciting and exotic qualities of women Phillips met in his travels in the tropics with French common sense and the feminine qualities he admired: "God knows, [I have] been picking women to pieces for years," he wrote; "she is everything I have been looking for . . . everything American girls are not."

However, Simone was already engaged to one André Villemorin. "One of those damned arranged marriages," Phillips said, and proposed to rescue her. Simone's family was outraged. "The entire personnel of the families Guillot and Villemorin" bore down on Simone and carried her off to Béziers, where her mail was censored and she was watched night and day.

Mrs. Phillips had just heard of her son's intentions when he wrote again to say his engagement was off. "I am bitter . . . but I can continue to globe trot without domestic distraction." Simone did not give up so easily. She managed to get a letter to Phillips through good friends, telling him she was returning to her mother's home in Vichy, where they were going to marry her to André on April 30. "She told me to come and get her, and just how to do it. . . . It was not a day too soon. . . . The feast was spread, so to speak, the guests invited. I shall never forget that beautiful spring day, the 29th of March, there in the rolling fields along the Allier," wrote Phillips. "I went down to Vichy on the night train. At six o'clock [a.m.] I walked out in the deserted streets of Vichy, as nerveless as a Chinese god, fit for any conspiracy or brigandage."

Following Simone's directions to take an auto to the *école des jeunes filles* at St. Remy, the neighboring village where her mother lived and taught school, he hired "a rickety old boat that creaked along the bumpy roads, among the blooming pear trees, but pretty soon there was the school, and there was the lost Simone running down the path, throwing her arms about my neck and saying 'Phillips, Phillips! Phillips!! . . . Let me get my things and we will go,' she said, and came back with the housekeeper. It was pathetic enough, I tell you, Simone saying, 'adieu, Marguerite, adieu,' and me shaking the old lady's hand and trying not to weep. So we ran away. It was a strong mixture of joy and sadness to take her in that fashion away from the place where she had grown up, where all the village loved her, the place she was looking at, perhaps for the last time, but if you could realize how happy she is now, you would realize how little she regrets the affair."[37]

There was the problem of where Simone should live until the wedding, a civil and religious ceremony to arrange, an apartment to find in Paris, and what date to choose: "Not in May, clearly, that is unlucky. As soon as possible in June, then, when Koenig can come up to Paris to play for us."

Paul Koenig was the organist at the church of St. Pierre in Caen. Phillips went down for "bully weekends" while Simone was there. "The old town was peaceful and cool, the old room airy and the linden trees rustled outside the window and there were no sounds except the hourly bells from the steeple." They lunched under the lilac bush in the garden, visited Koenig's parents "who talked clear French," and Phillips could talk freely with them. They went up into the organ loft and listened to Koenig play; they climbed up in behind the organ "amidst the dust of centuries to look at the works, and afterwards out onto the flat roof of the side aisles of the church to look over the town." They took long walks and visited the Abbaye aux Dames, founded by the wife of William the Conqueror.

They spent a memorable day at the shore where the Koenigs had a summer villa and visited their friends, the Colniches, "aged folk of aristocratic origin. This was really an experience for me, both to get out in the Normandy country and to visit a Normandy interior. You would not believe the treasure house those old skin flints had crammed into that little old stone house—the handed on junk of generations worth thousands, perhaps hundreds of thousands of dollars. Among it was an authentic slipper of Marie Antoinette, lost on the way to the scaffold, and that I held in my hand and gazed upon."

They went back to town on a little railroad which "followed the shore for about ten miles, and then went up along the canal that leads in from the sea to Caen . . . a lovely country, [in May] fertile, deep in grass, made glad with trees, marked here and there with grey and secular towers, reminding me of the St. Lawrence between Montreal and Quebec. One could live there, it seems."

On their honeymoon, the couple left Paris and traveled to Granville, "and thence drifted along to Avranches, Pontorson, Mont St. Michel, St. Malo, Brest, and back up the Loire."[38] Then they moved into their apart-

Left: William Phillips before his wedding day. Photographer unknown. (Author's Collection)

Below: Simone Guillot Phillips on her wedding day, June 1924. Photographer unknown. (Author's Collection)

ment at 20 rue Mobitor while Phillips wound up his work at the graves office. Simone reveled in her new role. They entertained often and her husband was immensely proud of her skills as cook and hostess.

Madame Guillot was never reconciled to the marriage, although she came to Florida to visit her daughter and meet her American grandchildren, then jumped on the last boat back to Europe before the outbreak of World War II. She outlived Simone and never forgave her son-in-law for destroying her dreams for the French match.

PHILLIPS AND GIBBS had been receiving word of Olmsted Brothers' new project, at Palos Verdes, California. In April, Phillips wrote home, "Had a letter from Bill Munroe out in California, saying they need me there and outlining all sorts of advantages. I am very much inclined to go . . . whether they want me to stay here or not, if I can get a definite arrangement. I think Simone would like it better there than in the harsh climate of Boston . . . and I think there may be a future there which I have never discerned in Brookline."[39] Two weeks later he told his mother that he had heard from Olmsted, who was in California, saying "he'd be mighty glad to have me out there, so I guess we're still on good terms." Phillips knew that Olmsted had been angry when he left the firm for the graves job.

Gibbs also decided to give Olmsted Brothers another try. Gibbs had studied with Olmsted at Harvard in 1904 and was one of his "chief designers" in Olmsted Brothers, Brookline, from 1905 to 1914. He sent Olmsted, who had been a member of the Fine Arts Commission when the war graves plans were made, a full report of the activity in France. They had completed 150 plans, he said, all specs written by him, and had let out more than ten contracts involving close to eight million francs. Language and the "diplomatic side" of his job had caused him the biggest problem. He had tried hard, he wrote, to comply with the plans of the Fine Arts Commission: "Some changes were made over here rather against my advice and some . . . [were] made necessary by local conditions, but taken all together I feel that the work will be a credit to the U.S. . . . to the Commission and to the Quartermaster Corps."

He concluded by saying he was "anxious to know of any possible opportunities at home . . . [and] from my past experience I know you will be good enough to have me in mind."[40] Gibbs was generous in his praise of Phillips:

"Mr. Phillips has been a great help [and] my chief helper on walls and fences, planting and grading. . . . I hope he will stay on till fall at least to help with the engineering and inspection work in Romagna and supervise all of the cemeteries planting for there is lots to be done."[41]

The request from Gibbs that his chief helper remain in France created a dilemma for Phillips. "I can't make up my mind. . . . It would be stupid work . . . and I ought to get back into something more in my line. On the other hand, I'd have no rent [here] and could save money," and he knew that Simone wanted to stay in France a little longer.[42]

But by August, the problem was settled. "[Phillips] is worried about the quota question (for Simone) and does not like the idea of being marooned for a season, so I fear that plan may not work."[43] That month Phillips wrote home, "I have received and accepted an offer from Dawson to work in California @ $300/month. I have said I would get there early in October. It looks like a long stay . . . a several years operation. The Gibbses are going, too."[44] The Phillipses left Paris on September 13, taking a month to reach Los Angeles, with stops in Spain, Portugal, and the Azores—"a trip of no little inspirational value."[45]

RETURN TO THE UNITED STATES

Phillips's return to the Olmsted office was made difficult in ways he had not anticipated. His mother, recently widowed, accompanied her "dear children" to Redondo Beach, California, to help her daughter-in-law with a language that Simone spoke fluently, and continued to direct the least details of her son's days and lean on him for financial and domestic advice. Simone looked to her husband for guidance; he was not immediately aware of the extent of his mother's interference. Simone found herself in a new country under great emotional pressures, and her health, already poor, declined. Although her whole life was centered on Phillips, there were times when she longed for her family, and signed her letters to them, *"loin des yeux, pres du coeur"* [far from my sight, close to my heart]. Dr. Beaman Douglas, Phillips's family physician and close friend, who met Simone in Paris before the wedding and several times afterward, diagnosed her as having secondary anemia and "hysterical exhaustion" brought on by family scenes and her guilt over the many lives she had disrupted in her determined fight to marry Phillips.[46]

Simone Phillips in America. "I remember her very high but soft French voice, her dark eyes and hair drawn back, and the adoring way she looked at Uncle Bill," said Phillips's niece, Nancy Kimball Dunlap. (Author's Collection)

The California project was to be another planned community at Palos Verdes, financed by the eastern banker Frank Vanderlip and his brilliant young protégé, Harry Benedict. At first look, it seemed preferable to Phillips to the moribund Brookline office. Vanderlip and partner Benedict purchased 16,000 acres and hired Olmsted Brothers to create an exclusive colony with all the necessities and amenities.[47] The vast inland acres not desirable for residential building were sold and part became the famous Rolling Hills Golf Course. The job was a plum for Olmsted and kept the firm busy until the Depression. Set on the Pacific coast, the plan was grand: millionaire homes on generous acreage with lavish planting. Olmsted built a house for himself in the Malaga Cove area, and Phillips had land which he later sold.[48]

Despite the project's importance and success—Phillips said that Olmsted "did his best work there"—Phillips became increasingly dissatisfied with his professional as well as his difficult personal situation. Not since Balboa had he been his own master, enthusiastic and creative. The American suburban development, the special province of all of the Olmsteds, to which John Charles especially had contributed so much, now seemed to Phillips to be distressingly set in concrete, a standardized design for all sites and seasons. Here at Palos Verdes, with plenty of opportunity and money for real creativity, he found himself once again doing "mostly humdrum office work under people whose talents never impressed me, on subdivisions, gardens, parks."[49]

"Palos Verdes was never developed according to the original grand plans, due to the Depression," Harry's son Russell Benedict said. "Our house, for example, remained on the drawing board and we moved into the servants' quarters, which had, by the way, six bedrooms and a four-car garage. We were a bigoted lot, to be sure, but believed our servants should live well." After World War II, Palos Verdes boomed into a large, freer-to-the-public community with a wider economic range.[50] Phillips remained on the job until December 1924. During that time he had a "memorable trip over the road to Seattle where I laid out and tied down a subdivision of about 100 acres. Into the Yosemite on the way back."[51]

In December, Phillips left for a fifteen-day trip to Boca Grande, Florida, stayed for three months, and "worked out a subdivision plan for the entire island. . . . [It] came to nothing when the owners, the American Agricultural Chemical Company, decided to quit the real estate business."[52] At the close of the job, Olmsted asked Phillips to continue in Florida as his representative, on a planned community in the making at Mountain Lake Colony, Lake Wales. It was March, and Florida was at its best. Simone, who was with him, agreed they should stay. "But you must remember," Dr. Douglas wrote to Phillips, when he heard they were going to move there, "[while the] primitive conditions [of] a pioneer life . . . seem interesting to a man . . . [it will be] very strange for [Simone to be] planted down in the hot Everglades away from everything she knew."[53]

PART III

Lake Wales, Florida, 1925–1933

A period of real accomplishment.
WILLIAM LYMAN PHILLIPS[1]

THE MOUNTAIN LAKE COLONY was originally planned and administered in 1914 by a Baltimore and New York developer named Frederick Ruth, and later his brother Tom, as a membership organization holding title to unsold land and also owning and managing citrus groves. The colony was to be in effect a club, a private enclave with restricted membership, following the practice of many private American suburbs created during the first decades of the twentieth century: closed to Jews, Negroes, the Irish, and Poles. Olmsted examples include Forest Hills Gardens in Queens, New York, Roland Park, and Palos Verdes.[2]

Ruth put together an inviting prospectus and invited F. L. Olmsted Jr. to suggest initial lot divisions and create an overall expandable plan for his new colony, so that as more lots were sold, it could grow without disturbing the basic concept and design. He chose Olmsted based on what he knew of the Olmsteds' work for Roland Park in Baltimore, where Ruth had grown up; Ruth saw it as a possible prototype.

The land was divided into estates, for prosperous, often distinguished winter residents who were captivated with the area and the bonus of buying into the groves. They were equally delighted with the tax break from growing citrus, and the promise that on a purchase of ten acres of the orange grove, they would get their money back and make a profit within six years. The corporation provided caretaking services for members and looked after community grounds: roads, golf course, and the Colony clubhouse and its restaurant and pool. Prospective owners were introduced to architects and builders recommended by the Olmsted firm.

Ruth was already involved in several large real estate enterprises on the East Coast. He was an excellent salesman and something of a visionary. In 1907, he and his brother Tom had been offered thirty-five dollars an acre for their two thousand acres in Polk County, Florida, which their father had purchased in 1885 for $1.25 to $1.65 an acre.[3] Ruth took his lawyer and went down to see what he had.

It was not the orange that had brought the first investors there but the vast deposits of phosphate discovered in 1883, which stimulated a man named Henry Plant to build the Tampa-Jacksonville Railroad in the same year. By 1911, the Atlantic Coastline Railroad came to Lake Wales, bringing materials for turpentine manufacture and taking the product back out to market; there were thousands of acres of virgin pine woods in the vicinity. Lake Wales grew out of this activity and by 1914 had a twenty-five-room hotel, a newspaper, and Tampa–St. Petersburg air service.

When Ruth and his attorney made that first trip to Florida, they drove eighteen miles from the town of Bartow by horse and buggy over sandy trails through the pines, past occasional lakes and ponds surrounded by hardwoods. To Ruth's delight he found a sportsman's heaven: bream, perch, black bass; dove, quail, wild turkey, and duck; deer, bear, Florida panther, and twelve-foot alligators. He also found a sawmill, strings of lakes, citrus groves, and the smell of orange blossoms everywhere.[4] Ruth did not sell.

In 1916, Olmsted made a preliminary plan for Mountain Lake Colony, in which the lots and groves were laid out to take advantage of the paths and trails to the lake made by hunters, animals, and fishermen. Although Olmsted designed the clubhouse, the architects, Charles R. Wait and Franklin Abbot, were commissioned to design many of the colony's houses along five miles of lakefront. Internationally acclaimed expert Seth J. Raynor was hired to lay out the Mountain Lake golf course for the 1916–17 season; an instructor and stable of horses were available for riding on the miles of roads within the Colony grounds, and the tennis courts were built of special resilient material by the same man who had done them at Forest Hills.

By the end of 1918, Mountain Lake Colony comprised 2,800 acres; by 1930, the area had grown to 3,500 acres. Twenty-one houses had been constructed by 1923. After Phillips came in 1925, there were twenty-one more; by 1930, another thirty-two. A 1950 brochure map listed seventy-three resi-

Mountain Lake Sanctuary, Lake Wales, Florida. Looking toward the Bok Tower from the Mountain Lake Colony road, 1950s. (Author's Collection)

dences at Mountain Lake Colony, many of which were occupied by a series of owners who wanted Phillips to design and produce instant gardens.

The Phillipses settled at Mountain Lake for seven years. As Olmsted representative for Mountain Lake Colony and the Mountain Lake Sanctuary, Edward Bok's dream park, Phillips was extremely busy: "Very much on my own for the most part, and often without office help, I laid out and supervised the execution of many gardens and estates."[5] He was designing, keeping a labor force occupied, keeping clients happy, answering for Olmsted to clients, making decisions for Olmsted, answering to Olmsted.

This arrangement was often farcical and very time-consuming for Phillips. He was required to send daily reports and wires to Brookline; their replies were delayed when Olmsted was in transit. He put in his daily time sheets once a month and submitted bills for hired labor and materials. Phillips received a salary of two dollars an hour ($360 per month plus expenses) from 1928 to 1931; Olmsted Brothers billed the clients five to ten dollars an hour for Phillips's services, plus costs, plus Olmsted's time whenever he came to the job or for his time writing reports. Over the years Phillips would get fed up with the whole arrangement; Olmsted would recommend him for an overseas job or send him out on a scouting trip. In 1931, he sent Phillips on a quick visit to Europe, but so far, Olmsted had never let him go for long.

MOUNTAIN LAKE COLONY occupied only part of the Ruths' holdings in Lake Wales. Immediately adjacent to the estates was Iron Mountain, sacred ground to the Seminole Indians and the highest point in south-central Florida at 324 feet above sea level; in Florida, this was considered a mountain. The Seminoles and their religion were not uppermost in anyone's mind; at the time they were considered—if at all—as curiosities, wrestling alligators or selling their crafts in colorful dress in "Seminole villages."

One of the earliest residents of Mountain Lake Colony was Edward William Bok, author and editor of the *Ladies Home Journal*. He had married into the Curtis family, noted for its high-minded commitment to education and philanthropy, and had lived in Philadelphia until his retirement. In 1919 he bought a winter home in the Colony. He was enchanted with central Florida and the mountain property. He soon acquired fifty more acres of mountaintop and slopes from Ruth for the purpose of creating a beautiful, serene sanctuary: a refuge for "birds and small animals and humans." The preserve would also fulfill his grandmother's injunction to her family to make the world "a better or more beautiful place for having lived in it."[1]

Bok had met Olmsted at Mountain Lake Colony prior to his purchase of the parkland and thought the landscape architect was a perceptive designer who could help him achieve his dream. He asked Olmsted to walk the property he had just purchased and to discuss the project with him. The idea of a sanctuary filled with indigenous plants for native and migratory birds appealed to Olmsted, too. Olmsted described his vision of the sanctuary in letters to Bok, but construction had to be delayed until the war was over. The sanctuary site would remain a "pine-clad hill with a rough tangle of under brush" well into 1923, when Hans Koehler was sent from the Brookline office to do the first planting.[2]

After a few visits to the area before Koehler arrived, Olmsted called for a pond and nature trails and suggested a plan to bring thousands of plants from the surrounding Ruth land when the time came, to augment inadequate nursery stock and make what he called groves, thickets, and bushy pastures. Olmsted, like his father before him, did not draw plans. He gave suggestions and directions on-site, made notes for future referral, and left the drawing to his office draftsmen and designers. However, he was always directly involved in engineering requirements. He designed an extensive road and irrigation system and agreed to provide preliminary estimates for parking areas and necessary boundary and road changes when additional land was acquired.

Phillips was asked to assume the supervision of design and planting at Mountain Lake Sanctuary when he became Olmsted's representative at Mountain Lake Colony. "I was in immediate charge of the later and more striking developments at the Mountain Lake Sanctuary of Edward W. Bok, on which, however, Mr. Olmsted exercised close oversight."[3]

From the outset Bok announced his intention to make his sanctuary for the public, but the original grounds were open only to him and his friends and neighbors at the Colony: the access was private, from the Colony side. The scale of the parklike sanctuary was intimate—appropriate, Phillips wrote, only for residential grounds. A path, cleverly curved for best "dramatic impact," wound up through woods on the north slope of the mountain, bordered with a dense screen of cabbage palms and other native growth, to the manmade pond on the hilltop. Now, to the west, a terrace had to be built to command a broad view; the mountain top would be transformed into a plateau, with a "classic grove" of live oaks to be planted, and the pond greatly enlarged to make a reflecting pool for the future tower.

In 1924 the first planting of many to come included over 1,000 live oaks, 10,000 azaleas, 100 Sabal palms, 300 magnolias, more than 500 gordonias, the southeastern "Black Laurel," which grows to a large tree with yellow-centered white flowers, and 10,000 sword and Boston ferns.

The first planting was dense. Live oaks and magnolias in small size were set in with masses of predominantly laurel cherry, gallberry, and *Cattleya*

Mountain Lake Sanctuary. A woodland path bordered by lilies and ferns, azaleas, cabbage palms, and hardwoods, 1950s. (Author's Collection)

guava; planted trees and shrubs thrive best in a close community. The specific intention was that, "by natural process and human intervention," the density would be reduced, a long-time procedure to create natural or quasinatural scenery. Olmsted called for this procedure to provide the quick effect Bok expected, confident that Phillips would thin out and remove excess planting when the time came.

With Olmsted's approval, Phillips introduced many "exotic" plants, including jasmines, especially *Jasminum mesnyi* (primrose jasmine from China), *Bauhinias*—the orchid tree, *Durantas repens* (the pigeon berry and golden dewdrop from the West Indies and Martinique), cymbidiums, ginger lilies, several varieties of vines (especially the red flame vine, *Pyrostegia venusta*), palms, azaleas, camellias, and acacias. Phillips was particularly enthusiastic about the Australian acacia varieties, which were handsome and would grow well in the comparable climate. The plant list Phillips compiled for the sanctuary contained 60 families and about 185 species, all of which he had observed in growth and knew to be successful in Lake Wales.

FROM THE MOMENT work on the sanctuary gardens began, so did construction of the singing tower, the Bok Tower carillon, modeled at Bok's request on the four-hundred-year-old tower at Malines, Belgium. Of Georgia marble and Florida coquina stone, fifty-seven feet wide at the base and thirty-seven feet at the top, it achieved the height—two hundred and five feet—needed to give the necessary sweep for the sound of the bells. The tower stood in the center of fifty acres protecting the area from unwelcome noise. Completed, it "immediately dominated the composition [of the garden]," Phillips said, for placed at the center and at the summit of the grounds, it rose to five hundred feet above sea level. Sabal and other palms surrounded the

Mountain Lake Sanctuary. Open parkland, 1950s. (Author's Collection)

Mountain Lake Sanctuary. Bok Tower, facing the moat. (Photograph courtesy of Bok Tower Gardens)

Mountain Lake Sanctuary. The moat from the opposite end, 1950s. (Author's Collection)

fifteen-foot moat, in which grew water iris and spider lilies, designed and planted under Phillips's supervision. First he oversaw Olmsted's plan, and later he "corrected the math" so that the whole tower was reflected dead center in the pool.[4]

To transform the sanctuary into a public park, an admission booth, additional roads and parking space, a gift shop, restaurant, restrooms, and offices would be needed. Phillips designed a new parking lot on the east side for Colony residents, sanctuary director, and carillonneur, increasing the existing shrubbery masses for greater privacy to allay Colony management fears; they were paranoid about wandering tourists.

Enlargement of the sanctuary began in 1926 under Phillips's direction. Olmsted studied Phillips's plans, usually when he was on the train between other jobs, and sent back his opinions, usually sound, sometimes an inspired flash, then left his representative to think it through. This had gone

Mountain Lake Sanctuary. The oak grove. (Courtesy of Bok Tower Gardens)

on for years between them, Olmsted searching out the big project, Phillips filling in the details and correcting the composition. The challenge for Phillips was to retain the intimate scene while extending the existing private place to accommodate many visitors, while enlarging the park and adding new features and facilities—the Resurrection garden, Tower Grove of live oaks, designing and creating a wildlife pond and new reflecting pool—and while developing panoramic vistas to the east, south, and west. He wanted to retain the special atmosphere which would be, he said, "agreeable . . . the refreshment of greenery and water in a somewhat parched land, the oasis effect, shade and play of light. . . . The effect was achieved by differing size and shape of masses, and all of the openings varied in size, orientation, surface modelling, inclination."[5]

Bok was frankly ambivalent about strangers in his once private preserve, in spite of his original high-minded resolve. Although he deeded the sanctuary in 1924 to the American Foundation, which he created and endowed for future direction and maintenance, he remained in control for the present.

And while he appreciated the garden's beauty and serenity, Bok was no gardener and had no idea of the costs and maintenance required.

On February 1, 1929, President Calvin Coolidge and entourage came to Lake Wales to dedicate Mountain Lake Sanctuary in all its beauty to the people of the nation for visitation. It was a culminating moment for Bok, who believed that now the park could be maintained with just a few men to clip borders and trim the paths.

Increasing irritation set in about the monthly bills from the Olmsted office. When the firm sent down from the north a carload of plants that proved unsuccessful, Bok blamed Olmsted and more specifically Phillips, who was directly on the scene. He was "fed up," Bok told Olmsted, and tired of spending money on "filling vacancies." Not too much was ever said, however, about the depredation by imported birds, which Bok did not want to enclose in pens; the flamingoes were eating up all the new vegetation!

Other disputes had erupted previously. In the summer of 1927, Bok purchased in Camden, Maine, sixteen pink horse chestnut trees, which he ordered the director, retired Major H. M. Nornabell, to plant on the east side of the sanctuary plateau—the very heart of Olmsted's plan—"at regular intervals of 20 feet apart, alternating with *Parkinsonia* . . . in a fairly straight line." Nornabell asked Phillips to "mention [it] to Mr. Olmsted."[6]

Olmsted was furious that Bok, without consulting him, had gone far beyond the usual client-designer relationship, with no regard for the composition of the sanctuary or the integrity of its design. As Olmsted wrote and told him, Bok was about to ruin

the artistic unity of conception in the several compositions of the Sanctuary for which I have striven so hard . . . the beginning of the end of the Sanctuary as a worthy work of art.

I have been from the first deeply interested in guiding the work on the Sanctuary, so as to make it . . . a highly beautiful expression of ideas which I derived from *you* and have always been happy to comply with [your suggested] improvements [developing and modifying] my original conception, based, again, on [your] ideas. [Therefore,] if I seem to be reacting more feelingly and more strongly than the nature of this proposal seems to you to justify . . . it is because no one who is not himself a

practicing artist in any given field can realize what apparently slight
touches of detail . . . [make the] difference between good art and bad. . . .

In order to continue to produce such a work of art, [I must have]
artistic control over the artistic expression of all the details in the picture. And in the last analysis, you will have to take it on faith from me
. . . that this proposal, unless it has been radically misinterpreted to me,
simply will not fit in.[7]

Three months later, Phillips reported that the "18 pink horse chestnut trees
sent down by Mr. Bok were planted in the original Sanctuary grounds,"
not where Bok had wanted them, but "in an area centering about 400 feet
to the northeast of the tower." Phillips had quietly saved the day, but the
relationship between Bok and Olmsted had cooled considerably.[8]

Edward Bok died in 1930. His widow and son took control and seemed
to underrate Phillips's contribution. Mrs. Bok frequently asked Olmsted if
it were really necessary to have an expensive landscape architect supervising maintenance work. Olmsted said yes, it was.[9]

By 1931 the expansion of Mountain Lake Sanctuary was complete. Phillips made the map, and as he noted in 1956, "The layout was firmly established in 1931, and has persisted to this day without change in any essential
feature."[10]

Phillips and Simone at Lake Wales, c. 1926–28.
Photographer unknown. (Author's Collection)

PHILLIPS WAS NEVER disturbed unduly by the attitude of the Boks or by any Mountain Lake Colony client. He was at this stage of his life almost overproductive; indestructible as a rock, he knew his own worth and was satisfied with the quality of his work. He was happy with his wife and, soon, two daughters; they were all he desired. In spite of the two Mountain Lake projects, which consumed much of his time, he was concurrently doing a good deal of independent work.

On Olmsted's behalf and often with Simone at his side, almost as soon as he arrived in Florida Phillips began a private enquiry into state park possibilities in Florida. He was on the board of the Roeblings' Highland Hammock Park at Sebring, consulted with Ernest Coe on the latter's campaign to make an Everglades National Park, and explored possibilities for Olmsted and Bok to purchase land at Tiger Creek, beyond Mountain Lake Sanctuary. And having crisscrossed the state so many times, he "became very familiar with the scenery and the major features of the floristics." Also for Olmsted, he "laid out two or three subdivisions, made a town plan and report for [the rapidly growing town of] Lake Wales, designed small Inman Park Cemetery for the Winter Haven Garden Club, and Tony Jannus Park, of some size, for the Tampa club; did a planting improvement on a boulevard at Tampa and located a river down there."[1]

Phillips soon received requests from clients to design gardens for them, independent of Olmsted Brothers. These commissions came to him through word of mouth, his garden club work, and socially. Phillips's cousins Amy Phillips and her sister, Mrs. Gertrude Manigault, came to Palm Beach every season and Amy often wrote for the society page of the *Palm Beach News.* She knew everybody and the Phillipses visited often.

Casa Alejandro, Palm Beach, Florida. The terrace side of the house, c. 1929–30. (Author's Collection)

Casa Alejandro. Tiled pools along the central axis, which runs directly from the bas-relief above the door to the bottom of the garden. (Author's Collection)

Casa Alejandro. Entrance court-yard. Phillips makes effective use of Florida coquina paving, laid in a seemingly random design. Hibiscus massed against the stairway, bougainvillea vine, and lush green planting cut the glare. (Author's Collection)

Casa Alejandro. Side garden. Profusion of citrus and shade-loving flowering plants in tubs. (Author's Collection)

The first contract, the result of cousin Amy's "wanting to give me a personal boost," was with Mrs. George Alexander McKinlock of Chicago, Palm Beach, Saratoga, and the Ritz (New York). Widow of the organizer of Chicago's Electric Company, donor of McKinlock Hall to Harvard College—in memory of her son, G. A. McKinlock Jr., killed in World War I—and involved with various charities, she was the first president of the Palm Beach Garden Club and remained in that position for years. A long-time member of Palm Beach's "real Old Guard—an autocratic widow matriarchy," she wanted William Phillips to design a garden for her.[2]

Phillips explained his connection with Olmsted Brothers. She was unmoved; she wanted Phillips to do her garden. He took the question directly to Olmsted, who wrote to the Brookline office from Palos Verdes: "Note the inclosed [sic] correspondence with Phillips. This matter of outside personal work is an old story. I think Phillips's voluntary action in re-

Casa Alejandro. The bottom of the garden. A tangle of palms and native growth with a clear view out to sea. (Author's Collection)

Phillips, left, at the patio and pool he designed for the Holland Inn. Photographer unknown. (Author's Collection)

McKee Jungle Gardens, Vero Beach, Florida (c. 1930?). Amazing reflection at the naturalistic swimming pool. Having hacked his way many times through overgrowth to make a clearing, Phillips enjoyed helping to create a jungle. (Photograph courtesy of Indian River Land Trust Save McKee Committee)

McKee Jungle Gardens. The arbor, past the long avenue of royal palms, was often used for weddings. (Photograph courtesy of Indian River Land Trust Save McKee Committee)

porting to the office the time he spends on such outside work is a very good way for handling it and I think such a method should be encouraged by not charging a man up for the time so reported unless it proves to be a serious matter. If it is kept as a separate memo account and not passes [*sic*] through the books unless it proves to be serious, I think it will save trouble all around, don't you?"[3]

The letter went the office rounds for initial approval and signature: "Seems a good way in P's case but not for general use," was the consensus.

"Is this all right for you?" Olmsted wrote to Phillips. In a rather convoluted way, he outlined a suggested plan whereby Phillips would owe an amount of hours to Olmsted Brothers; anything that cut into this would be charged against his salary. With Phillips on a creative roll for the firm as well as for himself, Olmsted did not want to cut him loose.

According to Olmsted, however, at the end of 1926, the record showed Phillips behind in hours for Olmsted Brothers, and his salary was docked $18.40. Phillips protested, which he rarely did, but Simone was in the hospital and he was worried: "It is true I took a long vacation last fall but I don't know [that] anyone who has put in two successive summers work in this climate would consider it too long," he wrote to Whiting.[4]

Whiting answered. "Mr. Olmsted (who is away) was going to talk . . . with you, but apparently he did not. I have now looked into [it] more carefully and find that your hour class . . . on the books is somewhat higher than . . . the men . . . doing similar work. This seems to me to be entirely unreasonable and would of course account [for your dropping] behind in the yearly total of hours. I am therefore dropping your class to 2150 hours/year which will . . . straighten things out. And furthermore I am destroying the bill . . . because I think Mr. Olmsted did not fully realize the situation."[5]

Winter Haven, Florida. Corner of a private patio. (Author's Collection)

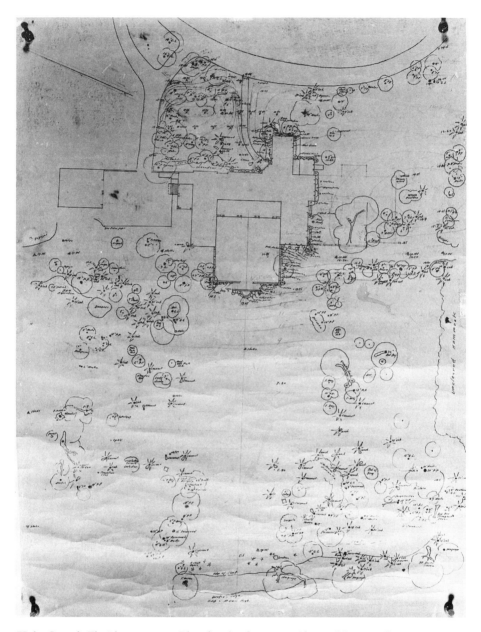

Hobe Sound, Florida, 1929–30. Plan for the former residence "Corsaire," now a private club. (Courtesy of Otto G. Richter Library, Special Collections, University of Miami, Coral Gables, Florida)

It was an agreement that marked a great change in the Olmsted-Phillips relationship, and they both knew it.

Mrs. McKinlock's stunning garden was all that the Garden Club president could want: "[She] lives in the Vita Serena area in a cathedral-like villa named Casa Alejandro . . . with a beautiful garden patio shaded by palm and banana trees and separated from the rest of Vita Serena by a high wall trellised with ivy and bougainvillea."[6] The terraces were laid in an ordered pattern of native stone on different levels, a large open space with a central fountain on the lowest, a small fountain pool with raised edge for pots on the smaller patio, which faced the ocean. Grand, indeed; nevertheless there was also a likeness to the typical comfortable architecture of Florida's early days, with porches on both floors to catch prevailing breezes, a style Phillips much admired.

Nor was this all. As Phillips's resume sums up other work in this period, "Did, independently, hotels and gardens elsewhere in the state; also, independently advised on McKee Jungle Gardens at Vero Beach, a spot which has achieved some local fame."[7]

AS MORE HOUSES were built in Mountain Lake Colony, demands upon Phillips increased; his work load was phenomenal. He continued to receive rave reviews from clients: "Dear Mr. Phillips—The charm and beauty [of my] garden is beyond my expectations . . . even in its unfinished state, and when the trees and shrubs are grown and the hedges clipped it will be simply perfect."[1]

Gardens for the winter estates seemed often lavish, on relatively small lots of one to three acres. Neighboring clients living side by side wanted and expected Phillips to provide them with elegance and one-of-a-kind landscape design. He was ingenious at making houses and grounds appear different from each other, although much of the available plant material had to be the same: palms, citrus, semitropical shrubs and vines, and longleaf pines. His driveway designs were long and winding or came straight up to the doorway that faced the Colony road or lake. He often used sharply defined plants—yucca or agave—and handsome terra-cotta pots to dramatize an entrance. He excavated sunken gardens and created shaded patios of grass, rolling lawns, swimming pools, and fountains. For the most part, Colony houses were tinted stucco, pale coral, or white with Spanish tile roofs. There were exceptions: ranch houses with simple gardens that preserved native pines around them and shuttered white New England–style houses with sloping lawns bordered with great beds of flowering annuals.

In his designs for Mountain Lake Colony landscapes, Phillips paid particular attention to the need for privacy. As the winter "cottages" became ever grander, the plots on which they stood seemed to shrink. It was hard to maintain privacy and beauty within a given space that would be distinctly individual and yet compatible with the gardens on either side.

Lake Wales, Florida, 1925–32. Five miles of waterfront view for Mountain Lake Colony residents. (Author's Collection)

Mountain Lake Colony. Phillips always saved the longleaf pines (*Pinus palustris*) wherever possible. Here he leaves the large lawn clear of other planting to suit the proportions of the house. (Author's Collection)

Mountain Lake Colony. A long, dramatic entrance drive, with free use of cabbage palms. (Author's Collection)

Mountain Lake Colony. This owner requested thickly planted flower borders along the curved entrance drive. (Author's Collection)

Mountain Lake Colony. The garden behind the house on page 94 (*bottom*). The stone figures line the boundary wall. (Author's Collection)

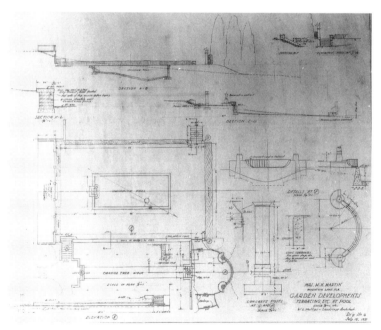

Mountain Lake Colony. Plan of the garden developments at the residence shown on page 94 (*bottom*) and this page (*above*). (Courtesy of the Otto G. Richter Library, Special Collections, University of Miami, Coral Gables, Florida)

Above: Mountain Lake Colony. "Design notes": Phillips drew on photograph of the house front for the new owner, showing his plan for trees and shrubs at full growth. (Author's Collection)

Left: Mountain Lake Colony. Phillips's continuing design notes, side view of the home above. He paid particular attention to future vines, corner and foundation planting, and hedged walkway. (Author's Collection)

Under his direction, plants harmonized from one garden to the next, and if the view from one lot was better, Phillips would design something especially lovely for the other. Boundaries define possession, he said; in the case of adjacent properties, they must enclose the space to satisfy pride of ownership, without becoming claustrophobic.

Phillips's solutions came from regarding Mountain Lake Colony's houses as varying integrals in an overall context that contributed to the total design. It was this complete picture, which he saw so clearly, that challenged Phillips and made him very proud. He felt that he had created a whole

village, which needed all of his tact and patience when it came to ease-
ments, common fences, and the choice of decorative borders, which all
required agreement between the landowners sharing boundaries.

ONE OF PHILLIPS's major problems when he first worked in Lake Wales was
to acquire the thousands of plants necessary to implement his design
schemes. Plants go in and out of fashion, like everything else. Phillips was
always searching for new material and unusual species that would meet his
climate and soil conditions. Mountain Lake Colony and Mountain Lake
Sanctuary depended on his own informal nurseries on-site and his constant
encouragement and promotion of nurseries throughout the state. The list
included the Glen St. Mary Nurseries in Glen St. Mary; Royal Palm Nurseries in Onoco; N. A. Reasoner in Bradenton; Southern States Nursery;
Winter Haven Nurseries, Inc., and Mulford B. Foster in Orlando. Many of
the state's best growers came to depend on customers Phillips brought them,
on his knowledge, and on the seeds he collected from around the world and

Left: Mountain Lake Colony. Notes for same house, side view extending to wall at edge of
grass terrace, with Phillips's continuing design for the garden facing the lake. The size of each
owner's view and the amount of privacy often depended on the neighbor's planting. Phillips
draws another tall evergreen, right, to balance the one on left. (Author's Collection)

Right: Mountain Lake Colony. Design notes for a driveway coming off a shared Colony road.
It is hard to tell whether the shrub at the corner left is intended to close off the left road.
Clearly, the silhouette of a *callitris* at left and rounded canopy on right are for privacy. (Author's
Collection)

Left: Mountain Lake Colony. Phillips's record of developing a formal property: garden excavation. (Author's Collection)

Below right: Continuing development of the same property: elegant pool and arbor wall in place. (Author's Collection)

Mountain Lake Colony. Striking formal arrangement of garden beds and palms growing well since preparation. Note the special design of the clipped borders, requiring high maintenance to preserve. (Author's Collection)

shared with them. He propagated plants himself and encouraged others in the business to do the same.

Phillips's clients constantly wanted plants that simply would not survive in their climate. Azaleas, rhododendrons, the gingers, beds of blue plumbago, magnolias, and camellias were not enough; they wanted to plant outdoors all the exotics that grew in their conservatories, craving orchids, heliconias, frangipani, *Pachira* (white or pink shaving brush), glorious pink and yellow *Tabebuia* trees. It seemed inconceivable to many gardeners that where oranges flourished, as they did in Lake Wales, tropicals would not,

In vain, Phillips tried to explain that wherever the coconut palm and the mango grew—*that* was tropical—and no coconut or mango tree would exist in central Florida.

He was further challenged by northern clients who clamored for color in the garden. Proponents of natural Florida gardens (and Phillips often was) point to the subtleties of predominant grey and varying greens, drawing their compositional effect from their conjunction, differing textures, height and size of leaves, and muted colors.

Mountain Lake Colony. Elegant simplicity in outside wall treatment. Delicate vines (possibly *Thunbergia fragrans*) float down between soft-leaved trees; symmetrically placed jars with sansevaria and agaves widen the picture. (Author's Collection)

A dramatic thick-beamed arbor is an integral part of the residence. (Author's Collection)

In discussing his early Florida years, Phillips wrote to David Fairchild: "I could say horticulture in Miami in 1946 is not what it was in Mountain Lake in 1926. Then I felt myself to be somewhat on the frontiers of knowledge. We were breaking new ground, both figuratively and literally, in residence development. I had to work out a whole new technic, for structural materials as well as for planting. There is no doubt that I established practices which became standard. I was something of an authority. Now the sort of knowledge I had has become the commonest sort of knowledge."[2]

Mountain Lake Colony. Phillips, at the peak of his Colony success, beside a client's pool. Photographer unknown. (Author's Collection)

Mountain Lake Colony. Phillips's special fountain design at the end of a pool. (Author's Collection)

In truth, he was also partly responsible for some of the growth of south and central Florida's most rampant pests: Brazilian pepper, camphor trees, cherry laurel, casuarina, the beautiful silver-barked melaleuca. Phillips warned clients repeatedly that these untended plants would proliferate; during the Depression when gardeners were laid off, and with the man-power shortage of the war years, birds and seedlings spread the pests state-wide. Of the casuarina, which he was often directed to plant along state roadways, Phillips later wrote to William Vanderbilt, "I am less than en-thusiastic . . . it's a perpetual nuisance, very seldom a joy. Unless [for] a permanent windbreak. . . .[In other areas] strips of native hammock—sea grapes and cabbage palms—would be better."[3]

But of all Phillips's Colony gardens, the one upon which he lavished the greatest care, even passion, was El Retiro, his finest.

In 1929 the vice president of Bethlehem Steel, Charles Austin Buck, visited his sister at her Mountain Lake Colony home. While there, he pur-

Mountain Lake Colony. Phillips designed these cleverly turned stairs to make the distance seem greater from swimming pool to lake view. (Author's Collection)

Mountain Lake Colony. The swimming pool and surrounding area enjoy a broad view of Bok Tower across the lake. (Author's Collection)

Mountain Lake Colony. A private meditation bench with a table beside it in a serene corner. (Author's Collection)

chased about eight acres of land in the section of the development directly adjacent to Mountain Lake Sanctuary. On the basis of the residential land-scapes Phillips was designing for other owners, Buck decided to hire Phillips to work for him.

As a young man, Buck had worked in Cuba, and he wanted his house to reflect the easy Latin lifestyle he remembered, in which one moved easily from cool interiors to outdoor patios with palms and agaves and bright flowering plants in tubs, and where he could sit and look at the rest of his gardens beyond terrace walls. Phillips understood completely, from his own days in the tropics. He would work with enthusiasm to make Buck's dream a reality.

Phillips did not recommend calling in the architect, Charles Wait, until many basic landscape decisions had been made. An architect himself, he may have considered doing all of the plans as well as the landscape design; but presumably the press of other work stopped him. As it was, he had considerable input, dictating almost all of the basic decisions to Wait, and the house bears the Phillips stamp inside and out. Nonetheless, this trium-virate of two professionals and a passionate amateur gardener enjoyed a remarkable and unhurried collaboration until 1932. Wait was happy to work

El Retiro, later renamed Pinewood, 1932–33. Entrance drive from Mountain Lake Road. Phillips was committed to this house, from site plan to building to designing and planting the gardens, as if it were his own. (Author's Collection)

Above: Pinewood. First sight of house with great *tinajones* (jars) on either side of front door. (Author's Collection)

Left: Pinewood. The frog fountain on front terrace. Was it a copy of its twin in front of a residence in the old town of Panama, Canal Zone, now the French Embassy? (Photograph courtesy of Bok Tower Gardens)

with Phillips, who "added that touch which made each undertaking out-standing."[4]

El Retiro is considered to be one of the best examples of the Mediterra-nean revival style in Florida. Many of the Colony houses reflected the strong Spanish influence fashionable in Florida in the 1920s and 1930s, lavishly exemplified by Addison Mizner's ducal mansions in Palm Beach, afford-able only to the megarich. This influence had already been there since the founding of the state and before, but that highly colorful scamp of American architecture "helped create the modern Spanish trend in the state

Left: Pinewood. The moon gate garden. Phillips's plan called for a ligustrum hedge bordered by blue and yellow annuals. (Author's Collection)

Below: Pinewood. Facing the great lawn. (Author's Collection)

[Florida] of Spanish origin [and] was accused of inventing a style 'more Mizner than Spanish.' [He] combined Italian and Moorish and Spanish in his architecture and when combing the Mediterranean became too burdensome to accumulate doors, wrought iron and tile, he established a factory where he created these adjuncts 'in the Mediterranean manner'."[5] Mizner's glamorous rise and fall did not really impact Ruth's solid conservatives at Mountain Lake Colony, who spent their money quietly and dissociated themselves from the raucous side of the Florida boom.

Wait combined elegance and simplicity of form with livability—the result of thick stucco walls and cross ventilation. Care was taken to give the house an aged appearance: the salmon-colored exterior paint, chosen to cut sun glare, was smoked and mottled, and the fast-climbing creeping fig, *Ficus pumila*, soon appeared to have been in place for decades.

Phillips based his landscape design around a long central axis, beginning in a rondel of cypress pines (*Callitris verrucosa*) at the southeast boundary of the property near the entrance and running to a pond on the western

Pinewood. The house reflected in the pond Phillips made in "an otherwise uninteresting corner" at the bottom of the great lawn. (Author's Collection)

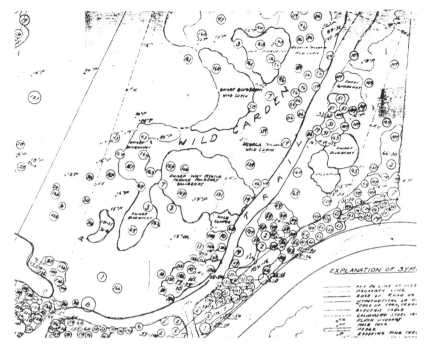

Pinewood. Plan of the wildflower garden. Phillips was not keen on it, knowing that such areas often become unkempt or simply die of neglect, but the owner insisted, so Phillips included in the varied planting hardy blueberries, wild coffee, and lupines in an area near the bosque and hoped for the best. (Author's Collection)

edge, which formed a long vista from the house. The line runs through the center of the house, which is set north-south. On the west side, house and garden are on the same level, doorsill to grass, producing the easy indoor-outdoor access that Buck sought.

At the lowest point of the property on this, the west side, Phillips carefully designed a "naturalistic cloverleaf pond," as he wrote to Buck in August 1930, "to make a view, which otherwise would be uninspiring." It was also an inviting stroll, down across the lawn with several 165-year-old longleaf pines (*Pinus palustris*), particularly saved by Phillips, or through the bosque—a wooded grove planted specifically for this purpose—encircling the great park. From the house could be seen a grove of sabal palms, a bench, a magnificent dogwood, two of the ten *tinajones*—big terra-cotta oil jars Buck purchased in Cuba to enhance the garden's Mediterranean appearance—and the pond, reflecting the house, tree trunks, and sky. Phillips imaginatively combined an English-style park with Spanish and Italian influences, to include even more eclectic features such as the moon gate, grotto, and Jekyllian borders.

A walled moon gate garden at the northwest corner of the house was conceived as an extension of the dining and breakfast rooms: within is a rectangular lawn bordered by paths and low beds of blue, white, and yellow annuals, backed by a ligustrum hedge. A small fountain was placed behind the octagonal gate. "The Chinese," wrote Phillips, "placed a decorated screen behind the opening to keep out evil spirits, who can only travel in a straight line."[6] But although Phillips recommended and Richard Bassett, former Olmstedian, now an artist, designed it, Buck never agreed to build the screen.

The front of the house, the east side, had the lesser view. At its far end, on a slight rise, Phillips situated an orchard of citrus in variety. The fruit trees marked the edges of allées—paths between rows of citrus or loquat trees—planned to divide the space into pie-shaped wedges meeting at a rondel.

Below this slope was the formal front entrance. Buck vetoed Phillips's original design, a covered walk to take visitors to the front door. "Your decision put me momentarily out of gear," Phillips wrote to his client, and he went back to the drawing board. "However, after considerable study, I've come to the conclusion that a good looking open arrangement can be made . . . [with] a revision of the garden plan as well as of the entrance itself." There would be a delay to accommodate the "growth of green screens instead of masonry . . . [but] I believe," Phillips added, "it will result in something quite satisfactory from a technical viewpoint, and more in line with your tastes."[7] Between door and orchard Phillips laid out a series of stairs with colored tile risers. A terrace of gray coquina—Florida oolitic limestone—was bordered with formal plantings and Buck's requested profusion of pots and flowering tubs, with agaves, *Strelitzias*, and tinajones marking the corners. A tiled frog fountain, a replica of one still to be seen today in a residential garden in Panama, was placed in the center of the patio between the French doors leading to the library and a grotto where water dripped down rocks into a pool encircled by ferns and dwarf cycads. By definition, a grotto is a cave, and this one was dug because Phillips needed dirt somewhere else. Ever practical, he excavated from this spot, then lined the inside of the hole with stones and planted the top with citrus.

Phillips achieved a harmonious composition at El Retiro, largely through a calculated repetition of plant types, including many groups of tall, columnar *Callitris verrucosa* and artfully placed specimen magnolias, camphors, palms, and live oaks. Most of the trees were already large when he planted them. He created long views, one of which stretched south to Edward Bok's newly built carillon tower a mile and a half away, and pure landscape views,

Pinewood. Partial plant list.

from house to pond, house to orchard, and through the trees to plantings on the slope. Such strong vistas in all directions made Buck's holdings seem many times greater than they were. Phillips wrote to Buck, "The place promises to have a very fine and a very livable appearance. Everyone, down to the dirt pushers, is enthusiastic about it."[8]

The landscape architect and historian Rudy Favretti hired as consultant for El Retiro in the 1980s tracked Phillips's work with enthusiasm and appreciation for "the styles he adapted, his ingenious devices and solutions to problems, and the strong statement he made." He concluded that the very eclecticism of the garden became Phillips's own unique style.[9]

Jonathan Shaw, president of the American Foundation and director of the Bok Tower Gardens, the new name for Mountain Lake Sanctuary, observes that Phillips "practiced an incredible *diversity* of horticulture. He experimented, he learned—unlike the narrow specialization you tend to see today. It is easy to say we don't agree with his plant selections now"— the cherry laurel and camphor trees Phillips used at Lake Wales have become rampant, weedy pests—"and overlook the knowledge he gave us."[10]

El Retiro's name has been changed. It is now called Pinewood, for the longleaf pines. It was purchased by the American Foundation in 1970, has been rehabilitated, and is on the National Historic Register, open to the public.

PHILLIPS MOVED FROM Lake Wales in 1932. "I stayed with [those] jobs and nursed them into impressive maturity," he wrote, certain that a part of his life was finished, but his leaving did not break the connection; no other landscape architect replaced him permanently. He was recalled time and again until the late 1950s to check the condition of gardens or to construct new ones for old and new clients.

When he came back in 1952 to work up and finalize plans for a new resident, he stayed in the Colony Club guesthouse, previously the home of millionaire August Hecksher, evidently willing to pay for discomfort. Phillips stayed in Hecksher's bedroom, close under the roof and very hot. He remembered that it had been designed by Olmsted and Wait, "way back . . . when architects got their inspiration from picture books. [This building] was an affair of gable ends, porticos, patios . . . and many stairways difficult to navigate—bathtubs under sloping roofs in which you cannot stand up."

Twenty-seven years after he and Simone had first gone to Lake Wales, Phillips wrote to his sister Florence: "Here I am among the scenes of my creative years. I wander around in gardens I built which have remained unchanged save for the prodigious growth of trees—live oaks, silk oaks, eucalyptuses, camphor trees, etc. The fountains and pools—stone, stucco, Spanish tile—the walls and stairways and terraces are here just as I drew them first on paper, and looking at them, they seem very much my own though some of the properties have changed hands many times."[11]

Authorship of the Mountain Lake Colony gardens, and who should receive design credit, has been a complicated and delicate matter. But it seems evident from the record that although when he first came in 1925, Phillips finished projects begun or outlined by Olmsted, the rest are clearly Phillips's own: "I looked over the photographs of Mountain Lake places [you sent]," Olmsted wrote in 1938. "The more interesting pictures, however, were all or nearly all of places which I had contributed very little to—That might indicate that the work you did with little or no interference from me produced more picturable results!"[12]

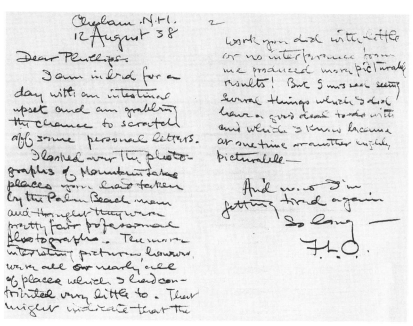

Mountain Lake Colony. Part of an eleven-page letter Phillips was proud to receive from F. L. Olmsted. (Author's Collection)

Doing easily what others find difficult is talent;
doing what is impossible for talent is genius.

JOURNAL, HENRI-FRÉDÉRIC AMIEL (1821–1881)

OVER THE YEARS, beginning in graduate school and ever after when he found time and inclination, Phillips set down his theories and methods for the practice of landscape design: in articles, memoirs, speeches, and when an idea set him off, in letters to colleagues and much correspondence with Olmsted. Writing, he said, helped him to clear his mind and think through a problem. He wrote a great deal, mostly letters, and published little, partly because he never pursued editors—what he did publish was usually by request.

Among his papers are three interesting essays in transcript, with no dates or indication of publication, that give insight into the way he thought and worked: "What Is a Garden?," "Character in the Garden," and "Sounds in the Garden." The first begins: "It is easy enough to say what a garden is. A garden, by the dictionary, is a place where plants are cultivated. If we went no further than that we should be soon talked out. But to say what is a good garden or a bad one, an interesting, beautiful one or a dull commonplace one, is quite another matter. On this point, happily for the writers and talkers, it is possible to go on forever."

Phillips decried strict adherence to convention: "It seems to be an irrefutable principle that the garden as an art form has to be an enclosed space . . . or give an impression of enclosure, yet following (the principle) blindly does not necessarily lead to a beautiful result." He derided those who put a bird bath on the lawn and thought they had done garden design "full justice," or who placed objects perhaps pretty in themselves into the enclosure to achieve beauty, but without plan. All they had achieved was a "garden-by-implication, by symbolism."

"[Other] people, and they are numerous," Phillips wrote, "are convinced that the quality of a garden is lifted from the ordinary by the number and quality of plants used; their attention is drawn to these *'features'* which they can sense and appreciate and so they become preoccupied with gardening and not with the art of gardens." This idea appears again and again throughout Phillips's career. As president of the Florida chapter of ASLA, an office he occupied twice, he had a national forum for fulminating against the erosion of his profession by architects and engineers, leaving little more than thoughtless planting, in his word, mere "landscaping."[1]

Phillips regarded the garden as an art form, and although he allowed many ways of approaching the subject, in the beginning, at "the moment of creation," he considered the garden a "problem." "To shrink the problem down so it can be grasped," three questions must be answered fully: "the purpose, the objectives and the limitations." At this point he viewed the client's input as all important: Would this garden to be a place to "stay in, to go to, or only to look on?" Would it be large or small, a sunny colorful place, or sheltered, "restful, pompous, romantic, other-worldly," or several of the above. And the limitations: Must the site be protected from wind and rough weather, salt spray, drought? Must the client's pocket be protected from cost—that is, would it be "little or much, must [the garden] go with little care or can it have care without stint?"[2]

Once he had reached this point with a garden, he wrote, "only the hard part remains." Phillips progressed to the "exquisite torture" of selecting the final design and the best relationship of integrals such as walls, steps, gates, pools, fountains, terraces, furniture, and ornaments.

> The problem [becomes] one of space-composition, of relationships of objects defining the spaces or to stand within them. The modes of thinking of the painter and sculptor can be invoked. There is as yet no question of materials, of plants. Though the materials available have to be known and understood, the problem at this stage is one of form alone. The size, shape and proportions of openings, the height of enclosures, the centers of interest, all such elements of the problem can be debated

without considering the material. There may be many possible solutions; they are all to be examined, to be weighed, and weighing may become so delicate a process as to be excruciating because you cannot gather the good things of all the possibilities into one solution.

When the composition is finally decided on [Phillips considered this point to be crucial], then plants may be selected which will best realize the intention; when the composition of the garden is established, the details, the minor plants which may be desired for cheer, for color, for intimate interest, may conceivably be of many sorts, may be varied in disposition from year to year, and yet the garden will retain its qualities. If it was beautiful in its concept it will always be beautiful, through change and even decay.

If the space-composition is successful the garden will be good and will be satisfactory. For, as one writer has put it, those who live in a well-composed space never tire of it and never want to get away. Aside from the observation [he could not resist adding] that this might be a principle more appropriate for prison architects than for garden designers, it still has the ring of profound truth for gardens.

Thus I maintain that the garden is a problem. What comes after this view point is gardening, horticulture, which has its own problems but is quite another thing. It is a *process*, whereas the garden is a *fact*, an entity which has an existence previously as an idea; it may come into being slowly, by the processes of horticulture, but it was all contained in the first solution.[3]

The principles noted so far would not in themselves have produced a garden to satisfy Phillips, without *character*, "by [which] we mean essentially individuality, some quality setting it apart from the common aspect of things of its kind. Without character the garden is negligible."[4]

Within the broad category of national styles in the gardens of Italy, England, France, Japan, and the United States, he said, it was simple to distinguish the regional character of each country, derived from native climate, vegetation, and use; the danger for the landscape architect to avoid would be literal translation of the style of one country to another. Yet unimaginative use of local materials—stone, earth, vegetation—would not alone suffice: "Distinction must be gained by the new definition of the usual forms, by the discrete introduction of new forms. Contrast is essential. A likeness in unlikeness."[5]

Phillips discussed two treatments of terracing, "subtle modifications of site which may sharply raise the garden out of the banality of a simple terracing." In the first instance, influenced no doubt by the Italian hills where site configuration is steep with splendid vistas, he writes:

In place of slanting paths offering slopes . . . to ascend, let there be successive terraces, direct stairways, agreeable promenades whereby you should oppose to the ever majestic spectacle of note, not naturalistic coquetries but a virile work, testifying to a strong and noble domination.

However, as it is important that the slope treatment offer an impression of security and stability, give to the terraces, turfed or in flower, proportions restful . . . then bind them closely together by ornamentation as well as by plan, endeavoring to lend to your garden a manifest cohesion. As for isolated trees and shrubs . . . choose those . . . drooping with thick foliage profuse and dark, in order that their compact masses may seem like the round heads of gigantic pegs fixing firmly to the ground of your superimposed terrace. Then at the edge (precipitous base) of a terrace place a columnar tree which by its vertical . . . will accentuate the natural slope of the ground and make more notable the horizontality of the terrace, and again, suppose a line of honey locusts with branches lithe and flexible as ropes . . . by their movements sinuous and careless will reinforce the impression of security (of the terrace) which you have sought to create.[6]

The second type of land configuration was all too familiar to Phillips in Florida with its monotonous miles of level ground. His design solutions were heartfelt:

If it's necessary to build a garden on a flat plain, do not raise up at great expense, a terrace and stairways which will bring no other result than to . . . confirm not only the absence of view but also the tiresome flatness of the region. You may sink parterres of a few steps descent to create a diversion to the precise horizontality of the surroundings, but it will be better assuredly to exaggerate, even to the point of a style the monotonous character of the country, and to profit by the levelness of the ground by planting avenues of trees which by their length (the avenues) and rectitude will express a feeling of continuity, grandeur, infinity. Direct such an avenue to the sunset, as at Versailles.[7]

Phillips considered sound an important element of garden design, involving both the desirable—bird song, animal and house voices—and the intrusive noise of contact sports and radios and cars that must be eliminated or subdued: "Color and form and light and shade a garden may have. . . . Lacking sound it will be no more than a pattern. . . . The thoughtful garden maker will seek to control [outside] sounds . . . and seek to introduce others more amenable to control."

He wrote of the sound of wind in the trees. He quoted an anonymous writer describing the sound of the old casuarinas in an Indian garden, like waves on the beach, and then the "slow swirl of dragging pebbles." He remembered the wind sounds in the high "leafless, rigid crown of the Quepo of the American tropics, like a harp. . . . In the aspen it is lively, [in] the spruce melancholy. . . . Has no ingenious person," asked Phillips, "analyzed the sounds of the different trees as to their ideographic significance? Here is a life work."[8]

Phillips's use of light in the garden was particularly distinctive. He played with light, separating it from heat, especially important in Florida. He set out trees where they would throw lengthening shadows across the lawn and created dappled bosques and allées where you could walk in comfort, and he placed benches, often of his own design, at strategic spots where one could rest and appreciate the scene.

"But of water in the garden," Phillips wrote, "who can speak enough?" If he played with sunlight on the landscape, he was masterly in his proficient use and control of water, in the pools, fountains, ponds, and lagoons that he built. This was his veritable signature: there was *always* water in a Phillips garden, for the serenity it imparted, for its wet look in sunlight, a mirror reflection of the surroundings, for the wind to ruffle, and for the sound.

If Phillips was, in truth, a genius in his field, as his peers came to describe him, perhaps it was because in practice his philosophy of design and true artistry rested on the particular strength of his mathematical prowess, his ease with spatial forms and perspective, his thorough knowledge of the materials of his craft to project beauty he held in his mind's eye. This, and his insistence that every garden detail be well considered and in harmony with the whole concept, were the golden nuggets in what he deprecatingly called his "bag of tricks."

EVERYONE SAID IT would be only a temporary recession; it was hard to comprehend immediately that the October crash of 1929 would bring on a depression that would be so bad and last so long. Many Florida fortunes had already been lost in the 1926 boom and bust provoked by hurricanes, freezes, and real estate scams, but the shock was temporarily postponed for Phillips. He had been working for most of his professional life for wealthy families and was still at the beginning of his three-year project for Charles Buck, who had not been unduly hurt financially. But Phillips's other clients eventually dropped off one by one, as each one said, until times get better.

Olmsted Brothers was retrenching heavily; it was a reasonable assumption that the far away "complete charge representatives" would be let go first. Julia Phillips wrote from Redondo Beach, "They tell me that the Olmsted office [in Palos Verdes] has not a bit of work but George Gibbs and Mrs. Eick are making a good thing writing reports."[1]

In February 1931, Olmsted, working hard to generate new jobs, made a business trip to Florida and took Phillips to Vero Beach, where there was talk of a small development "out on the shore a couple of miles above the Casino," possibly in connection with Ruth. "This job is hard on the feet," Phillips wrote to Simone, adding—perhaps to comfort her for his extended absence—that "considerable activity has started up on the selling end all at once and there is a bunch of prospects out today."[2] Nothing came of that project; much later, in June 1945, Phillips told Olmsted he was working on a "little subdivision job for a Negro beach resort on that stretch of lonely shore which . . . remains exactly as we left it back in [the early] '30s."[3]

Phillips gave Simone a temporary address in Vero and added a postscript: "FL seemed to think it a good idea for me to go to Europe this summer. He did not, however, offer to advance any cash." Two weeks later, he was still there: "FL insists on my staying here . . . until he himself goes. . . . I think he wants me to go look at that proposed Everglades Park with him." On March 9, Phillips reported that he and Olmsted had driven to Coconut Grove and visited David Fairchild, had driven the Tamiami Trail to the Everglades park, had seen millions of waterfowl "without exaggeration . . . then all over the Italian villa Deering [in Miami], itself, [down the keys to Matacumbe] until FL concluded we had seen enough," and they returned to Vero Beach.

On March 12, worn out with talk but resigned, Phillips told his wife that Olmsted was talking up business again, this time at St. Johns Island, where he took an investment tycoon out for a boat ride and was later observed in deep conversation with another prospect. "[We must] not be prematurely downcast. There are things stirring."

Phillips went home to Lake Wales and continued to work on the Buck estate, such other business as was left at the Colony, and mapped the final enlargement of the Mountain Lake Sanctuary. He went to Spain for two weeks in August with Richard Bassett, and they returned laden with pots and artifacts for El Retiro. It is not clear why Olmsted thought it necessary to send two men to Europe during these hard times and to help with the cost; possibly Buck underwrote the trip. Probably at the request of the Palm Beach Garden Club, Phillips also made a plan for the Palm Beach Lake Front in 1931 (signed O.B.). For the rest of the year he put out feelers through letters and visits to his Florida contacts, but there was no business. He got no further in California or in New York. Money was owed to Phillips from several accounts, but few payments were made.

Where to go and what to do? His Maine cottage was not winterized to enable them to stay past October, and there were no funds to install heat. Simone, their daughter Juliette, born on January 18, 1929, in St. Augustine, and the new baby, Mary, born on January 11, 1932, in Lakeland, would not be able to live out the depression there.

In April 1932, Olmsted wired Phillips: "Dawson can arrange for your supervision Neal Job Houston $300/month starting 1 May, 2–4 months. We pay transportation [you] pay own living expenses."[4] Simone flatly refused to stay alone so long. Olmsted wired again: "We regret this undertaking involves some personal difficulties [but] no other work in sight for you. . . . You are well qualified to handle this."[5] When company wives made difficulties, Olmsted called upon his own wife. "Mrs. O wondered . . . could not Simone see [this] was the best solution?"[6]

The job did not begin right away, which gave Phillips time to install his family in Maine. In June before he left for Houston, he received a letter from Ted Whiting: "I am wondering . . . if nothing turns up within the next two or three months you could afford to take more than a month off without compensation; and . . . whether you can or you can't—would you rather have the amount taken from your salary in one lump or distributed over four months?" Phillips chose the "lump," but there was no check until August.

In daily letters in June to Simone from Texas, Phillips vented his frustration over the irony of their situation: "I have never been so happy as with you and our little family in our cottage, when [you] placed the crib out under the birch tree on the south side where [the baby] lay happily, her vocalizations mingling with the birds; [why is it] these moments cannot last?" He wondered why J. Robert Neal, of the River Oaks Company, "somewhat in the manner of the M.L. Colony . . . should tolerate to have me here. He has a landscape department which appears to be competent to carry out the plans . . . [and is] more familiar with the terrain than I am—."[7] It was impossible to get around without a car.

"It seems so foolish for me to be down here," Phillips wrote, "leaving you alone. . . . I am irritated with the job in advance. I doubt if Dawson has done anything [for Neal] than [Neal] could not have done locally. A few pretty drawings, taken from points of view which do not reveal the weakness of the scheme, a bunch of useless plans, and a lot of needless expense. Then I arrive to struggle with a cockeyed thing which the client has doubtless come to regard as the word of God."[8]

Two days later Phillips was beside himself:

This job is the most monumental piece of OB asininity I have ever encountered. Immediately after my arrival he [FL] gets a bill for $2200. For what he does not know. He supposes it to be for plans, as he had already paid a big bill for "services." But it appears, in foolish conversation with me that I may have to revise some of these plans. This breaks him all up. However, we seem to have reached an understanding to go ahead, and he [FL] sets off to a director's meeting.

Meeting probably a glum affair for this morning he calls me up. Unable to get Dawson on the phone till Thursday, the latter being on the train. In the meantime, engage no labor, incur no expense. I think he wants Dawson to call him back to Brookline to get him out of this mess—he has been running around in a frenzy all day.

Can you think of a happier situation? I can only turn to the audience like Maurice Chevalier and inquire, "What would you do?" Particularly in Houston, where there is nothing to do, and it is too hot to do it. . . . I never felt so like a silly ass . . . and I have had that feeling very strong [at other times]. I see myself as just the victim of a lot of lack of judgement in Brookline.[9]

In two more days the job blew up and Phillips was on his way home with his friend Nick Saigh, who now had his own engineering firm in Texas and needed to come north.

EARLY IN OCTOBER, Phillips returned to Brookline for a day to discuss future plans. Olmsted summarized their talk in writing: Phillips could have all moneys coming from ongoing and future jobs at Mountain Lake until the economy improved and Olmsted Brothers could return there. Olmsted would write to assure the old clients that they would continue to have whatever benefits they felt they were entitled to from Olmsted's Brookline office. This was in part because Phillips had pointed out to him, and Olmsted had agreed, this was not a time when the homeowners at Mountain Lake Colony would write to Brookline when they wanted a small job done on the spot. This arrangement left Phillips connected, albeit loosely, with the firm. Olmsted rescinded the arrangement in 1937: "Only by special arrangement with Olmsted Brothers to the contrary in each instance will you accept direct employment by [new] clients or former clients of Olmsted Brothers."[10]

The agreement did not bring Phillips much financial relief, however, with dwindling clients, nor did it prevent the firm from accepting their fee of $250, in August, the "agreed upon charge" from the Tampa Garden Club, for the Hillsborough River Parkway Beautification Program, designed by Phillips and French.[11]

Back in Florida in the fall of 1932, Phillips decided to open an office at 412 Australian Avenue in West Palm Beach; he had been contemplating opening his own practice long before the Crash. Simone, who it turned out had never cared for Mountain Lake, was delighted. Phillips counted heavily on cousin Amy's connections and his past clients there, notably Mrs. McKinlock, but she urged caution: "Palm Beach needs Mr. Phillips but I do not know if they know they do as yet. It would be slow work."[12] It was.

In January 1933, Olmsted wrote that he and Whiting had decided Phillips should have a small check, since he had resigned from the firm out of consideration of the times. And, as the depression wore on, Olmsted offered Phillips a loan—"we have a fund for this . . . and as you stopped drawing a salary, of your own volition, to help us." Phillips refused at first but later had to take advantage of the offer. He was required to list his obligations[13] and to receive, with a small check, a shameful lecture on how to budget

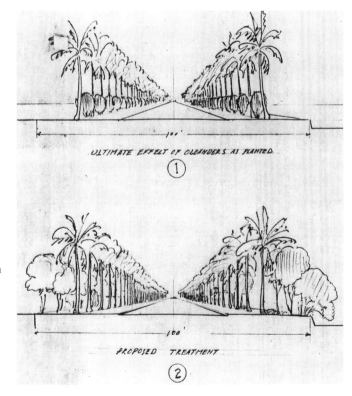

Venetian Way, Miami Beach, Florida, 1932. Proposed planting of oleanders and coconut palms for five causeways. "There would be in addition a general ground cover of beach runner, sea lavender, perennials, etc. outside the coconuts." Drawing by Phillips. (Author's Collection)

food, save on electricity, and "do you really need a telephone ? . . . not that I do it [budget] myself, Mrs. Olmsted handles all that for us."[14] Phillips never asked again.

ON MARCH 31, 1933, Congress passed legislation to create the Civilian Conservation Corps, or CCC, President Franklin D. Roosevelt's extraordinary program concurrent with the Works Progress Administration (WPA), to provide jobs and alleviate a potentially dangerous nationwide problem. On April 17, the first CCC camp of two hundred men was established in Missoula, Montana. Olmsted Brothers, other landscape architecture firms, and the ASLA chapters circulated information to their members who might want to sign on in supervisory capacities. The first Florida contingent of young men was due to arrive in November to escape a Montana winter in temporary shelters. Phillips applied for the position of project superintendent and was accepted.

Phillips became "Project Superintendent for Civilian Conservation Corps Camps in Dade County, ECW [Emergency Conservation Work], SP-1 (State Park), with advisory duties in Highlands and Munroe Counties." He

Venetian Way. Phillips's drawing of future mature growth. "Expected height of coconut palms 25 feet." (Author's Collection)

would be given one hundred men and sent to Paradise Key, near Homestead, at the entrance to the Everglades, to develop Royal Palm State Park.

He took the job reluctantly, wondering whether he had made a fatal error, for through French he had received and completed a commission to landscape the Venetian Causeway in Miami Beach, and although that project was over, other small jobs were coming his way. But as French, who was working in Sarasota, signed up with the CCC too and went to North Miami with his crew to start building Greynolds Park, and George Gibbs on the West Coast also accepted a project, Phillips went along.

He would be employed, which was better than most of his Florida colleagues could claim. Some, without work, left. Those who stayed took whatever work they could find. George Merrick, founder of Coral Gables, went to work on a road gang; former professors pumped gas, white-collar men were picking vegetables; everybody who remained counted on the climate and cheaper living to see them through.

Venetian Way. Mass planting at the old bulkhead. Drawing by Phillips. (Author's Collection)

The National Park Service and the Civilian Conservation Corps

Royal Palm State Park kept the beauties of Paradise Key as they had been,
a dark tropical jungle dominated by majestic Royal Palms.

MARJORY STONEMAN DOUGLAS[1]

ROYAL PALM WAS ONE of the earliest parks chosen by the National Park
Service and the Department of the Interior for Emergency Conservation
Work (ECW) when they began the countrywide search for public sites to
conserve and improve. It was chosen primarily because the mild winter
climate meant work could begin forthwith, whereas elsewhere crews had
to wait until winter housing could be provided.

It was also chosen due to the hard work and promotion by May Mann
Jennings of Jacksonville. Wife of the former Florida governor, she was
money poor but owner of several thousand acres of land at Homestead.
During her husband's tenure, she had persuaded a Florida Supreme Court
judge to draft a bill for the state to hold 329,000 acres of state land to be
turned over at the proper time for an Everglades national park; the bill
passed both houses in 1916. Mrs. Jennings then dedicated nearly four thousand acres of her own on Paradise Key, contiguous to the state land, to the
Federated Women's Clubs of Florida, to become Royal Palm Park, with
the understanding that they would deed it to the Department of the Interior as part of the Everglades National Park when Congress created this.
The state built the road into the park and now, with Mrs. Jennings as
chairman of the Royal Palm State Park enterprise, she and the Federated
Women's Clubs built the Royal Palm Lodge, a rustic hotel open to the
public. She maintained strict control over the lodge and used it during the
intervening years to invite interested dignitaries to join her vigorous campaign for national park status. Marjory Douglas knew and admired Jennings

from their work together on suffrage campaigns but believed the Royal Palm Park was Jennings's scam to sell her acres.[2]

Mrs. Jennings greeted Phillips enthusiastically when he arrived on November 14, 1933, with a group of young men totally unprepared for what lay ahead, for the first "stage" of six months. These increments of six-month stages were set up as a safeguard in cases of glitches because the program had no established guidelines yet. At the end of each stage another roster was set up in every park as more men joined the CCC and had to be moved to where they were needed most.

Phillips's salary was $220 a month. After all his experience, all the work, he was making less now, at forty-eight, than he had made in Balboa twenty years before. His wife tried to cheer him up: "Dear old William: . . . Why speak of failure when speaking of yourself? . . . You are not a failure, you are a success. . . . You are everything that a good man should be. . . . How generous you are, and sensitive and loving, so don't consider yourself a failure. Lovingly, Simone."[3]

Southern Florida presented a difficult environment for outdoor work of any sort: unremitting heat, mosquitos and snakes, scorpions, palmetto bugs, bees and wasps in numbers inconceivable to us now, regular bouts of malaria, dengue fever and prickly heat. For Phillips, it also meant living a goodly distance away from his wife and daughters in West Palm Beach, with little home leave; mandatory record keeping with detailed monthly reports; and answering to the National Park Service for every penny spent. Hard as it was for Phillips and Simone, it was also fortuitous. Neither could know he was now in the right place at the right time, nor could they know the acclaim and lasting appreciation that awaited him.

PHILLIPS'S CHALLENGE WAS to make a public park in an extraordinarily interesting part of south Florida: the Everglades. There is nothing like them anywhere in the world, Marjory Douglas wrote, "their vast glittering openness . . . wider than the enormous visible round of the horizon . . . their massive winds. . . . The light pours over the green and brown expanse of saw grass and of water, shining and slow moving below, that is the meaning and central fact of [this place]."[4] To which could be added the mangrove trees, bordering and containing the shoreline, with their astonishing and almost sinister tangle of roots above the ground and in the water, of paramount importance to Florida ecology.

Not so beautiful did all this appear to the CCC men, who often had to wade through the river of saw grass sedge (*Cladium jamaicensis*) in the course of a day's work, enduring slicing by the teeth that gave the sedge its name. To avoid getting soaked to the neck, they had to learn to negotiate the sloughs—shallow troughs in the limestone floor of the region, where drainage concentrates and forms a relatively permanent body of water[5]—and they had to go into the mangrove swamps, mindful of alligators, water snakes, and unseen marine life about their feet. It was Eden with ticks, heaven with the nightmare of inevitable hurricanes and fire, waiting for their moment.

The attractions for tourists were manifold, the chief among them being water birds by the hundreds and hundreds of thousands, including clouds of white egrets, ibis, roseate spoonbills, herons and limpkins, black and silver anhingas—"snake birds" that periodically sank for lack of oil glands and had to scramble to safety to dry their outstretched wings. In those early days it was also possible to see an abundance of deer, otter, raccoons, possum, rabbits, turtles, and the occasional Florida panther and black bear.

Available to Phillips for his plant palette was an embarrassment of riches, an infinite combination and variety of subtropical native plants as well as plants familiar all the way up the coastline—water lettuces and lilies, orchids and air plants (epiphytes), wildflowers and carpets of ferns, vines and shrubs. And there were splendid trees: pigeon plum (*Coccoloba laurifolia*) and coco plum (*Chrysobalanus icaco*), buttonwood (*Conocarpus erectus*) and oak, West Indies mahogany (*Swietenia mahagoni*), willow, mastic (*Sideroxylon foetidissimum*), bay, ash, mammee apples (*Mammea americana*), gumbo limbo (*B. simaruba*), pond cypress and maple, Florida dogwood (*Cornus florida*), palms, and the strangler fig (*Ficus gibbosa*), which wraps its branching trunk around its host tree like a boa constrictor and in due course kills it.

Phillips made up his mind at the outset that his overall park design would respect the history and enhance the magnificence of Paradise Key hammock, leaving as much as possible in its natural state.

The hammock—*hamaca* is the Arawak word—is another astonishing feature of the central and south Florida landscape. It is, in effect, a "tree island," a seeming oasis where the trees anchor roots below the shallow soil to the limestone ridge, speedily grow tall, and colonize thickly. The tropical hammocks of the Everglades look like ships afloat in the saw grass. They are made of broadleafed trees from the West Indies, their seeds carried over by birds—a mix of madeira, bustic (*Dipholis salicifolia*), torchwood, nakedwood, gumbo limbo, and paradise trees. Closer to Miami, hammocks may include live oaks, red bay, mulberry, and hackberry, beside some of the tropicals mentioned; in Big Cypress Lake they are a handsome combination of cypress and royal palms. All hammocks have a closed canopy and a moist interior that promotes growth of ferns and water plants, and often they can withstand drought.

Royal Palm State Park, Paradise Key, Florida Everglades, 1933. Explanation by Phillips of his plan. (Author's Collection)

Royal Palm Park. A Florida hammock. (Courtesy of Florida State Archives)

Royal Palm State Park. State-built road to Paradise Key. (Author's Collection)

Phillips was given to understand that Royal Palm Park would eventually become the entrance to the national park. The roads therefore had to be built for tour buses; access had to be provided for the airboat facilities and to reach the Seminole villages where Indian crafts were sold within the park. Land had to be allocated to make safe trails; boardwalks would be rolled out through the forest and over the marshes so that visitors might observe wildlife.

Before he could proceed, he was required to draw up plans without any maps or vital information and submit them to the CCC work inspector for approval—"A lively experience in design and administration in the midst of much confusion," he said.[6] It was a nightmare of bureaucratic entangle-

Royal Palm Park. Operation work force, men of the Civilian Conservation Corps. (Author's Collection)

ment and lack of material, and monthly allotments were always late. When the money did not come, planned work had to go on hold, yet Phillips had to keep his men busy. A motley group of green, unskilled men, they had no previous experience for the situation they confronted.

In urgent need of assistance, he began a training program of his own and was able to write two months later: "It is of interest to note that a plane table party made up entirely of CCC men has developed a reasonable efficiency in . . . mapping . . . and the weather conditions are ideal [for the work]." Phillips was not a born teacher, but he was practical. Wherever he found himself during and after the CCC days, in what he considered the "Florida wilderness" where men with no training set up as "Landscapers," he taught bright young men eager to learn how to use this fundamental surveying skill, and much else.[7]

By February, the men had completed the general cleanup, which entailed controlled burning, an absolutely essential first step in that country to ready the ground for planting. Then came brush cutting and clearing of roadsides and trailsides; tractor and drag scraped and prepared the rocky surface for smooth surfacing. Tree pits (planting holes) had been dynamited and staked over thirty acres for royal palms and other trees.

Royal Palm Park.
CCC men dragging
and clearing the site.
(Author's Collection)

Royal Palm Park. CCC men planting a royal palm. (Author's Collection)

Fire wells were driven, firebreaks were cut, and a lookout tower was built affording a panoramic vista of the glades. When a trash fire escaped—luckily it was contained very quickly—Phillips urged acquisition of better equipment, pointing out that fire in the Everglades could ignite the grasses in seconds and sweep through them with terrifying speed, "especially along a public road where cigarette stubs are very apt to be thrown."

The deer park was fenced, repairs were made to the lodge, plans for four service buildings were approved, and the first visitors' shelter "with authentic thatched palm roof" was constructed. A large lily pond was dynamited and ready for cementing. Phillips designed it to look as if it had been there always: free-form and at ground level with a hardly visible curb.

Royal Palm Park. Phillips directed the CCC to build the lookout tower. Faintly visible lines drawn within superstructure were Phillips's "drawing notes" to show future work to be done. (Author's Collection)

Royal Palm Park. View down from the lookout tower on the path already cut through the hardwood hammock gives a whole new meaning to the word *clearing*. (Author's Collection)

Royal Palm Park. The lily pool. Phillips was fond of using agaves, right foreground, as accents for many of his Florida designs. (Author's Collection)

Mrs. Jennings kept in constant touch and seemed to enjoy her visits to the park genuinely. She was always looking for new ideas for Royal Palm. She went to the McKee Jungle Gardens Phillips had designed at Vero Beach, which looked more like a lush tropical garden than zoo, with shaded pools, arched bridges, and a long driveway lined with royal palms. Mrs. Jennings was full of admiration and wrote, "I am fascinated by [the creek] and am wondering if the ditches you plan to dig to drain the yard that fronts the Lodge, could not be made the same way?"[8]

She told Phillips that on her visit to Dr. Fairchild, in Coconut Grove, he "was exceedingly proud . . . that you [have] charge of the work and told me to tell you that he would be glad to have you come in and consult with him any time." They were both anxious, Jennings wrote, to have a big grove of Florida royal palms to attract a crowd. "He quite approves of our using the Cuban Palms to be given . . . said they could be put towards the back of the burned area." The royal palms were pursuing Phillips, who had told Olmsted twenty years before how little he cared for those "feather dusters."

Planting began in March over the thirty-acre burned area, with royal palms, mahoganies, and ironwoods. Mindful of Royal Palm as the future entrance to the national park, Phillips concentrated on road planting. The roads and trails made a grand loop from and back to the tourist center, beckoning visitors into the very heart of the hammock where they could walk underneath the high canopy of shiny green leaves undersided with red—the satinleaf (*Chrysophyllium oliviforme*)—and under the coco plum and all the others crowding the trail. They could almost stretch out their arms and touch the trees, look down at the marsh pinks and swamp lilies as they listened to bird calls and the buzz, like chatter, of nearby small creatures. Along the way were the thatched rest shelters. To stop and feel the vibrance of the space before coming back into the sunlit open was an entirely new experience for most of the people who went there.

The Dade County Parks nursery in Miami and the Department of Agriculture station were inadequate to supply the needed plants. After Phillips exhausted them, a kind of door-to-door solicitation of indigenous trees and shrubs was implemented, with gratifying success, although the gift plants were not always the needed plants. Once the word was out, local gardeners were flattered to donate their plants to the state park—if the park would come and get them. This had a downside for Phillips.

Royal Palm Park. The CCC men built the Gladesview shelter. (Author's Collection)

"Ninety-five man-days were devoted to digging, loading, and bringing in Royal Palms donated by various individuals, another slow operation, since the plants have to be excavated by hand out of virtually solid rock." Furthermore, for planting out, the tree pits required proper soil, which was "usually brought in from the Glades by litter bearers. . . . Subsequent watering which has to be done with water carried in pails or other one-man containers, involves as much or more labor than the planting."[9]

May 1934 was a month of horror. Three weeks of unseasonable rains brought a record-breaking twenty inches. The water over the Everglades rose to near flood levels. All the landscape projects stopped; getting soil from the glades for planting pockets was impossible. Two miles of telephone poles—seventy of them—had been cut and set out by the men, across stretches of open glades, and "the wire pulling had to be done through water often up to a man's shoulders."[10]

ON JUNE 15, 1934, field operations ceased, the six-month stage over. Mrs. Jennings hated to see Phillips leave, but her influence did not extend to keeping him at Royal Palm. He was firm in his refusal; he had already told her so in his letter of May 30: "As for returning to Royal Palm in the fall, I can only say . . . I hope to be through with CCC camps sometime. . . . I don't need to conceal the simple fact that I would not continue to work [for this money] if I could see a safe opportunity somewhere to make more. . . . And I feel that the special contribution I can make to this operation has been made."

Mrs. Jennings asked if he would be interested in the job of landscape architect for the state road department. Yes, as a consultant, he answered, rather than as a regular employee, for "in [that] capacity one is not . . . confined, does not have to abandon all his other connections; he is able to limit himself to strictly technical work, not becoming involved in a lot of administrative detail, [and is] better paid for actual work done. . . . As a matter of fact," he wrote, apparently enjoying surprising her, he had been "in that status for some time for the Road Department" on one project (Brickell Avenue) in Miami.

"In a way I am sorry," Phillips wrote, "yet it seems to me best to leave any further treatment of Royal Palm Park to those who will determine the general policies and treatments for the National Park."[11] On 24 June, Jennings wrote of her deep appreciation of Phillips's "work and the splendid results obtained." Phillips replied with thanks, and agreed to continue to advise when he could. "I am honored," he said, "to be one of the Scientists Advisory to the Royal Palm State Park Committee, and am glad to accept the position."

In conclusion, Phillips listed the "major results of the operation at Royal Palm Park as a), a general improvement in the ease and comfort of visitation and a more impressive exhibition of natural features and landscape possibilities; b), a greatly enhanced orderliness and attractiveness of grounds about the Lodge, particularly on the west side; and c), a set of vastly better, more adequate, convenient, and durable service buildings located in a properly secluded service area. The effects of the planting work, though little evident now, should become impressive as time goes on."[12]

The Everglades National Park was dedicated by President Harry Truman in 1947. Although Royal Palm State Park became part of the national park, it was bypassed as the main entrance, thereby destroying Mrs. Jennings's dream. In time the whole park vanished into the sawgrass and hammock. All of it, the design and hard work of Phillips and the CCC, the lookout tower and sheds, trails and groves and pools were overgrown and lost in

Royal Palm park. Phillips beside newly built pump house, battling fatigue and fever. Photographer unknown. (Author's Collection)

impenetrable vegetation. The lodge, special source of pride and the setting for so many planning events and conferences, was removed and was said to be privately owned in Homestead. (Efforts in the late 1980s to find it were unsuccessful.)

In the 1950s a raging fire leapt firebreaks and and swept through the glades; only a few royal palms survived in Mrs. Jennings's Royal Palm Park on Paradise Key.

In the 1970s, Archie Carr wrote that "Paradise Key is an ideal setting. . . . There are parts in its interior where almost no one ever goes and where no man has left any trace of his presence."[13]

Only Phillips's photographs remain.

The forest of Highland Hammock is one of the oldest . . . in Florida and is now set apart as a park forever . . . a magnificent jungle. . . . In it are elms, oaks, cabbage palmettoes, marlberries, epiphytic orchids and ferns with a great variety of splendid subtropical vegetation.

CHARLES TORREY SIMPSON[1]

ALL THROUGH THE winter months of 1933 and spring of 1934, Phillips had been working with and training unskilled labor, dealing with all of the daily miseries at Royal Palm, and moonlighting where and whenever he could find other work, for the extra money and the boost to his professional ego. Although his design for Royal Palm Park had been a success, he realized now what another CCC project would involve: records, requisitions, no rest, bad food, and two or more jobs at a time. Yet there was no certain alternative in sight; he was discouraged and depressed. Prentiss French had resigned from Greynolds Park. He loathed CCC work and decided to try his luck elsewhere—anywhere. This left an opening; Phillips put in for it and was accepted. The park was nearer home and it would be easier to find and work on extra jobs. But before he could get started he was embroiled once more in an Olmsted complication.

Olmsted, who loved Florida and came often, for any reason, had appeared at the Royal Palm Lodge several times during the past January and February, to explore the Everglades rivers and involve himself in discussions of the future of the area with Ernest A. Coe, May Jennings, and others. A landscape architect in Miami, Coe had dedicated his life to persuading Congress to pass legislation to make the Everglades a national park. He became executive chairman of the Everglades National Park Association in 1927, and between these two prime movers, Coe and Jennings, and with the help of distinguished citizenry like Olmsted, CCC labor, and a lot of politics, the Everglades National Park would in due course become a reality.

But this time Olmsted had come particularly to ask Phillips to help him out of a difficulty he was in over a proposed botanical garden and arboretum in Sebring, Florida. The fact that Phillips was no longer an office representative almost appears to have slipped his mind. Nor, as it turned out, was he entirely clear in the early days as to how the CCC would affect his own practice. Work had dried up to such an extent for Olmsted Brothers that Olmsted was on the road constantly, seeking contracts. Nevertheless, it was something of a golden moment for him: his name was still synonymous with parks. The National Park Service was actively looking for public parks to develop and keep CCC men working. Olmsted saw an opportunity for his services that might tide the firm over the hard times.

A real possibility was to solicit private donors who could no longer afford to maintain their holdings and would be amenable to making a land gift for tax purposes. One such belonged to the banking and philanthropic family of New Jersey, the Roeblings, whose several properties included Highland Hammock Park in Sebring, Florida, which they had already opened to the public as a nature preserve. The Roeblings were quick to seize the opportunity of giving their lands for new parks to be developed

The Everglades. William Phillips and Frederick Law Olmsted at left, with their host (unnamed), exploring Lost Man's River, Ernest A. Coe on right, n.d. (Courtesy of the National Archives)

with CCC labor and government funds. Olmsted and Phillips had been included in discussions about the area since early Mountain Lake Sanctuary days; Phillips was listed on the Highland Hammock board in 1931.

C. A. Ray Vinten, a 1922 graduate of Massachusetts Agricultural College, was employed by the Roebling Company in the "acquisition, preservation and limited development of Highland Hammock State Park," and then became project superintendent when the CCC camp opened in 1934. Olmsted was listed as an advisor. When the Roebling gift was finalized and the National Park Service established the CCC camp there, the park was renamed the Highland Hammock Botanical Garden and Arboretum at Sebring. Harry Baker of the Florida State Forestry Service was engaged to develop the arboretum, and Olmsted evidently thought he had been called in as a paid consultant for the overall design.

Olmsted made himself available at Sebring, to give his first impressions on the ground. He attended preliminary meetings and wrote up his findings; he intended that Phillips would implement his ideas. Further, he could see the advantage for Olmsted Brothers of Phillips's CCC supervisory position and the labor force he commanded, a situation that would work so well later for Colonel Robert Montgomery at the Fairchild Tropical Garden.

During the winter of 1934, when Olmsted was still under the impression that he might have a contract for Olmsted Brothers with Phillips as representative, Olmsted pulled strings to free him from Royal Palm without asking if he were willing to come to Sebring. He had even summoned Phillips there a few times in the latter's precious free moments, disregarding the fact that Phillips was committed to his government job.

Olmsted knew the top men in the National Park Service and had heard that there was a policy under discussion to make it possible for a senior project superintendent to be responsible for two or more places at once—a policy born of necessity because able supervisors were scarce. He saw no reason why Phillips could not design a park at Greynolds and be advisor to Sebring as well; Olmsted virtually accepted on his behalf: "Dear Phillips," he wrote happily, "I was glad to have the directors fall in at once with the suggestion that you should be made free to take a hand, very much at your discretion in steering the operations [at Sebring]—especially from the point of view of design while continuing as superintendent of the other camp at

Greynolds. . . . I [told them] that I thought you were the best landscape architect for [this] bar none."[2]

BEFORE PHILLIPS'S STATUS was official, Olmsted was already conferring at Sebring on how to combine tree plantings in "rectilinear plots" with a handsome botanic garden, which would educate the public about suitable plants easily grown in the Florida climate.

Unfortunately, no agreement was possible between Baker at the arboretum and Vinten at the botanical garden; animosity grew and never let up. Olmsted forged ahead and argued against the idea of placing boxlike plots of trees of all ages, sizes, and hardiness to run the length of the park on the roadfront. Instead, he suggested separate mass plantations of trees throughout the park and as an occasional background for ornamentals, citing the Arnold Arboretum in Boston, for example. He found himself in the middle of heated discussions about the logical entrance to the park, the parking area, and whether the CCC was capable of building a permanent, fireproof records building.

In May, as the list of unresolved disputes increased, Olmsted finally recognized that there would be no money available to his firm from the historic works progress movement that was running on depression economics. The National Park Service regarded his work for them as the same pro bono publico involvement he had formerly had with the Fine Arts Commission and the War Department. He withdrew gracefully but pushed forward his Florida representative, who was no longer his representative, to keep the Olmsted name involved. He telegraphed Sebring: Since the "allowance to . . . district officers for services [was] very limited," he was willing to consult by correspondence "within reason" but unwilling to make regular supervisory visits.

Was Olmsted really trying to be a "district officer"? No record was found. Would an Olmsted even have entertained the prospect of "going on the dole," as it was considered by the Republican party, of which Olmsted was a staunch member?

Olmsted's wire went on to note that Phillips, attached to the Greynolds camp was a "first rate designer in such matters though as such he ought to receive something more than merely CCC foreman's pay."[3] To Phillips he wrote: "I feel a definite sense of responsibility for protecting that enterprise from botching through lack of professional help of good quality and I feel immensely relieved that you are going to be able to steer it. . . . It is up to you now and I breathe a sigh of relief; even though I have some twinges of conscience about dumping it on you."[4]

PHILLIPS WAS NOT quick to cooperate with Olmsted, who had blandly offered him up for double work. In light of all the difficulties at Sebring, for which Phillips held Olmsted partly responsible, he wanted none of it. Barely two years had passed since the fiasco with Olmsted in Texas; Phillips was reluctant to rejoin forces with him. And there were, indeed, some extra jobs filtering in. A Federal Aid State Road project on Brickell Ave was reactivated: "They want me [to do the final plans, specs, contracts]," Phillips wrote Olmsted, "and supervise the execution of the planting, [and will pay me] on a professional basis . . . for work to be done *and* the work I did last winter."[5]

But when Olmsted bowed out, and it appeared that Phillips might after all earn some extra money more reflective of his talents than was his CCC salary, Phillips changed his mind, with a proviso: "[I] assume senior rating carries increased pay for increased duties, if no prefer to remain [only] at Greynolds."[6]

The administration agreed and he became senior project superintendent for both parks. At first, he tried to be optimistic. He wrote to an old friend, Winton Reinsmith, a forestry foreman whom Phillips had come to know when they were both involved with McKee Jungle Gardens; Reinsmith had joined the CCC for the same economic reasons. "I was at Sebring Wednesday," Phillips told him. "Mr. Olmsted succeeded in unloading onto me some of the advisory functions they wanted him to exercise. It does not seem to be a very heavy duty, for they are quite well supplied with technical help of various sorts over there."[7]

He was wrong on all points, for hostilities never ceased. It became clear almost immediately that he should never have accepted. He was at a loss to understand and could find no rational explanation for the bad blood between the two directors, other than bad chemistry. The "landscape problem [has turned into] a nightmare."[8]

Phillips was angry that he had to keep spending five to six hours in the CCC pickup truck coming from the Miami coral ridge to the black muck of Sebring, only to find "that on this job there has been a great deal of discussion about principles and alternative solutions and very few paper studies"—plans, in other words, to get to work on. He was tired of the Olmstedian consultant role; he wanted to talk less and draw more.

In his capacity of district officer consultant, Phillips was under orders to oversee and approve plans presented to him, but as of August, the principals were arguing away the CCC's six-month stage. "[As] there is no aesthetic purpose in the stuff [plans presented to me]," Phillips finally said, "I therefore step forward with the very rough sketch enclosed which, however crude it may be, does represent, I think, an approach to the scheme in toto."[9]

He was aware that his solution would please neither faction, but he held to it, determined to preserve the hammock with only selective clearing for the paths and trails he sited. He concluded that Baker's trees would be

Highland Hammock Park, Sebring, Florida, c. 1935. (Courtesy of Florida State Archives)

planted to curve "in a belt two or three hundred feet wide along the north and east sides, with a border road . . . skirting them on the inner side." He determined the location of the main entrance to the east and established the parking area close by. He delayed work on the park's main feature, a big "garden-development with pools." It was to be built on low-lying ground requiring an extensive drainage system to prevent flooding in heavy rains. "There is more useful work to be done," he said, until they received the next allotment.[10]

Phillips had a case of dengue fever in October and did not come back to Sebring. Finally, in answer to unceasing complaints from Baker, who had transferred his hostility to Phillips, the district officer consultant responded with the "historical facts."

He had accepted Olmsted's request, Phillips wrote, to handle the design at Sebring as a consultant, while acting as superintendent of Greynolds; he had accepted on the presumption that it would be a viable cooperative effort. "Actually, I found the project here to be in a much less well-elaborated condition than I supposed, and the work made heavy demands on my time. . . . Instead of easing up . . . the pressure [is] increasing. I [can't] give any more time to [Sebring]. All plans ought now to be well along towards being met. . . . After a year's service I have not yet succeeded in collecting a red cent of travel reimbursement, and am now pretty well surfeited with this business. The Lord knows how many days, possibly weeks I have wasted making out these claims and revising and running to the notary with them and resubmitting them, but until at least one voucher is paid I don't want to get into more such hopeless proceedings."[11]

Vinten answered, "It is distinctly to [our] advantage to have the benefit of your advice in matters of design. . . . Your connection with this project [is] valuable even if only continued [to] check plans submitted."[12]

Phillips's input on Highland Hammock State Park Arboretum and Botanical Garden was a marked contribution, but it was always a headache. The postscript to the whole affair at Sebring was the deadlock predicted by Phillips, but he had seen to it that the botanical garden was left alone after the pools were completed. The "educational arboretum" was played down. What remain are trails and roads through the hammock, still beautiful, unspoiled by the plethora of cooks preparing the broth.

[Phillips,] I think your outlook mount and tower are corking. Congratulations! The silhouette of the main body of masonry reminds me strikingly of the Chateau of Murols (or Murol) in Puy-de-Dome or thereabout, though of course on a very much smaller scale. That has no significance and is merely amusing. But the thing itself seems to be a fine piece of constructive design; suitably theatrical and arresting but very refined in line and composition. More power to your elbow.

F. L. OLMSTED[1]

GREYNOLDS WAS DESIGNED and built as a pleasure park in north Miami. It was at first considered too far away from the town center to be used by Miamians, but after the opening in 1936, it proved so popular that rest rooms, camping, and picnic facilities had to be doubled. The largest portion of the park, the original 110 acres, was donated to the county by A. O. Greynolds, owner of the Ojus Rock Company. The land had been mined for ojus, a coral (limestone) rock, which was crushed and then used in surfacing roads throughout Florida. There were several abandoned quarry pits on the property, a number of old trucks and other machinery, and natural hammock land abutting the Oleta River. And extending a quarter-mile into the park site on a gradual rise was an abandoned spur of the Florida East Coast Rail Road, which had originally been used to bring in gondolas to take out the rock. With the rails removed, the old road bed, hard packed, became the base for the new road, creating a long vista from the main entrance to Phillips's "mound."

Phillips took over at Greynolds from Prentiss French, who had not coped well with the same dismal living conditions and lack of skilled labor that Phillips experienced. In their six-month stage, French and his men had built a fine rock entrance gate out of hand-cut oolitic limestone in blocks

Greynolds Park, North Miami, Florida. The mound. (Courtesy of the National Archives)

of different sizes and faced on five sides with hatchets, but Phillips still had a park to build. He made some significant alterations to the master plan left to him by French, rearranging the space to feature the mound, "but mainly he brought new life to the project," said the director of parks, A. D. Barnes.[2]

Under Phillips's direction, the CCC men built two miles of roads through the park, winding in the same flow pattern as the river and lagoon; four parking areas, small, and made remarkably unobtrusive with planting; and bridges over the streams. He cleared extensive trails through the hammocks, removing underbrush and debris and leaving the hammock in its natural state, augmenting it with more native plants. He set about similar clearing and replanting just inside the main south entrance, where a group of messy casuarinas had taken over too much space. From there was a view of the long lagoon; between it and the river was a wide open area for buildings and picnic areas.

Phillips transformed the quarry pits into "meandering lagoons," creeks, and a lake. The rock ridges left from the quarrying operation formed geometric protrusions above the water line, with some submerged. Through judicial use of dynamite, a small drag line, and a great deal of hand labor, "islands" and wider areas for planting were created. Phillips cleared the edges and wound a trail around West Lake and the rookery in it, which remained undisturbed by visitors and still harbors a quantity of cattle egrets, herons, anhingas, and many other local and tropical birds.

Phillips and civil engineer Raymond Ward cooperated on the siting and construction of the buildings and shelters. Ward, who had formerly had his own land surveying and engineering firm, worked in this capacity for the CCC until 1942 and with Phillips on all the Dade County parks; they met on this job and became close friends for thirty-five years.

During this period, park architecture throughout the country was standard government-issue plain. Plans were available from several manuals drawn by the National Park Service—"Park Facilities and Structures" was one—and other Government Printing Office texts were available. They contained practical directions for using minimal and cheap materials. This

Greynolds Park, North Miami, Florida. The mound. (Courtesy of the National Archives)

was one of the principal reasons for French's defection—he was discomfited by the banality. But Phillips had worked with government-issue tin shacks in Balboa and had learned enough to delay building the garage at Royal Palm until lumber from the temporary sheds could be salvaged for it; he came to regard such strictures as a challenge.

The mail-order park plans included approved construction details that had to be followed. Under Phillips and Ward, "only slight revisions were made by the Dade County Park Department," Barnes said.[3] The main structure, alternately called the pavilion or boathouse, was made of the same native oolite limestone on the property used for the entrance gateposts, again hand cut in varying sizes and faced by hatchet. The roofing was of hand-split shakes from cypress logs, an early style common in Florida and south Georgia and known to Phillips's supervising foreman on the project. It was a simple, handsome two-story structure facing the lagoon and built on the edge of the old rock pit. On ground level were the refreshment areas and a wide observation deck. Below, at water level, was the large kayak storage area, reached by outside rock stairs. Kayaks were hung on racks

Greynolds Park. Looking toward the mound through the picnic grounds. Photograph by Madelene Charles. (Author's Collection)

Greynolds Park. The pavilion/boathouse, from the woodland path. Photograph by Madelene Charles. (Author's Collection)

attached to the support timbers and there was plenty of head room (designed by a tall man). Later, more shelters and camping areas and rest rooms were built to the east of the pavilion.

The largest lagoon in the park is now connected to the Oleta River. High tides from Biscayne Bay backed up brackish water into the river; salt water from another, privately dredged project came upstream and made a large area of saltwater vegetation along the river front of the park and lagoon. The smaller lagoon, opposite, was a freshwater lake and the two were separated only by a "shallow aquatic weed-clogged ditch." When the CCC widened the ditch and built one of Phillips's elliptical bridges over it to connect the nature trails, the waters met. After heavy rains the water levels rose and drowned most of the new planting along the small lagoon.

Phillips built a culvert to drain surplus fresh water into the large lagoon and river, and a flapgate kept out the brackish water from Biscayne Bay. Now in the fresh water, with handouts from CCC lunch boxes, bream and bass multiplied. Soon an alligator arrived; dubbed Joe, he was fed, too. When the park opened and the boys moved on to their next workplace, the Greynolds custodian continued to feed Joe at regularly announced intervals as a park attraction until one day, uninvited, Joe cleared a fresh-laid picnic table and on another occasion made off with a visitor's dog. In the ensuing public hullabaloo, Joe was banished to the zoo. However, Florida is a vast network of drainage ditches and steel culverts, home and passage to quantities of alligators, which continue to show up at Greynolds Park.

Barnes was thrifty and enterprising. The picnic tables beside the river (and more were made for other Dade parks) were fashioned out of salvaged creosoted railroad ties; the charcoal grill shortage was solved with galvanized buckets lined with fireclay, available to picnickers for a small deposit.

Phillips cleverly solved the problem of how to get rid of the abandoned cars and accumulated metal junk and other debris, too expensive to move. He ordered all of the scrap metal and old concrete footings to be collected in the center of the park on top of an old rock crusher. The whole mass he covered with fill and sod, making a large hill, and he built a coral rock tower on the new "observation mound," often called the castle. Concrete steps in the coral rock wall circle the tower as they climb. The flag flies at the forty-two-foot summit, the highest point of land in Dade County.

The sight is much photographed by the Park Service and the public. When Olmsted saw a photograph of it, he sent a memo to the Brookline staff. "Post on bulletin [these] pictures of Bill Phillips's very remarkable

Greynolds Park. Footbridge. Phillips enjoyed building bridges. In later years, when hurricanes destroyed them they were replaced by plain steel "walk-overs." (Courtesy of the National Archives)

Above: Greynolds Park. Stone bridge with the trap to keep fresh and salt water apart. Deep-sea fish observed on the bay side. (Courtesy of the National Archives)

Right: Greynolds Park. Phillips's plant list. (Author's Collection)

PLANTING KEY AND LIST

KEY NO.	NAME	QUANTITY
1	Alectryon subsinervum	
2	Arenga Ambong	
3	Bucida buceras	
4	Bursera simaruba	
5	Canella Winterana	
6	Coccolobis floridana	
7	Crescentia alata	
8	Elaeis guineensis	
9	Eugenia confusa	
10	Hibiscus tiliaceus	
11	Ilex cassine	
12	Inodes exul	
13	Krugiodendron ferreum	
14	Lysiloma bahamensis	
15	Melaleuca leucadendron	
16	Mimusops kauki	
17	Pongamia pinnata	
18	Roystonea regia	
19	Sabal Blackburniana	
20	Sapota Achras	
21	Schinus terebinthifolius	
22	Swietenia mahogani	
23	Torrubia longifolia	
24	Terminalia arjuna	
25	Thrinax keyensis	
26	Thrinax Wendlandiana	

and successful observation mound. It is a fine piece of work."[4] It was "Dade County's first *planned complete park*, when Matheson Hammock was just a picnic area with hammock trails."[5] In October 1983, the central part of the park designed by Phillips was approved and designated an individual historic site by the Dade County Historic Preservation Board chairman and earned a place on the National Historic Register.

Intelligent people are beginning to ask if it's wise to utterly destroy
everything nature has so lavishly given us merely for the sake of gain.

CHARLES TORREY SIMPSON[1]

Although Phillips still felt trapped by onerous duties and shortage of funds, his personal situation had improved. In 1934, he and Simone bought a house at 529 Northeast 129th Street, Miami, and moved in with their two daughters, now five and two. It was a small "Mission architecture" house on a corner lot, where Phillips immediately laid out a back garden and planted large trees.[2]

Simone had been diagnosed but did not evidence the symptoms of her terminal tuberculosis; there was, instead, a renewed sense of hope. The geography of home and jobs was more closely connected, there was a steady trickle of incoming moonlight jobs, and as the favored Park Service landscape architect, Phillips was designing all the major parks of Dade County.

Matheson Hammock, ultimately 630 acres south of Miami, is bounded by Biscayne Bay, Snapper Creek Preserve and Canal, several private homes, a girl scout camp, and Fairchild Tropical Garden. The park includes one mile of frontage on Biscayne Bay, with an extended area of sandbar at low tide that tapers from the north to a sand-fringed mangrove shoreline on the south end, still popularly known to county mothers and small children as the "wading beach." The total acreage is bisected by Old Cutler Road, a much-frequented artery running south-north, which has tended to make the western side underused and unpatrolled. The land conveyed and purchased included considerable areas of natural growth: rockland and "transitional oak hammock," salt marsh, mangrove, saw palmettos, and Dade pine and scrub surviving on soil so dry and thin that it barely covered the

Above: North Miami, Florida. The Phillipses' new home on the corner of 129th Street. His planting of avocados, mangos, and other large trees eventually hid the house from view. (Author's Collection)

Left: Simone Phillips with Juliette and Mary. (Author's Collection)

A glimpse into my study
and sleeping room, showing
the perch where if I am
not up betimes the birds
assemble with great
demonstration. Just under
the plunn are the orange and
black (the female orange are
grey) siskins from Venezuela

Australian diamond
doves and the lowest
on the podocarpus,
an African cordon bleu
I raised.

Exterior of Phillips's study, with notes on his bird visitors. (Author's Collection)

oolitic limestone ridge on which Miami is built. This was the land of the fifty-cent plant and the four-dollar hole. Even for small plants, south Floridians had to use a grubbing hoe or an iron "digging bar," taller than most men, tapping gently up and down until a piece of rock broke and could be removed. For his large-scale work, Phillips had to use tractors and rock scrapers—the rock plow, a powerful and devastating tool in the hands of future land developers, was not yet available—and he had to be knowledgeable about dynamite. Phillips was an expert; without it he could not have created the grand expanses of green lawns, plantings, and lakes in the pine barrens.

Commodore William H. Matheson's gift of eighty acres was the first parcel in Matheson Hammock donated to the county and the first for public use. It was the direct result of Dade County park system Director Douglas Barnes's invitation to the American Institute of Park Executives to hold their annual meeting in Miami in 1932. Barnes, newly appointed procurement officer for the National Park Service, was the facilitator and director of the Dade County CCC program, an offshoot of the County Roads and Bridges Department, in which the work force consisted of convicts and men from poor farms. Barnes's guidance of the new program and CCC work force "brought a whole new explosive change to the small Park Division." With admiration verging on awe, he recognized Phillips's design talents immediately and used them to the fullest.

The true importance of American park development in the 1930s was often obscured by criticism of the CCC as a boondoggle to employ the indigent lazy. But Barnes's organizational skills and ability to seize the opportunity presented were key to the proliferation of major Florida parks in record time. Eager to keep the CCC in the county, he looked out for more work opportunities—the secret was land acquisition by purchase or donation. Barnes walked the visiting park officers through the woods at Matheson Hammock, then boated them over to Key Biscayne and gave them a chowder party on the beach under the coconut palms and the Miami moon. The visitors were mesmerized.

Matheson's land came with stipulations that it be properly supervised at all times by a custodian, never be sold, and be "kept preserved and protected as a botanical preserve for the perpetual use and enjoyment of the public." No commercial concessions were to be allowed and, most important, "the destruction of vegetation shall effect a breach of conditions of this conveyance."[3] Matheson heirs donated additional land, County Commissioner Charles Crandon acquired more by purchase, and other donors made the final total of 630 acres.

Before the CCC arrived in 1935, the land gift was a mixed blessing to Barnes. The trails were unsafe, with sharp rock outcrops, long runners of thick vines, above-ground tree root systems, and standing water in low areas after heavy rains. The air was black with mosquitos; nightfall brought

Above: Matheson Hammock Park. Path through the native hardwood hammock. Photograph from the Romer Collection. (Courtesy of Miami-Dade Public Library)

Left: Dade Metro office at Viscaya, Miami, Florida. A. D. Barnes and Phillips. (Courtesy of Fairchild Tropical Garden. This photograph also appeared in the *Miami Herald* and [Dade] *Parks and Recreation*.)

"no-see-um" biting midges. The custodian and a small crew of prisoners from the stockade cleared and leveled the trail with pickaxes and hauled in limestone sludge to surface them and fill the low spots. In the process, the custodian was attacked by a bobcat, which he shot and killed. While the prisoners with machetes cut out saw palmettos too close to the picnic area for safety and comfort, he and the prison guards "shotgunned a number of rattle snakes."[4]

"A major part of my duties," Phillips wrote, "was to lay out and design the various work projects."[5] These included an overall plan of roads, bridges, ponds and spaces, gateways and walls, and building storage and construction sheds, often the first step in a park project. The park was to be left as "natural" as possible, protecting the hammock by preserving native growth of coco plums, the black, red, and white mangroves, buttonwoods, and mahogany. Phillips designed handsome arched bridges throughout the park, which were replaced after several hurricanes with plain serviceable spans. Under his direction, the men built coral rock boundary walls and gateposts for the main entrance drive, which was bordered with columnar palms.

Two unusual construction techniques were used at Matheson. The first, to acquire the necessary masonry blocks for park buildings, was the "wire saw" method of cutting the limestone rock. Instead of a blade, cutting was done with a three-strand wire. A mixture of sand and water was poured on the work for abrasion and cooling. Local sand was not hard enough, so Phillips sent Dade County trucks to purchase sand from Lake Wales.

The second involved a dredging operation. A high-capacity pump was installed on a barge at the site to power the hydraulic excavation for the

Matheson Hammock Park. Series of retaining walls and dikes across the lowlands to the beaches. Photograph from Romer Collection. (Courtesy of Miami-Dade Public Library)

Left: Matheson Hammock Park, 1938. Black mangrove on the "wading beach." Miami Beach skyline eight miles away just visible. Photograph from Romer Collection. (Courtesy of Miami-Dade Public Library)

Below: Matheson Hammock Park. The popular atoll beach. Photograph from the Romer Collection. (Courtesy of Miami-Dade Public Library)

Matheson Hammock Park. The picnic shelter. Stairs lead to open dance space under the stars. (Author's Collection)

harbor and atoll pool. A "ladder" was secured at the front of the barge to hold a suction line and tip. Water jets were installed near the (suction) tip to stir up the bay bottom, placing sand and muck in suspension so that they could be suctioned up and conveyed by a floating pipeline to the land.

The result was a large lagoon for bathing, contained and enclosed by a sandy atoll planted with coconut palms reaching to the bayside. A trademark "Phillips vista" vignette is best seen after driving in from the entrance gate to the first parking area on the left, then crossing over to the wide greensward planted with palms encircling the man-made lake, a mirror for clouds and tall trees. On the opposite shore the roof of the shelter is visible, behind the willows. Phillips left the rest of the land in its natural state, except for the planted drive and clearing for nature trails and roads.[6]

Provisions always had to be made for overall safety, with cleanly maintained firebreaks and, where possible, protection against wind and storm damage, vandalism, and bodily harm. Shrubbery as hazard was a serious consideration recognized early by Phillips. He voiced this some time later when he interpreted his design for Tony Jannus Park in Tampa: "You will

Above: Matheson Hammock Park. Royal and coconut palms on south bank of man-made lake. Photograph from the Romer Collection. (Courtesy of Miami-Dade Public Library)

Right: Matheson Hammock Park. Royal palm "avenue" trail. Photograph from Romer Collection. (Courtesy of Miami-Dade Public Library; same photo in National Archives)

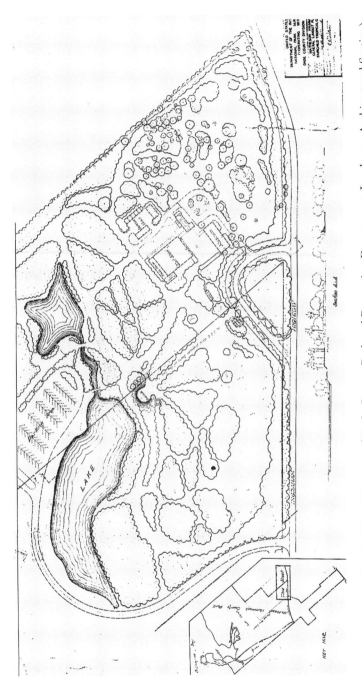

Matheson Hammock Park. Plan. (Courtesy of Dade County Park and Recreation Department, Landscape Architectural Section)

notice that the foliage in the background border is either above or below eye level, which is important for the preservation of views from the houses [nearby] and also in the interest of public order and effective policing. In general the planting is designed to avoid any thickety condition or opportunities for concealment; shrubs, except azaleas . . . are few and either small or well separated."[7]

But at Matheson, and later at Crandon, in the prescribed lush natural setting and in the newly planted nursery site, much damage occurred. As soon as they could, Barnes and Phillips had arranged to move the Parks Department nursery of shrubs and trees from the Miami County Poor Farm, where they were struggling in bad soil and drainage, to Matheson Hammock. Replanting was in the grove section near the custodian's house on the west side of Old Cutler Road, where there would be more control at that time and plenty of room to expand. It was a little botanical garden in its own right and became a popular walk for locals—around the lake, across a meadow, and through allées of growing royal and Alexander palms, colorful white and purple orchid trees *(Bauhinias)*, and yellow trumpet trees *(Tabebuia)*. Some time after the custodian left and was not replaced, young vandals came in, tore down his house, and set fire to the outbuildings. Nor was this all.

An earlier project, fulfilling a mandate of one of Commodore Matheson's covenants to preserve native plants in their natural environment, was the Matheson Hammock Botanical Identification Project, ongoing and open to the public as the park grew. It was headed by botany professor Dr. A. W. Gilbert, laid off when the University of Miami cut back. He offered his services to Barnes for a stipend and the help of one laborer and one assistant—none other than George Merrick, whom Barnes spotted working on the road and transferred him to Matheson.

Gilbert and Merrick set up a contact station at the entrance to the trails. Their exhibit "was to cover everything, trees, shrubs, vines, ferns, mosses, lichens, etc.," Barnes wrote. Gilbert was to "prepare a herbarium and a collection of the native woods. . . . Suitable glass cases were built. . . . [It] attracted much interest [until] vandals broke into the displays and destroyed many of them. It was an irreparable loss; no attempt was made to build another collection." [8]

Matheson Hammock was designated a historic site by the Coral Gables Historical Society in March 1992.

William Phillips created the closest thing there is on the coast of North America to the fabled tropical beaches of the Caribbean or South Seas: Crandon Park on Key Biscayne. Two miles of crescent beach, fringed with clusters of coconut palms, thatched-roof shelters on sun-brilliant white sand, and five miles of winding roads through tropical settings, Crandon was fat white cloud formations, bright moons, soft winter air, and love at first sight. Floridians rarely swim in January, but vacationers from North Dakota did, and they often watched cameras roll for the annual beauty pageants and movies made there.

Named for Commissioner Charles Crandon, the park owes its being to the munificence of the same Matheson family who gave Matheson Hammock to the people of Dade County. William Matheson's three heirs each donated a share of their coconut plantation for the great park, stipulating that a causeway be built from Miami to the key; the only access was by water. Men, construction materials, and plants had to be transported by barge; work was complicated by delays caused by shortages of steel, wire, concrete, and manpower during the war years.

Phillips began to research and design the park in 1941. That year, Crandon sent Phillips and the county architect to Jones Beach, New York, to study parking and traffic facilities, access roads, and cabana and refreshment areas. Phillips used coconut palms, which above any other plant spoke to him of the tropics, in masses of ten thousand—all over the beach, planted directly in the sand in clusters or singly, and bordering the roads and lanes, as he remembered them in Panama along the sea. He placed thatched-roof shelters at intervals between the picnic areas at either end of the beach. Pale green cabanas, away from the shore and nearer parking, blended into the surrounding sea grape (*Coccoloba uvifera*). He made a series of group

Key Biscayne. Aerial view. (Courtesy of Fairchild Tropical Garden)

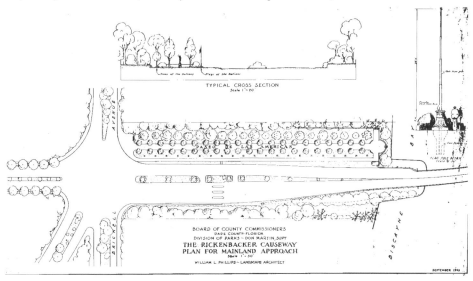

Rickenbacker Causeway. Plan. (Courtesy of Dade County Park and Recreation Department, Landscape Architectural Section)

Crandon Park. Coconut palms planted on the shoreline. (Author's Collection)

Crandon Park. Picnic grounds on opening day. Photograph from the Romer Collection. (Courtesy of Miami-Dade Public Library)

Crandon Park. Florida clouds; coconut palms planted on the beach to infinity. Photograph from the Romer Collection. (Courtesy of Miami-Dade Public library)

planting studies for Crandon: "marginal and various" referred to sizes, quantities, and shapes of plants he specified for the design. Fifteen hundred "broad-headed" tall native shade trees were raised in the county nursery and planted twenty-five feet apart in the center screen for some seventy-five parking strips in the parking area. They included masses of native black olive (*Bucida*), pongam (*Pongamia pinnata*), West Indies mahogany (*Swietenia mahagoni*), China flower (*Adenantheras*; should be *Adenandra*), and Tahitian flowering almond (*Terminalia*) were planted along the access road to the parking. They were surrounded by marginal planting, by which Phillips meant plantings of various sizes and textures as borders. These included oleanders (*Nerium*), *Bauhinia, vitex, ixora*, the gold shower tree (*Cassia*), Southeast Asian *Radermachera*, and Brazilian Pepper tree (*Schinus*). He used as the backbone, the integral part of his design, the old road built through the center of the key for harvesting the coconuts on the original plantation there.[1]

The two "separate but equal" beaches for whites and blacks, at Crandon and Virginia Key, were planned first. Virginia Beach was smaller, accessible on the bayside point before the causeway. Now that beaches are no longer segregated, this one has been closed off for the marine biology installations

Crandon Park. North on the old road through the coconut plantation. Photograph from the Romer Collection. (Courtesy of Miami-Dade Public Library)

Crandon Park. Cabanas on the beach. (Author's Collection)

of the University of Miami. Next was the wonderful children's park with its miniature train carrying children and parents through the natural hammock, augmented with planting to become a tropical jungle. The four-mile Rickenbacker Causeway, with inviting stopping places for fishing, bathing, or launching boats, was built after 1945, and last came the zoo.

By the time of opening in 1947 there were facilities for picnics, barbecues, and golf; spaces for 5,000 cars with plans to accommodate another 15,000; and promises for many more future delights. The cost to that date was $11 million for the park and $6 million for the causeway, paid for by revenue bonds.

Phillips was proud of his design and gratified by credit given to him for it, which was too often overlooked. "Crandon Park has been opened with much publicity," he wrote to Olmsted and Jack Wister. "Mary [his daughter] and I had an airplane ride . . . as guests of Captain Eddie Rickenbacker, in connection with the dedication goings-on. In the main my layout has been adhered to, and I think it has some merits, though the design of beach parks has become a stereotyped problem; the main concern is to provide people ways to drive in and out safely and to park their innumerable cars, and to get something to eat and drink; and it is a question of how far an esthete should or can involve himself in such consideration."[2]

THE CRANDON ZOOLOGICAL GARDEN, an adjunct of the park, was begun in the early 1950s. Its first director was Julia Allen Field, a lion tamer who caused a sensation when she stepped into the cage and put on exhibitions with the big cats she brought to Florida.

She and Phillips designed the cages and animal ponds together, and he designed an exquisite garden for them, on a circular plan with cages on the circumference surrounding lakes and a park. He included lush tropical vegetation and extensive use of open air habitats, but the animals soon showed where design improvements could be made. Phillips wrote:

> The tortoises tend to lie close to the barrier in the shade of a large Mahogany tree I planted at the West end where they can be easily poked and slapped. . . . I think an inner barrier that would keep them out of reach of the pokers and prodders would be desirable. . . .

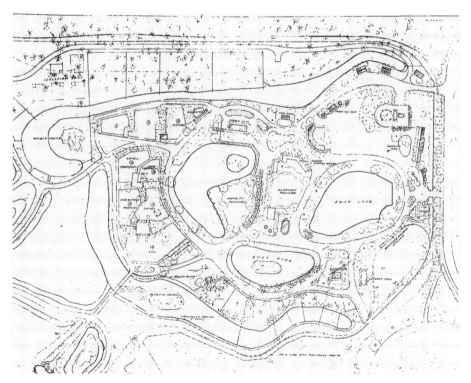

Crandon Park Zoo. Plan. (Courtesy of Dade County Parks and Recreation Department, Landscape Architectural Section)

Nor do the east pens appear wholly satisfactory. In the old ones [seen from all sides, all] the animals were . . . constantly running around and making a show. Now they can get away from the people, and they do. . . . They lie quiet . . . in the remotest corner; the Anteater and Wallaby are . . . scarcely to be seen—Yesterday, [I saw] only one deer . . . across the moat in the farthest corner. The others may have been below the near bank . . . or lit out as you suggested they might. Evidently we should have more animals in the pens, or smaller pens. The goats, however . . . because they are more numerous, are well displayed and amusing. They use the rock work picturesquely. . . . They have, by the way, quite consumed the Spanish Bayonets [*Yucca aloifolia* L.]. We should get some artificial ones, made of a stainless steel.[3]

The park suffered vandalism as well as interference with animals. Barnes's worst nightmare occurred on opening day when "in just an hour or two Phillips's plantings of Coconut Palms and clumps of spider lilies on the median strip of the Park entrance drive worth thousands of dollars were yanked out or stolen" in the face of four park police patrol cars and two park trucks trying to get them back.[4]

Not long after its opening, the zoo fell on hard times and was moved to South Dade. The area is locked except for special public occasions having nothing to do with animals, but it retains its quality, its lovely lines, and an ineffable sadness. It has been used since for art fairs; the Key Biscayne Garden Club "refurbished" it to their taste, without a plan; and in July 1991, there was a movement to bulldoze the whole area for a basketball court.

Crandon Park and Key Biscayne have changed immeasurably since the original planning: County Parks men could not foresee, in their wildest reckoning, the massive influx of all-year-round vacation and retirement hotels, condominiums and malls, another park opened around the old Cape Florida lighthouse, or the traffic glut of the annual Lipton Tennis Cup series. With the increasing demands for new roads, the original road through the center of the key, which Phillips considered an integral part of the whole design, has been irrevocably altered.

And where, importantly, is that design? Dade County landscape architects who are studying Crandon with an eye to restoration would like to know, but the plans seem to have vanished. In Dade County, I was told in February 1992, "After 50 years the records are purged."

The Master Work

Fairchild Tropical Garden, 1938–1954

The plan of the Garden aims at presenting the trees and other plants as botanical species, and, at the same time, as elements of garden scenery, "informal" for the most part, "formal" in certain passages, but not necessarily naturalistic. The area has been divided and subdivided to the end of producing a great extent of walk and lawn borders, and of shores, along which the specimens can be disposed and viewed. Variety of conditions for plant life has been sought, and variety, constant change of scene for the visitor. The policy is to form collections (groups) based on the plant families, but no attempt is made to arrange the groups according to any botanical system. Other groupings are made on horticultural characteristics—vines, ground covers, etc.

WILLIAM LYMAN PHILLIPS[1]

The Fairchild Tropical Garden exists due to a serendipitous coming together of a nucleus of experts, all world-class in their chosen fields. Their appreciation of Florida may have been all the greater because none of them was born there. They came, like Ponce de León, and their dream was to build a tropical botanical garden on the only piece of land in the United States where a wide range of tropical plants can grow and flourish, in the ground, in the open air.

The key member of this group was plant explorer David Fairchild, founder of the Seed Collecting Division in the U.S. Department of Agriculture and chief of this division and the Office of Foreign Plant Introduction when he retired in 1935 after twenty-five years with the USDA.[2] Now in residence at "The Kampong," his home in Coconut Grove, he was enjoying his "third life": writing, corresponding, planting, and still periodically going off on seed and plant collecting trips to the far corners of the world.

Fairchild Tropical Garden. Main entrance. Looking through gates to the overlook. Photograph by William M. Houghton. (Courtesy of Fairchild Tropical Garden)

David Fairchild on Great Inagua, West Indies, 1932, holding sprays of a ground orchid *(Oncidium)* species six feet long. O. H. Dorset–Alison V. Armour agricultural expedition. (Courtesy of Fairchild Tropical Garden)

Fairchild's great contribution was the introduction into the United States of more than eighty-five hundred kinds of useful plants and exotic ornamentals, especially those that would grow in south Florida, at the Chapman Field Plant Introduction Center, and at his home. He tested potentially edible tropical plants—without restraint; he made himself ill on several occasions. Plants, especially fruits, came to him from all over the world to be evaluated, to have their strain developed and improved for durability, better taste, appearance, and commercial potential and then sent back to their country of origin for large-scale planting.[3] He was much honored and bemedaled, by the National Academy of Sciences and many other societies; he was on the board of the National Geographic Society and was president of the American Genetic Association.

Few of the activities and people engaged in south Florida agriculture, horticulture, or park development escaped the attention of this charismatic and dedicated man. He knew and had worked with all of the important botanists and planters of his day and was well known and respected by them. Generous and open-hearted, he enjoyed bringing people of like interests together to foster knowledge.

The vital force in the creation of Fairchild Tropical Garden was Colonel Robert Montgomery, a self-made dynamo and highly successful lawyer and certified public accountant. Admitted to the Philadelphia Bar in 1904, he became a partner in his own firm, Montgomery and Lybrand, and was president of the American Association of Certified Public Accountants in 1912. He held important national positions: a place on the War Industries Board in 1918, with Bernard Baruch, Hugh Johnson, and General Goethals, about whom he and Phillips would later compare notes. He was appointed to the United States Shipping Board in 1921 and served on the War Preparation Commission in 1930, with Dwight Eisenhower.[4]

Imposingly handsome and gregarious, Montgomery never hesitated to call on his friends whenever he needed cooperation and donations for the particular enterprise currently dear to his heart. He became an enthusiastic amateur plant collector, concentrating at first on conifers at his Cos Cob, Connecticut, home, the greater part of which collection he gave to the New York Botanical Garden in 1949. The director, William Robbins, when accepting the plants, said Montgomery "spent years collecting unusual specimens of larches, yews, junipers, pines, firs and spruces. . . . This collection of rare evergreens . . . is unrivalled in this country and probably in the world."[5]

Early in the 1920s, before Phillips went to Lake Wales, Montgomery bought property in Mountain Lake Colony, where he began his first collection of palms and cycads. He visited Dade County often enough to get to know Tom Fennell at the Chapman Field Plant Introduction Center. Fennell became his mentor and helped him select and buy plants.[6] He also met Dr. Fairchild and County Commissioner Charles Crandon. While he was interested in seed propagation, Montgomery did not have the patience for it himself and was content to encourage others. But he was fascinated with seed collecting and took several "searching" trips around the world with his wife.

Unfortunately, the Lake Wales freeze of 1926 wiped out his incipient collection. Furious at having wasted so much time in the wrong geography, the colonel sold out and considered trying again in Palm Beach. However, thanks to Fairchild's persuasiveness and Fennell's urging, Montgomery came to south Miami in 1932. Fennell chose the property for him where, wrote Fairchild, "With the possible exception of Queensland [Australia], this is the only area on the globe which has an essentially tropical climate where an arboretum of tropical plants could be built."[7] At the colonel's request, Fennell helped him to acquire his ultimate collection, which became the Coconut Grove Palmetum.[8] From then on, tropical plants were one of Montgomery's ruling passions.

In 1934, Dr. Fairchild's friends began discussing the need for a place to display examples of the advances in tropical plant growth and research Fairchild had instigated and watched over in the area for years. Montgomery heartily endorsed the idea; he wanted to supplement such a collection with part of his own, which had outgrown his palmetum. Generous with his time and money, Montgomery was the catalyst and prime mover of the new enterprise. In December 1936, he formally expressed in a legal document filed at the Dade County clerk's office his intent "to create a botanical garden on privately purchased land in south Dade County, of approximately eighty acres." Montgomery had originally bought the property adjacent to his palmetum for a friend who reneged on the deal; here was a far better use for it. The charter was granted, and Montgomery and his wife Eleanor founded the Friends of Fairchild.

Marjory Stoneman Douglas, journalist on the *Miami Herald*, author, and great environmentalist, wrote an inspired argument for the new project.[9] In stressing the importance of arboreta and botanic gardens to industrial and cultural development, she pointed to the introduction of vast numbers of what are now considered "*native* oaks, conifers and ornamentals," by Boston's Arnold Arboretum, and then wisely quoted Dr. Fairchild's proposal for a tropical garden in the

> warmest spot on the Florida peninsula with suitable soil conditions . . . where much tropical material can be . . . grown to maturity, furnishing seeds and pollen with which new forms can be made (and studied).
>
> Crops now growing in America whose beginnings are chronicled in the Inventories of the Plant Introduction gardens have a value of several hundred millions of dollars . . . in annual crop returns. . . . Tropical fruit industries of the future will have to depend [on the U.S.] for the germ plasma to create new and valuable varieties.
>
> The value that such a tropical garden and arboretum would have to the [educational and] cultural climate of south Florida cannot be over emphasized. Its scientific value [for research study] to the growing young University of Miami would be inestimable.

Finally, Fairchild pointed out that Miami's proximity to the Caribbean and great tropical plant gathering areas combined with its excellent transportation systems would ensure success in moving rare species.

Their proposed garden site adjoined Matheson Hammock, where Phillips was already working with CCC labor. The CCC men could work only on federal, state, or county land dedicated to public use; every step of every project had to be reviewed and approved by the National Park Service. Montgomery conceived a plan with park authorities Barnes and Crandon to make CCC labor available to the Fairchild project; he abandoned his idea of a privately owned venture and signified his intention to donate sixty-nine of the eighty-three acres contiguous to Matheson Hammock for public park development. Half of the remaining privately owned land would be set aside for his palms.

Petition was made to the National Park Service to include Fairchild Tropical Garden in the development of Matheson Hammock. Justification was submitted and approved. The agreement stated that "maintenance and operation of the Garden is a cooperative affair with the county largely responsible for the maintenance of the grounds only and the furnishing from time to time of equipment such as tree movers. . . . The Garden is responsible for the administration, plant collections and their records . . . for all operations . . . [of future] buildings [which will be] located on the portion on which the Garden still holds the deed."[10]

This in effect created the impossible situation of one garden—the Fairchild Tropical Garden—with dual ownership, two-thirds public and one-third private, and with solicited membership and an entrance fee. Barnes thought the Arnold Arboretum ought to be their model. Phillips disagreed. While the city of Boston had leased the arboretum land to Harvard for one thousand years, Harvard was to be in sole control. Fairchild Tropical Garden was to be under joint public-private ownership and management, the county supplying labor and Phillips's oversight but the Garden, represented by Friends of Fairchild and a newly formed Garden board, supplying funds for plants and architects for park buildings. Phillips looked down the road and worried what would happen when there was a change of personnel; the Sebring experience was fresh in his mind. He gave Barnes a copy of Olmsted's 1934 recommendations to the Florida Botanical Garden and Arboretum, covering these very points, and he wrote to Charles Crandon when Fairchild Tropical Garden was attracting international attention, suggesting a revised agreement between county and Garden and outlining how it could be done.[11]

As soon as the project was in place, Phillips wrote to Montgomery's friend Noel Chamberlin, a New York landscape architect who had been invited to Florida to discuss the feasibility of the Garden project and might be interested in planning it:

> I banged out a Plan so that the Association might have immediately a plan suitable for publication. There is no pretense that the scheme has been given close study . . . to precise location of lanes, openings, masses, etc. etc. or . . . kind of plant groups. . . . You will observe that I have indicated yourself and myself to be co-authors of this plan. . . . I have understood that Col. Montgomery . . . expressed the intention . . . that you should be retained as consulting landscape architect. . . . As for my

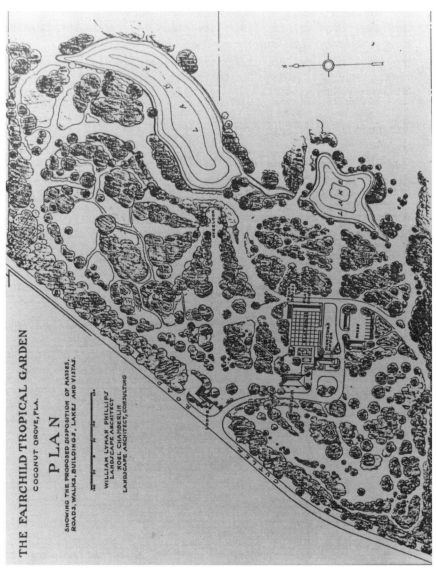

"I banged out a plan." The Garden becomes more than an idea. (Courtesy of Fairchild Tropical Garden)

own status, it has been vague and unsupported by any authorization. . . . Now that County participation in the Garden development is assured . . . I shall doubtless be able to do some work on the plans in my capacity as project superintendent.[12]

Montgomery always wanted two opinions; perhaps he was not sure of Phillips. But Fairchild was, and Chamberlin, who met Phillips during his visit, agreed. Phillips really wanted to design this garden and was willing to be a collaborator, but Chamberlin would bow out at the start; his only connection was the Hibiscus Garden, in his memory.

Phillips may have "banged out" the plan, but some years later in conversation with Nixon Smiley, he "recalled that he completed a rough sketch of a design for FTG six weeks after discussing overall plans with Colonel Montgomery. 'The Garden today is not essentially different from that first sketch,' he said to me, 'although many details have been changed, some new added'."[13]

Dedication took place in April 1938, on a "hastily cleared piece of land under a sapodilla tree."[14] Dedicatory mangos, palms, and avocados were planted, and in honor of Dr. Fairchild, a baobab tree. Dr. Robert Merrill, director of the Boston Arboretum, gave the main address, promising from his tandem position as chief of the Atkins Institute in Soledad, Cuba, immediate gifts of many rare species of trees and plants.

*I consider him one of the best authorities anywhere on the use of the palm. . . .
The Fairchild Tropical Garden . . . is a masterful piece of work. I don't think
there is anything like it in the world.*

FREDERICK LAW OLMSTED[1]

WHEN IT CAME to the creation of the Fairchild Tropical Garden, Phillips
wrote, "once again, [I] broke new ground and established practices."[2] He
was in complete charge of the plans from the moment that actual design
and planting started. There was token supervision of his work on county
land, but his plans were approved as drawn and followed to the letter, and
he would have twenty-five years of continuous involvement.

During those years I exercised a close control over most of what went on
throughout the Garden.

I recall no positive help from anybody regarding the character the
Garden should have. Colonel Montgomery expressed no opinion other
than that there should be "a garden rather than a park," that there should
be palms on one side and "flowering trees" on the other, and that palms
looked best standing on a smooth lawn. . . .

I, myself had no previous experience with botanical gardens, [having]
visited few . . . taken little interest. It seemed to me, however, almost
axiomatic, that a botanical garden is distinguished from a park by two
things: first, that it attempts to exhibit a wide range of flora, and second,
that it does this in an orderly way, by groupings that illustrate botanical
relationships, either taxonomical or ecological. It may look like a park or
like a garden—if one cares to make such fine distinctions—and it may
give more consideration to beauty than to science, but the scientific pur-

pose will be present in some degree at least, even if only by the labelling of species.[3]

In his preliminary study, and in an effort to solicit input from the directors, while marshaling his thoughts for the design scheme, Phillips had made his own list of reasons for establishing a botanical garden:

1. To make an exposition of systematic plant relationships.
2. To exhibit conveniently the flora of a region, with or without ecological relationships.
3. To exhibit new species having economic or ornamental value, such as is done by a plant introduction garden.
4. To demonstrate the garden or park-making values of familiar or unfamiliar plants.
5. To display with the greatest possible completeness certain groups of plants.
6. To make a collection of oddities and rarities, without much regard to their scientific significance or usefulness.
7. To demonstrate a dominantly esthetic motivation.[4]

Phillips decided from the outset that groupings by families were the logical and right procedure. Not everyone agreed. "Dr. Merrill," Phillips wrote, "[didn't] seem to think it important to group the families; in nature you rarely found several species together, you found them scattered and intermixed with other things, and he saw no reason why genera and species should not be intermixed in a botanical garden. Still the group system seemed to me to constitute one clear motive for design in a collection which was to be built up gradually through the years."[5] Phillips "clung to this idea," he said, "and never felt it had been less than an advantage."

It was still to be decided how many plant families, large and small, could have a place in the scheme. The Garden's private land threatened to become a tight squeeze, with half used for Montgomery's plants and the rest filled with the museum–library–gift shop, auditorium, offices, and public facilities. Some families would get little more than token representation.

Phillips identified the list of plants growing in the botanical garden of the Atkins Institute in Soledad, Cuba, to be of "immediate assistance, containing as it did a list of genera according to families, growing in a region

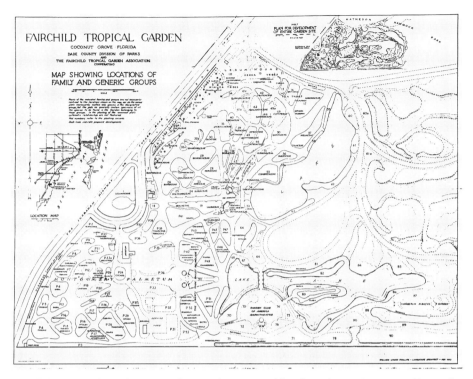

Fairchild Tropical Garden. Map showing locations of family and generic groups. Drawn by Phillips. (Courtesy of Fairchild Tropical Garden)

of cultural possibilities much like our own." Of the 160 families on the list, the Leguminosae and Moraceae included enormous ficus and other very large trees of "almost unlimited growth," which would make further pressing demands on the Garden's restricted space; some of the other families of more modest size and number of genera could be planted as undergrowth.

"The problem," wrote Phillips, "was to evolve a unified plan for the overall tract [of public and private land] without distinction of ownership, within the severe space limitations existing." At this point, the county had about sixty acres, the garden and the Montgomery palmetum thirteen each. Later, land was deeded back to the Garden for much-needed space for buildings. He decided first to acquire as complete as possible a collection of palms, cycads, and pandans for the Montgomery palmetum; the county-

Fairchild Tropical
Garden. Preparing
the cycad vista.
(Courtesy of Fairchild
Tropical Garden)

owned part of the garden would hold a wider range of trees and shrubs, grouped according to family.

The westerly end of the parcel lay on the Miami rock ridge, which Phillips called the "upland," or mainland, in his memoir, in order to distinguish it from the quite different "lowland" or marine salt flats, roughly eighteen feet below it. The upland had "a strong slope or escarpment face one hundred to two hundred feet wide joining it to the Lowland. It is in reality the edge of an ancient marine terrace which appears as an abrupt cliff at other points along the Biscayne Bay." Phillips considered the escarpment the property's boldest topographical feature, "which strongly influenced the planting." His ultimate solution to all of his technical and aesthetic problems was directly influenced by the terrain, "the plot of ground that had to be dealt with." He always determined the central long axis of the property as the base for the rest of his spatial design. At Fairchild Tropical Garden he opted to use more than one axis, because the land was so clearly divided into upland and lowland areas by the escarpment.

"The main features of the plan for the Upland were a more or less well-defined peripheral road, and the Overlook walk which, crossing the peripheral road just inside the entrance, where strong views open to left and right, continues to the Overlook terrace from which radiate lines of movement and vision."

The vista presented along this wide and straight grass path, from the gate lodge at the entrance to the overlook on the escarpment, was splendidly effective for its sense of surprise. At the beginning of the long walk, bordered by flowering shrubs, only a bank of distant trees was visible, then slowly a view unfolded: water came increasingly into sight in front of the trees until, arriving at the Overlook—an area octagonal in shape bordered by a wall on three sides—it was and is possible to look down on the created Pandanus lake with royal palms on one side and pandans on the other. There is the impression of great height: Phillips's magic at its best, for actually the drop is but fifteen feet. The lowland was "constructed around two long views related to two standpoints on the upland," this being one of them.[6]

Fairchild Tropical Garden. Looking through the pandans to the lake. (Courtesy of Fairchild Tropical Garden)

Above: Fairchild Tropical Garden. A magnificent vista. Photograph by William M. Houghton. (Courtesy of Fairchild Tropical Garden)

Left: Fairchild Tropical Garden, 1947. Phillips took photographs to record progress. Near the overlook. (Author's Collection)

Perhaps the most extraordinary aspect of the Fairchild Tropical Garden lies in the way Phillips confidently developed an apparently complete lack of uniformity and predictability into a cohesive entity. Study of the plan shows that nothing matches, nothing is the same: plant specimens vary in mass and height and orientation in beds of totally different sizes. But the beds reflect the curve of the terrain and subtly relate to one another. The lowland lakes and islands that Phillips designed and built with CCC men differ utterly in size and shape, their beauty doubled by their reflections of the plants above them. Likewise, there is variation in the great open spaces, Phillips's "voids," which were as necessary, as essential to appreciating his plan, he said, as the mass plantation. The whole garden is a network, a web of paths enabling views of the beds from all sides, paths laid out to present a sequence of views planned as carefully as are the vistas from the Overlook and of Bailey Palm Glade.

The sumptuous unifying effect depends upon the seemingly endless tones of green, the wide expanses of grass throughout, the great variety of plant textures, and the sky, punctuated by palm fronds and from February to April by exotic flowering trees.

UNDER PHILLIPS'S DIRECTION the CCC force did the original clearing and selective cutting. New topsoil was brought in to cover the rocky land, pipelines were laid for irrigation, a pump house was constructed, holes were dynamited. They excavated the lakes, spreading the resulting fill on the surrounding marshlands for later planting. They built the coral rock boundary wall facing the main road, stretching from Matheson Hammock to the Garden, and then, named for its donor, the Semple vine pergola, which ran along the Garden side of the wall for 560 feet. Mrs. Semple provided the plants and organized the first Fairchild Garden volunteers, the lifeblood of the Garden to this day.

Designed by Phillips and architect Clarence Dean, the pergola was made of a double row of high stone pillars connected by poles with crosspieces of pipe and treated wood to hold the vines. Masses of colorful vines were selected to bloom seasonally throughout the year, including red and purple bougainvilleas, white *Thunbergia*, Herald's trumpet (*Beaumontia grandiflora*), Coral vine (*Antigonon*), Christmas vine *(Porana)*, woody Scarlet climber *(Combretum)*, and many others. This planting was always tricky—the vines fought for space, the strong ones overrunning the more delicate, and then came hurricanes and pests and decay—but it is still one of the most popular sights. Phillips and the CCC also completed the Overlook, the Garden amphitheater, and most of the original terracing, as outlined on Phillips's master plan.

Phillips located all of the buildings, and he designed some himself. The first was the Gate Lodge, on which he collaborated with architect Mont-

Fairchild Tropical Garden. Building the vine pergola on the county side of the Garden, enabling the use of CCC labor. Ray Ward and Phillips, left and second from left. (Courtesy of Fairchild Tropical Garden)

Fairchild Tropical Garden. The completed vine pergola with initial planting. (Courtesy of Fairchild Tropical Garden)

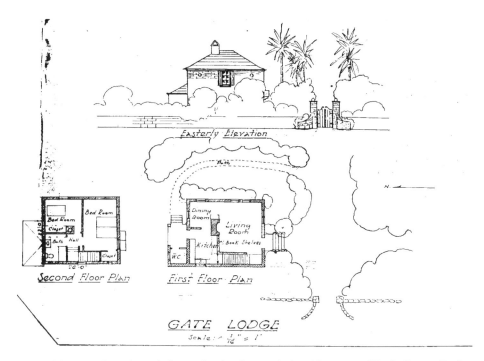

Fairchild Tropical Garden. Phillips's plan for the gate lodge. (Courtesy of Dade County Parks and Recreation Department, Landscape Architectural Section)

gomery Atwater. The two-story stone house was built with limestone quarried at Matheson Hammock; the colored floor tiles were composed of "pulverized Key Largo stone." After his years in the tropics, Phillips favored simple, wide and square houses sited for best air circulation, set beneath tall shade trees, with wooden shutters to keep out the sun.

Phillips collaborated with architects Robert Fitch Smith and Russell Pancoast on other Garden buildings. As an architect himself, he did not hesitate to ask questions of his design partners. About Robert Fitch Smith, who was designing the Garden House, he wrote, "I could see that insofar as he was concerned, my being in the show saved him no work or trouble. It was more likely to cause him more work. What we have here is a client-architect relationship in which I am attached to the client in an advisory way, and not to the architect in a designing capacity. I am concerned mainly with seeing that the building shall be suitably located in the Garden, and shall have appropriate relationship to its surroundings. The job of actually designing the building is Smith's, regardless of any suggestions I may make."[7]

Phillips's attitude toward Smith may have been intensified by his anger about a general encroachment by architects and engineers into the field of landscape architecture, against which he fulminated to all who lent an ear— among others Fairchild, Wister, Olmsted, Owens, and the Florida chapter of ASLA when he was chairman during the 1950s: "They leave us nothing but plants."

Smith designed the museum–library–gift shop in 1939–40 and the Garden House in 1946; Russell Pancoast designed the office building in 1952 and the director's house in 1953. Phillips designed the public rest room building between the Garden House and the museum, the Hambley patio, and the Founders' court in 1953 and 1954. Patio and court, with their wide coquina terraces, cover the entire space between museum, Garden House and rest room building, as Phillips wrote, to "join up in a satisfactory architectural way and add a special kind of interest to the Garden. The 'free forms' of the Court were strongly indicated, [to] accommodat[e] the movement of pedestrians, and for reconciling the slight but troublesome differences of level [throughout]."[8]

The Hambley patio, nearest to the auditorium side of the Garden House, is an intimate, sunlit open room with stone bench and fountain. In the center of the court Phillips built an octagonal lily pool with a wide raised rim to sit on and look out toward the palmetum. The local architecture, in postwar revolt against "boom Spanish," was really no-style, Miami 1940s, tropical bland. But the one-story, white and cream Fairchild Tropical Garden buildings, the museum of local stone, and the court are remarkably compatible and understated. The Garden House faces a wide lawn with quiet elegance.

Phillips made drawings for the Eleanor Montgomery orchid house, in 1941, and did a good deal of the building himself. There was an interesting technological problem it pleased him to solve for the special growing needs. He came up with an innovative roof design that allowed an even flow of light and air to come in at all times. It was an ingenious series of inverted triangular cypress slats under a fiberglass-coated screen and placed north to south, "and the shape allowed the same amount of light to pass through as the sun moved from East to West—with ordinary slats there was less light except at midday. When the orchid house was redone much later and they were discarded, the slats were used elsewhere, and were still as good as new forty-five years later." Phillips also drew up plans for the rare plant house, which was not built until after his death.[9]

WHEN PHILLIPS BEGAN to design the Garden, he asked for and received agreement from Montgomery that the Garden live up to its name and plant only *tropical* plants. An Acquisition Committee was formed, of which Phillips was a member. He drew up a plant "wish list," as he did for every public park project eligible for donations,

> to find out what is wanted, what can be had and [from] where. . . . I am making for each family a data sheet. . . . On this I list all the plants of each family that I know of or can find any reference to, if they seem to be of interest. I note opposite, the characteristics (large tree, small, shrub, vine, etc.) and the spread of its canopy. I run through the Garden and County Nursery inventories and donation lists and when I find such a source I note it. This is laborious, slow work. . . . The initial listing really needs library research. It is extremely important to get this information organized in some such systematic way. . . . Mere alphabetical listing of names and characteristics is not sufficient.[10]

Phillips was flexible and tireless in searching out substitutes for plants that did not please him or Dr. Fairchild in their growth or flower- and fruit-bearing habits: "I think I've discovered another highly salt-tolerant palm *(Copernicia gigas* and *cop. bailiana)*," he wrote to Fairchild in 1941; those he referred to are tall, robust fan palms with a smooth trunk and round crown of glossy leaves. Among the trees of Puerto Rico, he came across matchwood *(Didymopanax morototoni)*, which he described as a sixty-foot tree with a trunk of six to eighteen inches, and he reminded Fairchild "to ask Wal-singham to send some seeds. . . . It grows all over Cuba, and must be in his back yard. . . . Lynch has an *Enterolobium cyclocarpum* . . . a *guanacasta* ripening a crop of pods. . . . I knew this tree on the Isthmus and it always interested me."[11]

Phillips saw the danger of planting every gift received in the diminishing space available and warned Fairchild about it on several occasions, but to Fairchild each gift was exciting. He went right out and found someone to help him plant it wherever he saw a spot, without consulting Phillips and without regard to design, and beamed at Phillips while agreeing they must be careful of overplanting. So great was his enthusiasm that had he lived another decade, the Garden's major open spaces might have been in jeopardy.

There were other threats to the open spaces in Phillips's design. Early in 1941, when the Garden was well established, Fairchild announced that he wanted a palm glade to honor his idol, Liberty Hyde Bailey, world renowned horticultural authority and author. Fairchild wanted it to be a spectacular space. And Montgomery had come up with a request of his own. He told Phillips he wanted a view from his office window at the Garden. He would like "to have a cut made through the oak woods (the oak hammock on the escarpment slope) so that he could see the lake on the lowlands from his desk in the end of the museum wing." This, too, involved encroachment and shifting existing open space. Phillips solved both requests in one ingenious design.

Until he found a solution he was loath to make the unattractive cut into the existing woods. It would have had an angular relation to the lake axis and would not have been "a very attractive piece of planning." But as he looked over the map with a view to providing something that could be called a palm glade, it occurred to him that by making two symmetrical cuts to the south on an axis extending down to the south lake, and by clearing away the woods between,

> I would have a trapezoidal opening with some suggestion of design. . . . The narrow east end could not let in much of the unwanted northeast wind, and the broad upper end [of the trapezoid] could make possible a standing place where people could take in the view down the lake. . . . By cutting through the woods two diagonal avenues centered on the viewing position (the northerly one of which would give Colonel Montgomery his view) the whole plot could acquire a certain integration, and then might be regarded as a palm glade. The sides of the trapezoid could be lined with palms, and the avenues as well and the oak woods could be underplanted with shade-demanding species of palms."[12]

On either side of Phillips's "standing place" were rock stairs to the lowland and the formal sunken garden, cut in the same trapezoidal pattern but

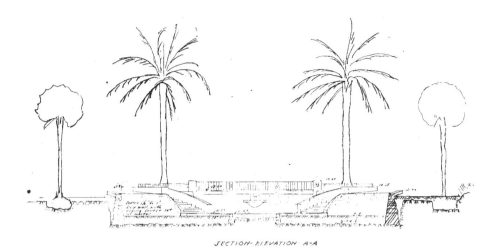

SECTION-ELEVATION A-A

Fairchild Tropical Garden. Bailey Palm Glade. Elevation. (Courtesy of Dade County Parks and Recreation, Landscape Architectural Section)

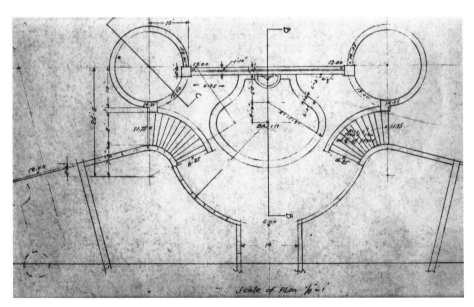

Scale of Plan ⅛=1

Fairchild Tropical Garden. Bailey Palm Glade. Detail plan of stairs and walls. (Courtesy of Dade County Parks and Recreation, Landscape Architectural Section)

in reverse—a mirror image of the one above—all grass, and bordered with palms and lilies. Instead of focusing on the lakes, the main view here was facing the stairways with a grotto between them.

Whereupon Phillips tore open the whole center of the flourishing three-year-old garden and brought in his heavy machinery. As the CCC could not work on the private part of the garden, convict labor was used. Fairchild's and Montgomery's thoughts as they watched the destruction before reconstruction of the Garden are not set down. It is more than likely that neither had any idea what his request entailed; but once the orders were given, who would have dared to say a word, voice a doubt? What if that tall, quiet, very independent man decided he had simply had enough and walked off, leaving them with that unholy unreconstructed mess?

Phillips spent the next year making a palm glade with view. Fairchild watched it grow with delight: "The little palms newly planted . . . are doing well and the view which was in Phillips's imagination begins to be evident to one with my modest amount of the imaginative stuff. It's going to be an outstanding piece of landscaping when we fill the broad lowlands back of the Amphitheater of the Garden Clubs of America with African wine palms, Costa Rican *Raphia taedigeras*, *Nipas*, and perhaps *Oncospermas*, the view from the crest of the hill back of the Museum will be a thrilling landscape."[13]

The Liberty Hyde Bailey Palm Glade was dedicated in February 1942. Bailey, then in his eighty-ninth year, was there for the festivities. Many people thought the Bailey Palm Glade outshone the Overlook, but the "palm people" at the Garden considered it a waste of space and had some palms planted into the grass on the lower level; on the upper part the cycad collection and other planting gradually encroached on the open space. Later, when Nixon Smiley became director of the Garden, he asked Phillips to explain "why there are no palms in the Palmglade," and why when palms were planted there and full grown, Phillips had them removed:

> These questions come from thinking that the Palmglade is only the formal opening in the woods between the terrace and the lake. But it was my intention . . . that the name should be applied to the entire hillside. There was a certain degree of arbitrariness in that decision, but . . . there was a degree of arbitrariness in David Fairchild's choice of the term; he could not say what a palmglade might be; hence I concluded it might be

any arrangement of palms. The opening would be, I thought, an important and desirable feature of the Garden, and I certainly never intended that the central low portion should be blocked up with tall-growing palms. . . . Some flowering herbaceous plant seemed to me to be clearly indicated, and I think the Crinums and Hemerocallis are about as good as can be found . . . which produce a floral display lasting for weeks . . . welcome recourse when visitors plaintively inquire, "where are the flowers?"

Hence, if anyone insists on regarding the formal opening as The Palmglade, making use of a sort of poetic license, he is on safe ground so long as he accepts the opening—an opening flanked by palms in a mixed wood of oaks and palms—and cherishes it. Compositionally—and without composition what have you?—no other course is thinkable.[14]

Smiley was delighted. It was the "Palm [Society]," he wrote, who were giving him grief because they "frankly admit they're not interested in vistas or open areas; they want only palms, palms, and more palms, and they are quite jealous of any area that is planted to grass rather than palms. They would even go so far as to put floating islands in the water in order to cover the entire Garden with these Phallic symbols. Your letter," he wrote, "solves my problem once and for all, and I shall put it in the record."[15]

Fairchild Tropical Garden. The palm glade from the lake. Drawing by Phillips. (Author's Collection)

Fairchild Tropical Garden. Garden Club of America Amphitheater. Elevation, planting study. (Courtesy of Dade County Parks and Recreation, Landscape Architectural Section)

MONTGOMERY GAVE AWAY open space on an even grander scale. A practical businessman, he considered donors a top priority, to be fostered and warmly thanked. A case in point was the Garden Club of America Amphitheater.

Fairchild Tropical Garden's exhibit of tropicana in "Gardens on Parade" at the 1939 World Fair in New York was seen by garden club members nationwide. As a result, the Garden was presented with the Garden Club of America Founders Fund for 1940. Mrs. Joseph Cudahy, member from Palm Beach, came down to the Garden to see what ongoing Garden project should receive their support. At the meeting, Phillips suggested that an "outdoor meeting place which might be called an auditorium or amphitheater would be a decided addition to the grounds."[16]

As it was built on the county-owned lowland, the CCC began the excavation of the south lake and the rock retaining wall bounding the semicircular amphitheater, and completed the speaker's dais before they left for war in 1942. The dais was a raised ashlar platform, twelve by twenty-four feet, with a stone screen wall behind it and a round pool in front.

Phillips carefully planted against the Garden boundary line and around the amphitheater a special collection of palms, including royals, Washingtonia, fan palms (*Coccothrinax acuminata, Thrinax crinata, Elais guinensis*), and oil, thatch, and sabal palms. But when Mrs. Joseph Cudahy wanted more shade around the area and suggested coconut palms, Montgomery instructed Phillips to give her the desired palms. In this case, Phillips's original design was lost and not restored for a decade: "I never conceived the thing [the Amphitheater] as a horticultural showpiece," Phillips wrote then, "but only as a passage of quiet formal scenery, a contrast and change from what prevailed elsewhere in the Garden. The attempt to get shade over the sitting space, by planting *Cocos plumosas* and *Bucidas*, destroyed the formality by filling up the open hemicycle, without creating any compensatory fine effect."[17]

About the other memorial buildings and elements in the Fairchild Tropical Garden named for special dignitaries and donors, Phillips wrote that "the Colonel is much inclined to this sort of thing as a way of interesting people and getting contributions. It might, however, result finally in a sort of horticultural Westminster Abbey . . . not an objective I should ever think of." One of these, the Chamberlin Hibiscus Garden, was planted out on the lowlands at the east end of the south lake with a magnificent collection of hibiscus and a handsome gate and gateposts. Dedicated in 1943, it was demolished in 1945 by a hurricane that brought in ten feet of water from the bay. Some of the ground remained persistently salty and this memorial had to be replanted higher up.

The Moos Memorial, dedicated in 1948, was built in and around what is popularly known in Florida as a sinkhole, more delicately a "sunken garden," a prehistoric sea-washed declivity or weakness in the limestone floor, with crevices in the rock wall excellent for planting. There had long been talk about doing something "especially fine" on this site. In 1948, the opportunity arose. "The sink was deepened to the extent thought possible without running into drainage difficulties," Phillips wrote. "The sandy sides were steepened and stabilized with rock work—little natural ledges having been uncovered [to create] a damp, sheltered spot bordered with massed tall palms, where a particular lushness of vegetation would be possible": an abundance of air plants and orchids all over the host live oak, and ferns (*Asplenium nidus, Polypodium popolypodiodes*), anthuriums (*aroids*), and philodendrons.[18]

AFTER PEARL HARBOR on December 7, 1941, when the CCC was preparing to close down to go to war, Phillips became a consulting landscape architect to the Dade County Park Department. Barnes tried to persuade him to sign on full time when Park Service employees went on the Civil Service rolls, but Phillips refused to become any part of it. "But Bill," Barnes said, "you'd have all the medical and other perks; you wouldn't have to punch a clock for me, who would know?" Phillips said, "I would know."[19]

Phillips wrote to Fairchild:

I slipped quietly out of the CCC two weeks ago and have gone to work with the County on the new park developments. This, for some reason, is hush-hush business. You are the first person down that way to whom I have told it. . . . The change will not weaken my relationships with the Garden, but may on the contrary strengthen them. Temporarily, I am having to concentrate on the new jobs, but I am sure that I shall be able to continue to make the kind of contribution to the Garden that I am fitted to make. This job has been just suited to my opportunities, and I am deeply grateful to you for getting me into it.[20]

In the following year federal funds for park maintenance dried up, and as the CCC and able-bodied convicts were called up and available labor dropped to almost nil, Phillips's county job was eliminated.

Before he went to work at "local military establishments,"[21] Phillips expressed his thanks to Colonel Montgomery: "Of all the things I have done at Miami the Garden has been the most satisfactory, and largely because

Fairchild Tropical Garden, 1947. Evaluating the Garden's development along the escarpment in nine years. (Author's Collection)

of the appreciative attitude held by you and Mrs. Montgomery [and] Dr. Fairchild." Phillips said he particularly appreciated being "able to work in a professional way, to some extent at least, without having to think about charges, a luxury which, ordinarily, is only available to people of great means."[22]

Montgomery answered immediately by offering Phillips a job as consultant to Fairchild Tropical Garden, "on a professional basis."[23] In February, he wrote to Commissioner Charles Crandon: "I have been fortunate to arrange [continuing work by] Mr. Phillips. Tropical gardens grow so fast that if not properly laid out they lose most of their beauty. . . . It requires a master mind to know what a tropical garden will look like in 10 or 20 years. Mr. Phillips is the only one who has the whole picture in his eye."

Crandon guaranteed that the Dade County Park Department would honor Phillips's authority at Fairchild Tropical Garden. With this, the colonel ensured the Garden's future; Phillips remained as landscape architect until 1954 and returned in 1956 until his death. Thus, with some bumpy interludes, the Garden had the benefit of a master for twenty-five years.[24]

SIMONE HAD CHOSEN Christian Science to control her tuberculosis. Her condition forced Phillips to return from Jacksonville, where he had been the designing engineer of airport facilities, drawing plans of runways and aprons for Reynolds, Smith and Hills.

He remained in Miami throughout the war, but he did not lack for war work. He was a full, if silent, master partner with Prentiss French on the plans and layout of Camp Shelby, Mississippi, during 1941 and 1942. French lived at the camp and paid Phillips out of his pocket. "Dear Doc—Shelby has materialized. Your letter . . . that you might help me out fills me with enthusiasm. Really this job scares me to death, but if you were on hand I should feel quite differently. . . . It's a fairly rich job and I am sure *we two* [can] come to terms on the spot. . . . Could you possibly take leave of absence [to come to Camp Shelby] and help me? Have little doubt I can at least match Dade County remuneration and should be mentally relieved if you came."[1] A grateful French wrote, "I could never have done it without you, Doc."

The Fairchild Tropical Garden played its part in the war effort. In 1944, student pilots at the Opa-Locka Naval Base made "as many as 200 training visits each week to FTG . . . [to learn] skills for survival on tropical islands in the event of being shot down on combat missions. They were given the necessary natural materials, and were taught to identify foods such as coconuts, sapodilla, chayotes, Surinam cherries, coco plum, taro root, cassava, and the like. They were also taught how to make a fishing line by shredding a leaf of the sisal plant and how to tap the leaf bases of the traveler's palm for water. . . . The textbook used was written by Dr. Merrill, then president of Fairchild Tropical Garden, 'Emergency Food and Poisonous Plants of the Isles of the Pacific'."[2]

AS MONTGOMERY'S ESTATE, the Coconut Grove Palmetum, was adjacent to Fairchild Tropical Garden, Phillips thought of them as one design. Phillips rearranged the palmetum gates and entrance, and after supervising the lake dug by Ray Vernor, Montgomery's garden superintendent, Phillips designed a vista with willows and trees framing the lake, leaving plenty of sky and grass and low shrubs visible to enhance the view from the colonel's terrace. His charges for this work were so modest that his client was upset. Montgomery said he and his wife thought Phillips's services were "really above price, but in these days it is necessary to arrive at some price . . . and your bills should be in line with your services."[3]

"As to the size of my bills," Phillips replied, "I cannot charge the county people at rates unusual to them for similar technical services without creating jealousies and embarrassments; and it would be a poor display of gratitude to charge you at a high rate to make up for the other's low rate."[4]

On May 15, Phillips wrote and thanked the colonel for "two raises," and on October 1, "If you insist on paying me more than I arrive at . . . I suggest we go on a monthly retaining fee basis, you to decide . . . the amount. I could undertake to do whatever may be needed at your place and the FTG that falls within my field and talents, but I would not be bound exclusively to this service as I desire and intend to maintain an independent professional existence as long as it is at all possible to do it." He was, indeed, busy doing just that.

Phillips was at the apex of his career, and as he wrote to Fairchild, "I am actually enjoying myself despite the complex of duties thrust upon me." Beginning in 1938, he had been performing an astonishing juggling act. He finished up at Matheson Hammock and designed and supervised the planting of the Fairchild Tropical Garden—serving two masters, the county and the owners—while at the same time "making studies for [Baker's] Haulover [Beach] and Crandon Park layouts" in Miami and for two small parks, in Homestead and the Redlands, for the Park Service; he was Park Service consultant for the Overseas Highway to Key West project—his report on this last received national recognition and special commendation. He was an active partner in the building of Camp Shelby. Meanwhile, all his other tasks increased: the requests for drawings, designs, and plans for roads, private parks, and residences; garden club talks and flower shows throughout the state; and his huge daily correspondence.

And again, there was Olmsted. He had recently retired to California where, now eighty-six, he was involved with a campaign dear to his heart to save the remaining redwoods and gave his name to the firm only as consultant. He had continued to write to Phillips frequently on projects as they arose, whenever he "got stuck" or wanted a sounding board; their relationship seemed to take on a different tone. For a park job in Homosassa Springs, "about which you [Phillips] once wrote me an illuminating report," Olmsted wrote a lengthy description of the possible work and received several suggestions from Phillips; now he wrote: "Do you care, for the good of humanity to give me at your leisure any suggestions on two points?" Olmsted, although bristling at being caught making a poor choice for Florida—"Yes! I said Gordonias"—was in command of the situation as always, but, also as always, not wanting to do the final work. The "two points" covered the whole job—how and what to plant.[5]

In 1946, Olmsted wrote from Sacramento, California, "I am groping for help on a State Park general survey which I have been employed to make for the California State Park Commission in the next six months for a lump sum covering all expenses." The job would require much driving through the state. Would Phillips be interested in joining him? "I don't know anyone I would rather have for a helper." As an inducement, Olmsted said, "I also have a cemetery general plan, a job of considerable interest and a little park in Monterey, and other things may turn up which I could ease over on to you." However, Phillips "would have to park Simone and the children somewhere, and it is the devil's own job to find any lodging place." It is hard to believe that Olmsted did not know how ill Simone was, how impossible this made it for Phillips to leave.

Olmsted planned to "travel in [his] station wagon, generally with Mrs. O. with most of our household goods piled in the back . . . [and probably] have to sleep by the roadside occasionally—auto courts . . . are so crowded."[6]

COLONEL MONTGOMERY LIKED the idea of putting Phillips on an indefinite retainer. Even more generously, before the colonel died, he presented Phillips with a car and stocks.

"Do you know," Mrs. Montgomery said, "those two men would sit out on the terrace comfortably with a drink and not say a word for hours, if they didn't feel like it. [When they talked, it] was politics, the stock market, automobiles, books—Bob was concerned about Bill; the way he lived, his sick wife. . . . If not for the Depression," she said, "Phillips would never have been there to do the Garden." In better times, she and Bob agreed, "Phillips would have been working successfully somewhere else."[7]

To millionaire Montgomery, the now moderately comfortable Phillips seemed this side of penury. Montgomery knew vaguely that it took many jobs—although he did not know exactly what they were—to keep Phillips and his family solvent. He admired Phillips greatly for his recognized talents, for his independence and seeming disregard of money, but in truth he had little patience with a man so rich in intellect who failed to turn it into real income. "If you want to know the real story of a man check out his financial record," he used to say. Phillips never let on to the colonel that his experience in the Depression had made him resolve never to be poor again. A thrifty New Englander, he pinched to save.

In 1942, when Juliette and Mary were thirteen and ten, Phillips began caring for Simone at home, because she begged to stay with him and her Christian Science practitioner and not be sent away for treatment. Extraordinary precautionary methods prevailed for tubercular home patients, including a ban on hiring help; milk had to be boiled for the family, and for the next six years, Phillips was responsible for the physical welfare of his daughters as well.

He adored them. He boasted in letters to friends and family about Juliette's drawing, her prowess with horses, her dark-haired good looks and popularity, and he spoke lovingly of Mary for her music and quiet disposition. But parenting in these circumstances was a considerable burden. There was never enough time to do it all: to teach the girls routine family chores, oversee vitally important hygiene, homework, clothes. "I am swamped with domestic details," he wrote to Fairchild, "while I am trying to earn a living."[8]

Although Simone was never entirely well throughout their twenty-five-year marriage, the first ten years were full of love and hope for the future. There were family trips across the country to California, to Maine for lengthy summer stays, to the Carolina mountains for her health, and Simone had appeared pleased to settle in Palm Beach, where there were art galleries and sociability. She was an excellent mother of babies and small children until her illness. She wanted to raise perfectly mannered little French girls (although she never spoke French to them), but when her healthy American youngsters grew up and became normally rambunctious, Simone, now quite ill, lost control and her own behavior became irrational. A key to the incidents of her breakdown was the depression, which locked her and her children in Florida when Phillips had to be away from home for long periods. Miami was not Paris. She grew to loathe the enervating heat and storms, the cultural aridity, her homesickness. Simone was something of a snob; she rarely found a worthy friend; she built a lot of resentment.

She rallied with a long visit from her mother, which helped to normalize the household, until Madame Guillot rushed to get aboard the last boat to Europe after the outbreak of war, leaving Simone in emotional turmoil. She began to target the adolescent Juliette, whose exuberance and independence enraged her, with the direst threats to send the girl to a home for incorrigibles, and Simone cemented family differences with odious comparison: "Why can't you be more like your sister Mary?"

Whenever Juliette was "confined to her room," she simply stepped over the window sill and was gone. "I grew up thinking my father was a cold Yankee," she said. "I never appreciated him until I had [three] boys of my own and saw his pleasure in them. Mary and I never knew a thing about him; he never confided in us. I couldn't deal with my mother at all, so I found wonderful surrogate families through my riding and working on horse farms, with the parents of my high school and college friends, and my boy friends. I was luckier than Mary. She was younger and allowed herself to get stuck at home."[9]

Phillips smoldered, forcing himself not to release his anger at his wife's Christian Science beliefs, which precluded medical help. When Simone died in 1948, Phillips wrote to French: "Well, Simone is gone. . . . My head tells me it is the best thing that could happen, but my heart is very sore. The girls have been fine. Juliette especially has displayed traits of maturity and staunchness which have been very comforting. I will say no more beyond making a tribute to Simone's extraordinary stoical fortitude, which, of course, was due to her religious outlook. Nevertheless, there was bad judgement behind it. . . . A tenth of the fortitude which she deployed first and last, intelligently used, would have restored her to a tolerably useful and satisfactory existence."[10]

When Simone Phillips died in 1948, Phillips's remedy for grief was sailing, his lifetime passion. Photograph by Mary Phillips. (Author's Collection)

Mary Phillips at the helm, Biscayne Bay. She was her father's companion until his death—he expected her to want to sail. (Author's Collection)

Juliette Phillips MacGregor Coyle. Her passion while growing up was horses, but later she switched her allegiance and went sailing too when she returned for visits. Photograph by Mary Phillips. (Author's Collection)

After Simone's death Phillips could not lose himself in grief because he had to raise his children and work. According to the letters of his friends at the time, he spoke as little as possible, as if each word were a stone. To his sister Florence, he expressed his guilt about Simone's loneliness, her inability to cope with his life. For twenty-five years, Nell Montgomery Jennings said, "he had a young beloved; what he lacked was an American wife and partner to push him, to help him advance."[11]

THE DEATHS OF Colonel Robert Montgomery in May 1953 and David Fairchild in August 1954 dealt serious blows to the Fairchild Tropical Garden and saddened Phillips, who had enjoyed both friendships. The truth of the matter was hidden from all but two or three people: Phillips, at age sixty-nine in 1954, was in deep depression.

There was a further shock for him when the new president and acting treasurer of the Garden, Jack Corbin, discovered Phillips's monthly retainer from Montgomery and began to question the validity of continuing it. When Phillips learned of this, he returned the retainer check immediately. He wrote:

Col. Montgomery began these payments without making clear what obligation they placed on me. I always assumed they were retainers to assure advice and help when and as needed . . . or [to] secure my good will and cooperation as an influential person in the County Park Department, or merely as a pension in consideration of past services. . . . Up until recent months I [accepted, for] . . . even when I did not accomplish much positively, I at least kept people from doing foolish and detrimental things. I [had] fairly tight control over the physical aspects of the Garden. Having Col. Montgomery's trust, I had authority. . . . That condition no longer exists. . . . My connection with the Garden has . . . become impracticable, and I propose to end it. This I do with every feeling of gratitude towards a place that has helped so much to make my existence in Miami meaningful, and has contributed appreciably for such a long time to my support.[12]

His resignation was accepted. There was some mention by the Executive Committee that they hoped he would be "available in the future for advice and counsel. . . . Mrs. Montgomery will discuss [this] with you."

WEST ELEVATION

Above: Baker's Haulover beach, North Miami. Planting elevation. (Courtesy of Dade County Park and Recreation, Landscape Architectural Section)

Left: University of Miami, Coral Gables, Florida. Drawing notes for campus housing. Here Phillips indicates a spreading tree (left), perhaps a royal poinciana. (Author's Collection)

University of Miami. Phillips sought to brighten the contemporary campus architecture with large flowering trees such as yellow and pink *Tabebuia*—the most spectacular of all—the red-blossomed tulip tree (*Spathodea campanulata*), or the silk oak (*Grevillea robusta*), all growing to one hundred feet, plus the smaller crape myrtles and flowering orchid trees (*Bauhinia*). (Author's Collection)

Left: University of Miami. Planting study drawing. (Author's Collection)

Below: Miami International Airport. Drawing. "This airport is . . . such a large and complicated building, so much walking before you can get to the plane or from it to a car . . . but it is very impressive. Hardly beautiful. I don't see that my plantings are likely to make it beautiful. However, some day you'll land here and be able to say your dad had a hand in it," wrote Phillips to Juliette in 1959. (Author's Collection)

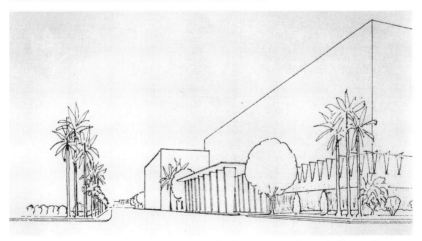

The Miami Herald Building. Planting study drawing. (Author's Collection)

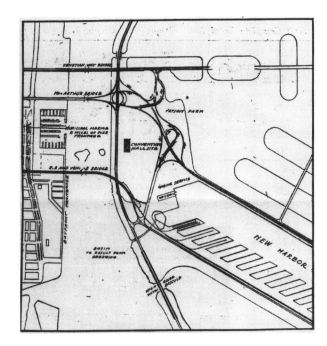

Phillips offers the city a plan for a new Miami waterfront: increased port facilities, new bridge and causeway, and redeveloped bay front. "No other city anywhere would have anything like it . . . [but] how odd, I offered a plan, gratis, [to be] carried out over 20 years, offering a lot for the money . . . and they chose to pay [someone else] $25,000 for [what] will ultimately cost tens of millions." (Quoted by Nixon Smiley, *Miami Herald*, October 23, 1955)

Mrs. Montgomery, in New Jersey and about to be married, was appalled when she heard what had happened, but Phillips had already left.

It was an ugly finish for a sublime achievement. He was sure that his days at Fairchild Tropical Garden were over—actually, it was to be only a matter of months before he was back—but in the continuing postwar boom there was a considerable amount of new work for Phillips, including public buildings, churches, cemeteries, and residential landscapes all over the state; many of them were clustered in South Miami.

Approaching seventy, he did not feel up to great swings and changes; he had lost interest. His wife and two special friends were gone. His daughter Mary, sister Florence, and close friend Ray Ward remained close by, but his older daughter Juliette was grown and leaving. French had moved to California. Former youthful sweethearts now widowed came to see him when they passed through Florida. It only made him feel worse: they had more money, energy, and health and more of a sense of fun. He may also have felt keenly disappointed by the great opportunity missed because of his responsibilities when he read the postscript of a newsy 1950 letter from Olmsted:

I withdrew from partnership as of December 31, 1949 . . . leaving the responsibility of carrying on to Whiting and Marquis (and such others as they may join with them as partners). . . . I wish they could get Zach back [but] he is firmly anchored in Washington. . . .

Looking toward future continuity of the Olmsted firm . . . in pursuance of its traditionally high ideals [we need] recruits of first rate ability and large caliber as designers. . . . You are one of the few men I know whose qualities as designer and grasp of sound principles in landscape architecture would unquestionably strengthen the firm.[13]

Phillips apologized for his delay in answering:

I have been . . . deeply touched by your expressions of esteem, and the implications of your suggestions. . . . What you say about me . . . comes with the force of an award of merit, a justification for having lived and worked. I treasure it more than I do the Barbour Medal given me . . . the other night.

You have guessed my probable attitude. . . . It is not that I think I am accomplishing very much here, or am likely to. Nevertheless I am strongly bound to the place. . . . All of my earth knowledge is of Florida, and my bag of tricks would be of little use elsewhere. . . . The idea of removing from this relatively simple . . . environment . . . [and] of moving . . . the young ladies—is too much for me to face.[14]

IN 1956, Edward Bok's son, Judge Curtis Bok, wrote directly to Phillips and asked him to do an evaluation and complete overhaul of Mountain Lake Sanctuary, "which he feels rightly has deteriorated, and in part has never been satisfactory for the kind of use it gets."[1]

Phillips was not feeling well. His back and his legs hurt; he complained about them a good deal, remembering how much outdoor work he had been able to do all his life. Besides, the last few years had been extraordinarily busy with residential gardens, state roadwork, big housing projects, traveling to Gainesville, Jacksonville, Tampa, Boca Raton, the Keys, and back to Miami. Several commissions were ongoing or on hold; there were more to come. He knew that if he took on this job by himself, there would be a great deal of walking and many trips for conferences and planting oversight. He did not wish to be reminded of the many changes in his life since he had first lived and worked at Mountain Lake Colony and Sanctuary, when Simone would come into the office on hot summer afternoons "bringing ice cream to the drawing boards while we mopped the sweat."[2]

He also did not want to divert income from his old firm—Olmsted Brothers had benefited from Mountain Lake activities for more than thirty years. And above all, he balked at putting his name on "Olmsted's work," because, he told Judge Bok, "certain ethical considerations" had to be observed. Phillips did not want to appear to step in and "erase" his old mentor, if by chance Olmsted remained interested in the project. "Olmsted has been ever generous in his praise of me," Phillips wrote, "and the last thing I would want would be [to be] . . . a credit grabber with respect to him. It is commonly thought to be highly unethical and the worst of bad form . . . to claim credit for the work of a principal. . . . The *conception* of the Sanctuary was F. L. Olmsted's, and all the professional attentions given it (by me, and Hans Koehler, before me) were supplied by Olmsted Brothers with whom I happened to be associated." Nixon Smiley, who was planning to do a story for the *Miami Herald*, asked Phillips several times what had been his specific contribution at the sanctuary, then and in the past, without getting a clear answer.[3]

Koehler had already assumed credit for the Mountain Lake Sanctuary and had been roundly and not altogether truthfully put down by Olmsted: Koehler applied to John D. Rockefeller for a job at the Cloisters, citing an article he wrote in 1940: "I did all of the planting at the [Mountain Lake Sanctuary]."[4] Rockefeller asked Olmsted Brothers for a reference and received a reply from Olmsted:

> Hans Koehler had nothing whatsoever to do with that job. . . . It occurs to me that if you see any possibility of using Mr. Koehler's services in any way you might like to have me prepare and send you an analysis of his abilities and qualifications, which are exceptionally good in certain important ways, and of his limitations; as bearing on his inability for different kinds of undertakings. . . . Even within the limits indicated . . . to you, he would be subject to handicaps that an employer ought to [know] . . . offset by his special qualifications in other respects. Koehler, whom I have known for 48 years [since Olmsted was 12!] is [so] remarkable it would take me some time to write an illuminating analysis. . . . I will gladly . . . if [you wish].

Mr. Rockefeller did not wish. Phillips, who had the best and longest claim to Mountain Lake Sanctuary work, wanted no part of such an argument.[5]

But Prentiss French thought his colleague's reticence went beyond ethics. "After all, [although] he put 'OB' all over the plans at Mountain Lake Colony, OB saw very few of the plans."[6] To Phillips he wrote: "I'd be happy to have you put my name on your work as you did for OB." French was more protective of his friend's reputation than Phillips was of himself. When *Town and Country* magazine published a photo feature on two Mountain Lake houses and credited only the architect—whereas, said French, the photos were all of the landscape—French wrote to the Allied Arts Commission to request that they take the matter up with the magazine and credit Phillips properly.[7] It was French, again, who urged Phillips to bring suit when Dade County architect Baxter put his own name on Phillips's plan for Baker's Haulover beach and published it in the *Miami Herald.* (Phillips had written an outraged letter to Commissioner Crandon, who apologized, but no correction ever appeared.)

"Doc," French wrote now, "I think you minimize the importance of the letter from Curtis Bok. . . . Of course you are correct to suggest there is a question of professional ethics, but I do hope you'll be able to take it on solo without OB. This is important and Curtis Bok is dead right that it should be restudied." French added, "This sort of thing should command a really tangible fee."[8]

THERE WERE MANY points for Phillips to reminisce about and mull over. It was proven that the price of working for Olmsted Brothers as a representative was well-paid professional anonymity, for those who stayed with the firm. Phillips had not stayed. He had left honorably, more or less with Olmsted's blessing (despite Olmsted's dislike of losing his men to independent activity), and with punishingly hard work on his own had made a name for himself. It had taken its toll. He did not want to work officially on Olmsted's behalf, again; but predictably, opening an old wound or simply out of habit, Phillips called in William Marquis, now a senior partner in Olmsted Brothers.

Although he had never seen the sanctuary and knew next to nothing of tropical gardening or terrain, Marquis was eager to step in. In answer to French's letter, Phillips admitted that while he was not anxious to spend much time in Lake Wales any more, he didn't think the job would be too pressing if he were a consultant, and he was certain that something would come of it; he was talking himself into it.[9] And so, with his reflexive dread of other hands on *his* designs, he agreed to be part of a dual arrangement: Phillips would do the groundwork evaluation and recommendations, and Marquis would handle the business end and correspondence with, as Phillips put it sardonically, the "admirably dignified, restrained and rational" Judge Bok. On July 2, 1956, they delivered "The Mountain Lake Sanctuary: A Report Prepared by Olmsted Brothers and William Lyman Phillips," written by Phillips.

However, Phillips found Bok uncooperative and almost impossible to please. The somewhat irrational proceedings dragged on for three more years. To Kenneth Morrison, the sanctuary director, Phillips said he was "just about nonplussed to know what to suggest that would please him [Bok]. If you have any idea I should be glad to know it."[10] Bok, Phillips wrote to Marquis, "can't tell why he dislikes certain suggestions. . . . He has merely vague feelings. He ducks, says he is only a layman and relies on expert advisors to tell him what to do. Yet when his expert advisors make recommendations he throws out 4 out of 5 . . . if not 9 out of 10. At the same time he has no hesitation about taking decisions on his own in matters he ought to refer to his experts. I am glad I am not alone in finding him a tough problem."[11]

Phillips finally told Marquis that while he had made it a point for the past forty years never to quit until told to leave—a lesson well learned at Balboa—it was absurd to carry on an elaborate correspondence, especially "when you [Marquis] purposely order out my replies." Tact was all very well, Phillips said, but "I want you to please send this next letter [in answer to a really insulting one from the judge] precisely as I have written it. I believe he will be angry, but I also believe he likes a good fight."[12]

He was right; Bok wrote to him to proceed and was adamant that he wished to hear only from Phillips. "My criticism of the existing [vegetation]," Phillips reported, "is that it presents a lot of trees and very little landscape." He recommended extensive cutting—not redesign but restoration[13]—to which Bok heartily agreed: "I am very much in favor of opening up and letting views in."[14]

Once the cutting back and clearing was under way, Phillips was satisfied to turn over supervision of the physical work to Joseph Hudak, a talented young man and the newest member of the Olmsted Brothers firm. Hudak had never worked with tropical plants, but Phillips, whom he remembered as a "cooperative personality willing to teach," would ask, "Tell me what you respond to, Joe," and walked the sanctuary with him until he was satisfied that Hudak could do the job. Hudak was impressed by Phillips and the "brilliant conversation." He stayed in North Miami with Phillips several times and remembered picking avocados from the yard to take home. When Hudak got to work in earnest at Mountain Lake, he was incredulous to discover that the plants were ordered from "*Michigan*!" a nursery Phillips had helped establish.[15]

Bok asked what could be done "to increase the flora in the Sanctuary?"

Drawing notes for Lake Wales road studies between Sanctuary and Colony. Same bend in the road with increased planting. (Author's Collection)

He wanted Phillips to provide new and interesting plants; he remembered the park with more color. True, Phillips said, it had been a handsomer park before "horticulture dried up [here]" for lack of maintenance and direction. As for new and interesting plants that would adapt to the climate and soil, it might still be difficult to please the judge: "Riding around Lake Wales I see nothing I could not have seen there in the '20s. . . . [Very few plants] having conspicuous and pleasing bloom . . . have shown up in my 34 years in Florida. . . . What you [Judge Bok] see at the Sanctuary represents the efforts of plant introduction to date."[16]

Phillips proposed that in the plant renewal program, they put more plants from Australia in the sanctuary. He was enthusiastic about acacias, which he had planted there years before, especially the golden mimosa (*Acacia baileyana*); the Sydney golden wattle (*A. longifolia*), fast growing, spreading, and fragrant; and the pearl acacia shrub (*A. pedalyrifolia*). While many varieties had been lost, the pearl acacia had gone to seed and sprouted in two unexpected places, dry and unwatered; it "plainly needs to be let alone."[17]

There were more than fifty varieties of acacias in over four hundred species that could be suitable in Florida.

Suddenly, on May 29, 1958, Curtis Bok wrote to Marquis terminating his arrangement with Olmsted Brothers, on the grounds that it was really a question of "our showing full confidence" in the new director [Morrison], and not letting him think we must have a landscape architect constantly in attendance." An angry Marquis wrote to Phillips, "What I can't understand is that Curtis Bok thought a trained ornithologist as qualified to be a good landscape architect and administrator as well. That was how the place slipped backward under the former incumbent and will probably do it again if you [Phillips] get a 'release,' too."[18] Phillips was invited to continue as consultant; Bok's quarrel was really with the firm, Morrison told him. Because Olmsted was gone now, Phillips told Marquis that he felt he could keep the job in good conscience:

> I will carry on this thing in my usual desultory fashion. People on one side or the other continue to keep me busier than I prefer to be . . . [but] how really silly it is to try to carry on a professional service single-handed. . . . I keep wondering if the world will not eventually find me out.
>
> Nevertheless, I feel uncomfortable over the whole situation—a team broken up and one member of it retained, cannot but leave the other . . . embittered. I hope you don't feel that way about it. . . . I suppose . . . that I happened to be the one in whom they saw more present usefulness. . . . Working with the old Office, with you, has been a pleasure to me. I shall, I fear, feel lonely without you.[19]

Mountain Lake Sanctuary was renamed Bok Tower Gardens, to avoid confusion with the private Mountain Lake Colony. Abandoning the word *sanctuary*, which describes the garden more aptly than any other, was a shame. The Boks kept an active hand in the garden's future until the 1980s; it is now controlled by the American Foundation.

This garden, as Phillips once wrote of it, affects "the senses of the visitor gratefully, creates a poetic mood, induces feelings of reverence, stirs the mind to rapt admiration. . . . A more striking example of the power of beauty could hardly be found; better proof that here beauty exists could not be asked for."[20]

Fairchild Tropical Garden, 1954–1963

He was a very unusual man. Independent, vulnerable, gruff. . . . He felt
keenly the lack of understanding of his efforts . . . when clients made changes
without consulting him . . . but often he was in a good mood when he worked
with me—he'd joke a bit if he knew you.

STANLEY KIEM[1]

IN FEBRUARY 1955, within a year of Phillips's having resigned as a consultant on retainer to the Fairchild Tropical Garden, Nell Montgomery, now
Mrs. Alvin Jennings, asked him to come back and advise. Always a prime
mover in the enterprise, she now took on the Garden as her main responsibility, giving it most of her time and considerable money. Reluctantly Phillips
returned, first clarifying in a letter to Jack Corbin that he would not de-
prive the acting director, Stanley Kiem, or any others "of all interest or
concern" but wanted "only to make it plain that any plantations or remov-
als are to clear through me." He was returning briefly, he said, because
Nell Jennings "was not pleased with the aimless planting."[2]

Young Kiem had come to the Garden in 1950 and had worked in the
orchid house. There being no director or other professional staff in 1954–
56, he said, "I was the horticulturist, botanist, plant recorder and nursery
man. I was responsible as well for maintenance and special events, and was
acting director during that time." And on his own, usually paying his way,
he traveled through the tropics collecting for the garden, mainly palms and
cycads.[3]

Apparently everyone at the Garden at this date had forgotten that Phillips
was still consultant at the Dade County Park Department and therefore
the consultant for the county side of the Garden as well. His resignation
from the "Garden side" had not removed him from his county role. The
irony could not have escaped Phillips's notice.

Fairchild Tropical Garden. The Rambler gives regular tours. Nobody would ever see the lowlands if people had to walk, Phillips said. (Courtesy of Fairchild Tropical Garden)

His preliminary study and planting plan for the Garden's lowland area had never been undertaken because of World War II; he turned his attention to it now.

When Phillips returned to the Garden, Kiem said, he was mainly concerned with

> the outlines of the plots and groups of plants . . . their size and growth habits, if he wanted to create a dense mass or a scattered arrangement one could see through. For example, [Phillips] was having trouble getting the plantings established on the lowlands. He seldom explained why he arranged plantings or what he hoped to accomplish by designing certain features, but in the case of the island plantings, of trees, he [told me] that if those he had originally scheduled did not do well there, I was to substitute whatever I had available [in the nursery] and thought might grow better; that what he was really concerned with was to create a dense and rather tall mass of trees, sort of a tropical forest, especially on the higher part of the island, with an understory of shrubs so that when viewed across the lake from the north, there would be unbroken foliage down to the water's edge with, hopefully, the crowns of several larger trees and palms rising above.
>
> In other words, I think that he was much more interested in the total effect than in the species of plants used. . . . He was always deeply concerned about the vistas, above all that they be strictly maintained and no

encroachment ever allowed with overgrowth from the sides, as he had designed particular plantings and features that were to be seen through these openings.

When Phillips gave orders for each job, Kiem said, "he was *clear* about it. As far as he was concerned, the original plan [his] prevailed, but his explanations were sketchy. You had to be alert to catch the explanations and comments—if you missed, he'd *remember* and come back at you abruptly; you got the definite impression that he had considered at great length and come to a certain decision of what he wanted."[4]

Kiem described a day in the mid-1950s when Phillips brought to the Garden a plane table, tripod, transit, and compass, and taught him how to work from a plan, to lay it out on the ground. He checked carefully until he was satisfied it was being done to his specs, and then made sketches of what he wanted. He wanted Kiem to work carefully from his plans for the newly developing lowlands; to locate correctly where to stake out the many plants scheduled for the new area, and to add the locations accurately to the existing plot maps.

Fairchild Tropical Garden. Phillips supervising planting of *Phoenix reclinata* palm. (Courtesy of Fairchild Tropical Garden)

In the beginning, Phillips "was still doing almost everything himself. He located all the plants, put out stakes, dug holes, labeled, etc. When we began to work together and Mr. Phillips began to be more comfortable with me, he began to delegate authority; his supervision of adding new palms and trees changed as he trusted me more. I worked up stake sites and prospective plants and we went over them together." As soon as Phillips was reasonably confident that Kiem really was familiar with the plot families, and "felt more assured of my judgment, he would say, 'if you can find space there, go ahead and plant it'."

Kiem recounted a major feat by Phillips when he returned to the Garden. He ordered his county workers to dig the lakes on the lowlands (on the county side) deeper than necessary, blasting to get the crushed rock to mix with marl for a better soil. This was a much easier and more economical way to provide necessary rock to build up the banks, rather than to send trucks out to quarries at some distance—if found. It was the season of the annual blue land crab march to the sea—Old Cutler Road was solid with them. It was hot and the mosquitos were wicked, but he stuck with the job to completion. When Kiem's soil test showed high salt content, Phillips had the county bring in wood chips from tree trimmings. This compact mix was to leach away salt as well as make for good drainage. "Even when it was covered with sea water for a number of hours [the mix] hardly absorbed any salt, with no long term effects," so they could plant.

Phillips had been spending time on the salt question around the state, most recently on the Gulf: "Over porous well aerated fill," he wrote, "is better than impervious; the salt will leach out very quickly. . . . [There will be] less erosion by wind and water. . . . Indian shell mounds are notably fertile sites. . . . They've had time to acquire organic matter, the shell seems to have an ability to take up water, and water is the critical need. . . . Grass can actually be grown on the most unpromising soils with fertilizing provided they're well aerated."[5]

Kiem reminisced. County nurseryman Ray Vernor, who had known and worked with Phillips for years, had said to Kiem: "That Bill Phillips is really something, isn't he? But let me tell you, he may be peculiar, but he's one smart man!" Kiem agreed with Vernor that Phillips was a gentleman who never raised his voice. He might not give a direct answer, Kiem said—"often didn't answer you at all—he'd be thinking, and in a week or two out

Fairchild Tropical Garden. The architectonic Bailey palms (*Copernicia baileyana*). Photograph by William B. Houghton. (Courtesy of Fairchild Tropical Garden)

of the blue would come his answer!" He laughed as he remembered how the work crew had thought Phillips "crazy, but they always did what he asked. He was a *stickler*; they never could be sloppy. They considered him odd, strange, sometimes sour and untalkative, but they joked about it, respected him. He would stand off to one side of a job, rolled plan in hand, and tell me," Kiem said, "what to tell the crew, instead of giving them the order directly."

All of his life, on a project or in his business correspondence, Phillips believed in and obeyed the chain of command; he would never overstep Kiem's prerogative. "One day," Kiem said, "he had the men move a big tree into position, contemplated it for a time, then told me to have them move it to another space. Same thing. On the third or fourth go he had them move it back to the original spot. 'Why couldn't he have left it there in the first place?' they asked me, but he was being as hard on himself out there in the sun as he was on them."

He was harder on himself. He was angry that there was so little he could do with Stanley Kiem and the present labor force to maintain the Garden. Garden administrators had allowed county assistance to erode, by default and through ignorance of the original charter agreement. He felt that his design, or any design for that matter, was no longer paramount, and lack of funds for sufficient maintenance was taking its toll; many important areas on his original plan had not been completed, some not even started, on the county side.

Every gardener knows that the more things change, the more they change. As Phillips observed how the plant beds walked; how overgrowth clogged and changed vistas; how storms knocked over trees and new ones— the same, substitutes, or perhaps lookalikes—replaced them, he knew all too well that owners or new men in charge had their own agendas. A bamboo grove here, a rain forest there, plants set out wherever open ground would receive them conveniently. It might be good enough for now—they might even look fine—but it was depressing. Did it remind him of Lake Wales when the Boks wanted to let their garden drift as it was?

Fairchild Tropical garden. Open spaces needed vigilant protection from encroaching beds. (Courtesy of Fairchild Tropical Garden)

*Every time I walk through the beautiful pathways you laid out in the
Fairchild Tropical Garden I bless you for your taste and skill.*

DAVID FAIRCHILD[1]

Between 1956 and 1963, Nixon Smiley became third director of the Garden while also farm and garden editor of the *Miami Herald.* Smiley was
handsome and humorous, with great charm and an incisive mind. Florida
born and with time away only for military service, he ranged his home state
depicting its natural and developing beauty in his column: the Everglades,
the "crop counties"—citrus, mangos, avocados, produce, cattle; beaches,
lakes, inland waterways. He wrote of the Florida pioneers, the history of its
cities, of out-of-the-way places and folk. An authority on Florida horticulture, he taught hordes of new Floridians how to plan and plant in the unfamiliar climate and difficult terrain. And always, he exhorted everyone within
reach of his pen to preserve and protect the environment.

When he made his first serious examination of the Garden, he was appalled. Lack of money was a given; funds would have to be raised. Of immediate concern was the lack of manpower. All of the beds had slipped
their boundaries, an abundance of seedlings becoming full grown before
anyone noticed. Palm trunks in the lawn were being seriously wounded by
mowers.

Smiley looked for guidelines for maintenance and development. There
were none. No log, no day by day written record. What county park system director Douglas Barnes had referred to grandly as the "master plan"
appears to have been Phillips's early drawing and the partial plans he sent
the Dade County Park Department for approval as he went along. There
were numbers of later detailed Phillips plans with full planting lists in

Barnes's office, Phillips's 1943 map of the Garden, and much correspondence between Phillips and the administrators, containing valuable information never shared with the horticulturists and superintendents. Smiley needed and wanted much more.

Providentially, there was Phillips himself, past seventy but still active, and Smiley had just heard he was picking up at the Garden again. "Bill," Smiley said, when he found him, "I'll do anything, take out trees, stand on my head, if you'll just come help us out on a regular basis."

What had inspired Smiley and had started him Phillips-watching even before he became Garden director had occurred when he went to Dr. Fairchild's Kampong in 1950, to do a story on Olmsted, who was visiting there. The conversation turned to Phillips. Smiley reported the ensuing dialogue in a letter to Phillips: "After hearing this . . . I was more anxious than ever to do a story about your work in the Garden."

"Dr. Fairchild," Smiley wrote, "began a monologue—and interesting," on the beauty of the palm and his affection for it. Olmsted agreed: "Only in the last few years have landscape designers learned how to use the palm effectively."

> FAIRCHILD: "You're right. . . . I think the first instance of the palm being properly fitted into the landscape that I have seen was in the Canal Zone."
> OLMSTED: "A pupil of mine did that work. He is doing some fine work for Florida."
> FAIRCHILD: "Everything [at Fairchild Tropical Garden] has grown amazingly fast. Phillips did a perfect job. I don't see how he ever accomplished what he did. He had absolutely nothing to go by, except his experience in the Canal Zone."[2]

The old ambivalence returned to Phillips when he answered Smiley: "Olmsted is a distinguished man, having greater mental powers than anyone else I ever knew intimately. [But] I was something more than his pupil. I worked for and with him for many years."[3]

Smiley eased Phillips into a weekly schedule of walking the Garden followed by a ritual lunch or dinner at his home with his wife Evelyn, a highly satisfactory routine. In between, he would fire off notes to Phillips in Miami, to "think about until we meet on Thursday." Phillips admired Smiley's capability, self-education, drive, energy, and humor and his me-

Mr. and Mrs. Frederick Law
Olmsted. (Author's Collection)

thodical improvement of the Garden. He wrote the citation and was the presenter of the Barbour medal to Smiley in 1956.

Smiley's questions were far ranging, from the practical to the philosophical. He asked about everything from unwanted seedlings to plant and plot maintenance; reconstruction of walls, pergolas, and paths; and new parking problems. He wanted design guidelines for the future from Phillips and was determined to get the older man to put his thoughts on paper. And there were the deeper questions: Is this the way you intended it, Bill? What was the idea behind this, originally? What is there in the Garden you would like to see revised—what would you do differently?

His main objective was a Phillips memoir. He began by eliciting written notes on a variety of subjects and collecting them for a future book. An example was the "wild area or small hammock" in the upland plot. "I agree with you," Smiley wrote, "that it should be preserved [but] there is some doubt in other minds regarding the value of a wild area in a botanical garden when Matheson Hammock, itself a wild area is near by."[4] Smiley suggested that one good reason to preserve it as it was would be in order to study the comparative growth of wild and cultivated plots. He asked for Phillips's opinion.

Fairchild Tropical Garden. Phillips at the Founders' court, which he designed. (Courtesy of Fairchild Tropical Garden; same photo at Francis Loeb Library, Harvard University)

"I have never thought that native plants had no place in the Garden," Phillips wrote. "The principle I tried to lay down was that the Garden should concern itself as strictly as possible with tropical species, excluding those not definitely tropical, that can be grown as well up-state. Our hammocks are, of course, definitely tropical, with the exception of the live oak component. And many of the hammock species have been planted (in FTG) as members of family groups."[5]

Smiley had decided to undertake a serious renovation of the Garden and asked Phillips if he would care to make a new plan. "I would not care to undertake personally to re-draw that map of F.T.G.," Phillips wrote. "It took weeks of labor and," he quoted from his favorite, Horace, 'I am not the man I was in Queen Cynara's time'—not the draftsman anyhow." But he took his original drawing on tracing cloth, now "wrinkled and discolored by lying around twelve years in this uncivilized climate," and showed Smiley how to stick on overlays to mark the Garden changes. This could be done "without unwholesome strain," he said, but if Smiley wanted a map on one sheet to one scale, Phillips offered to get a youngster in the Park Department to do it.[6]

"Bill," Smiley wrote in April of 1958, "this to remind you promised me a piece on how the Garden was made. Frankly," he wrote, "I have looked at the lay-out for a great many botanical gardens and I have looked in vain for a note of comparison between others and the lay-out of the FTG. I see a similarity between the lay-outs of all of these other gardens but somehow the FTG just does not fit into any category where there is room for comparison. On the other hand, I have never accompanied a landscape architect through the FTG who did not rave about the lay-out. One L.A. from California saw the FTG after a trip around the world during which he had seen all of the important botanical gardens. He considered the lay-out of the FTG above all of them."[7]

Phillips went to Maine for the summer and began his memoir.

*Design is more a matter of sheer physical labor than the uninitiated suppose. It
does not pop into one's head but evolves by repeated trying and discarding, a
process attended by doubt, discouragement, tedium and depression, with a total
absence of that joy of creation commonly supposed to go with artistic work. Such,
at least, is the impression I retain of it; I have not done much lately.*

W. L. PHILLIPS[1]

PERHAPS PHILLIPS, ever the record keeper, went to his files before he began
to write the memoir Smiley had provoked. There he would have found a
1938 letter to Karl Dahlberg, first Fairchild Tropical Garden superintendent.[2] In that letter Phillips set forth the principles he followed for designing the Garden, from which he never deviated. It shows how clearly he
envisioned from the first how it would be.

An informal treatment was envisaged throughout because the principle of informality would demand no specific form or character in the
vegetation masses. The growths could vary in kind and size through the
years without detriment to the general effect. Informality offered the
utmost freedom in the choice of vegetation, was compatible with any
stage of growth; whereas formality would limit the choice, would im-
pose demands for specific size and form. Certain formal elements were
later proposed—the amphitheater, the central panel of the Palmglade—
for what seemed to be good and sufficient reasons; but these illustrate
the point just made, that their realization demands a uniformity of vegetation which has little to do with the general purpose of forming a botanical collection. They do, however, demonstrate the use of particular
species for compositional purposes. . . .

The entire plan is essentially an articulated complex of openings. The necessity of open spaces was obvious for without well defined openings no sense of organization, no scenic effects, would be possible. They were necessary in order to assure light to bordering trees and opportunity for growth. Open spaces, furthermore, could be compared to rooms and corridors in a picture gallery, where the walls carry the things displayed. The more well developed, the more effective would be the use of the land. Space limitations on the upland . . . imposed a small scale of openings; to a great extent they could be no more than lanes or walks. Dominant openings were provided on both the north and the south portions (of the garden), but even these can hardly be called large. . . . The smallness of the openings was not thought to be disadvantageous aesthetically, for in Florida small landscape units and close views of vegetation are apt to be more attractive than wide views, and walks in shade more agreeable than walks in sun. By way of contrast, the proposed lakes on the lowland would provide much larger openings than any possible on the upland, and deeper, bolder views. The lakes, moreover . . . constitute inviolable open spaces.

Phillips knew that Smiley wanted what he was writing for an audience with a mixed appreciation of the technical difficulties and aesthetics of the landscape profession and for future directors who might otherwise, Smiley feared, spoil Phillips's vision.

The plan as it stands has no marked appearance of organization. To the casual eye it might appear to be a rather aimless scramble of lines and shapes. There are, nevertheless, clear purposes and principles underlying it, aimed at assuring certain aesthetic qualities regardless of what vegetation may be present, namely:

Variety . . . The openings (of different size) were and remain the vital elements of the plan. . . .
Consistency . . . The pattern, overall, is of a piece. The lines and shapes are dominantly free, casual, irregular, naturalistic, favoring if not absolutely assuring a natural randomness. . . . [It] aims at effects generically similar, specifically different.
Contrast . . . indispensable to anything normally regarded as landscape.[3]

In answer to a past question from Smiley, Phillips wrote that he would have liked to see the lowland area "treated as a wilder, more natural place than the upland, where, once things were planted, nature would be allowed to take its course, where spontaneous and accidental development of vegetation would occur, where even plants regarded as weeds would be allowed if their presence were not detrimental to the growth of planted material. . . . The lowland presents a truly unique opportunity. . . . [Its] exploitation warrants a very special effort."[4]

Looking back on his dual purpose design, he wrote:

Another principle I have tried to adhere to as basic is not to plant for a mere "landscaping" purpose, but always with some scientific purpose, either to exhibit a family group, or a type group (such as vines or succulents), or an ecological association. This I tried to do in such a way as to yield a good landscape effect as a side product. Obviously it was not a principle that could be adhered to exclusively, for various plantings were needed essentially for effect, such as the Overlook allée, the Amphitheater, plantings around buildings, etc., and a good deal of planting has been done, often against my wishes, merely because someone thought that more of this or that would look nice.

Phillips realized that the element of beauty is what brings most people to botanic gardens, that it is highly important for that reason, but that "unless some scientific motive is pursued concurrently you have no botanical garden, you have merely a pretty park, and no subject that can be presented to the public in a systematic, instructive and orderly way."

Smiley received the memoir during the summer and wrote to Phillips, "That really is a wonderful report you have done on the Garden. Remembering what you said, that it contained no brave ideas, I hesitate to suggest how really valuable the report will be to us."[5]

What has always endeared us to you is your philosophy of the quiet beauty of utterly unpretentious planting. Be sure, dear Phillips, it will live long after we are both forgotten.

DAVID FAIRCHILD[1]

PHILLIPS BEGAN THE YEAR 1960 with failing strength and pain; he was fighting cancer but had not told anyone yet. Smiley continued to pose work-related questions to Phillips, pulling him forcibly out of his gloom.

It would have been easy to dismiss Phillips at this stage as the crotchety old man, the quirky codger, the arrogant snob, part or all of which was true, but Smiley, who could not on occasion resist telling anecdotes about him, preferred to dignify him, give him his due. Smiley sensed Phillips's loneliness but refused to let him decline, continued to press him, to question, and to ask him to rethink plans, suggest new options. "[I had to] keep him thinking," Smiley said, "keep him alert, defer to his expertise. The man's body of knowledge and standards of excellence are so stratospheric, he belittles himself."[2] He followed Phillips up the road to Maine with letters, hoping he was "enjoying the breezy rock bound coast" and reminding him of the sketches he had promised to make for the Garden.

Again Smiley broached the subject of the Interama, in which he had been trying to involve Phillips for the past five years. Phillips, intrigued by the idea, had written of it to French:

I have been put on the Horticultural Commission of the Board of Design (for Interama). Interama is to be (the huge business) Inter American Trade and Cultural Center, a sort of permanent World's Fair. . . . [It] sounds preposterous but if they can sell an initial $27,000,000 of bonds it will go ahead. The site is terrible, a big expanse of mangrove swamp between U.S. 1 and the north end of Biscayne Bay where it narrows into the Intercoastal Waterway, south of the Sunny Isle which . . . crosses to the Beach a bit below Greynolds Park.

They propose to fill about 1600 acres of desert . . . the toughest sort of place to grow anything . . . yet the boys are relying heavily on horticultural embellishments to establish the fame of the place.

If it went ahead, he said, it would bring him good money over the next three years, but he did not want to get too involved with it because "such projects can easily drive a man mad."[3]

"Bill," Smiley wrote, "this is . . . a mammoth project, may be the largest landscape design job done in . . . years. Dr. Irving Muskat [director of the investing group] is . . . disappointed you [won't] take the job full time. . . . He would still like to have your services in *any* way. . . . The main problem is to find someone who can see through a big project such as this." If they finally had to get another man, Smiley wrote, suggestions had been made to replace Phillips with Brazilian Roberto Burle Marx, Garrett Eckbo, or Thomas Church.[4]

"It was a joy to receive your letter with its evidence that someone has been thinking of me," Phillips answered, since he had the inescapable feeling that he was out of the mainstream. Maine in August, with "a 'Canadian high' [clear, splendid weather] always on the way," was all one could wish. "The contemplation of these repeated, inevitable and quite-to-be-expected miracles occupies people's attentions to such a degree that scarcely any other thoughts ever arise in their minds. This explains perhaps why Maine always goes Republican on the national ticket, and Democratic on the state ticket." Phillips often digressed before coming to the point.

"What a source of glee," he continued, "if it should turn out that a landscape architect should finally propose a scheme . . . that would be accepted, after all the tries the architects have made. . . . I ought of course to respond with alacrity to Dr. Muskat's interest in me, and yours, and I certainly would if I were not so aware of my decline in vigor. It is hard, I suppose, for you to realize that." Concepts of design, he added, had "changed radically, leaving men of my generation way back behind. Nevertheless, I am . . . reluctant to decline all participation. After all, I must keep kicking, or sink."[5]

As usual, Phillips sent his news to French, who had just written to say he was thinking of retiring. Phillips told him to forget such talk: "I, who am older than you, still do not tell people that I am retired. . . . At Miami, it seems one of the biggest opportunities I ever had awaits me. . . . [Muskat] is . . . in a mood to put me into the thing in a big way, any way I want."[6]

The Interama was a good idea that failed for being too ambitious, for lack of funds and of agreement. But Phillips was inordinately pleased to have been so sought after. "The irony of the situation," he wrote, "is that at this late hour, Florida seems inclined to take notice of me."[7]

IN 1962, Phillips was still working with Smiley but at a slower pace. He began trips to the hospital in June. Smiley had accomplished, with Phillips's help, his "immediate objectives: to improve the Garden's image, gain support from the scientific community, and expand the membership." Smiley built up the educational programs, special plant collections, coordinated research with other botanical gardens, invited plant societies to hold their annual meetings at the Fairchild Tropical Garden, and started a seed and plant exchange with the Bailey Hortorium, New York Botanical Garden, Arnold Arboretum, Missouri Botanical Garden, and Atkins Gardens in Soledad, Cuba.

Before he resigned, Smiley led the search for his successor and paved the way for Dr. John Popenoe, the next director, to develop an internationally accredited research center. The self-styled Florida "country boy" with no academic degrees had placed Fairchild Tropical Garden in the forefront of the world botanical community.

Smiley wrote up for Fairchild Tropical Garden a charter that was unanimously approved by the board of trustees, to preserve Phillips's plan for all time from destruction by radical change. Smiley cherished his long association with Phillips; a close friendship, he said, with a true genius. Phillips's erudition, command of many languages, extensive reading, and wide interests captivated him. One of his own finest achievements, Smiley was pleased to say, had been to get Phillips to commit to paper his philosophy and rationale for this important garden.

In 1963, Phillips and Smiley left the Garden.

There is, nevertheless, a certain respect and a general duty of humanity that ties us, not only to beasts that have life and sense, but even to trees and plants.

MONTAIGNE[1]

DURING THE LAST three years of his life, which were punctuated by hospitalizations, Phillips methodically tied up the loose ends of long-held projects, made arrangements to be buried in the family cemetery at Searsmont, Maine, with Simone, and put his finances in order. He left his utterly astonished children houses in Florida and Maine, books, furnishings, Simone's jewelry, and something above $200,000.[2] He took his daughters on a short trip to Canada in 1964, and he and his daughter Mary went to Antigua and Puerto Rico in 1965. He corresponded regularly with old friends and faithfully mailed off weekly letters to his sister Florence.

He made an effort to find another landscape architect to succeed him at Lake Wales. He wrote to Edward D. Stone Jr., who had a practice in Fort Lauderdale: "I spoke to you once about the place and you expressed interest. . . . I was thinking of you or Walter Bradshaw."[3]

"I should hate to see any of my local members of ASLA fooling around up there," he wrote to Tom Ruth, still in control of Mountain Lake Colony. "They would probably propose something original and daring, some boulders scattered around surmounted by half stripped yuccas or whatnot. . . . I suppose," he added, "one has to step aside for youth to have a chance," but he was surprised to find that he was happier now than at many times in the past. "Once you let your skills and interest fade away, they might never have existed."[4]

Gone was the strain and pressure of running a one-man business, always overextending himself with too many commissions to earn a living. Now his former enthusiasm for the work "was at a very low flame." It all seemed far away, another life. Perhaps, he wrote to Florence, he should have taken the dares, picked up stakes and accepted the exciting new challenges when they came along, but in the end his professional opportunities were submerged by personal responsibility. He had few regrets; residual bitterness at Simone for refusing medical treatment or past professional slights had dissipated. Work had curbed his loneliness, stimulated him intellectually, brought him most of his social contacts; it was anodyne against the intermittent years of depression, grief, and guilt. Such troubles were past and gone, over.

He had always been introspective; now he became even more so. He became increasingly comfortable with himself, almost happy. It pleased and even "amused" Phillips to be known to the younger generation as the "Dean of Florida landscape architects," who were often in awe of him or thought him quite mad.[5] He enjoyed the telescope he had made, the music he listened to on his stereo, his old Renault, the almost daily company of Ray Ward. He was proud of his children and grandchildren—Juliette's three sons—and his honors and achievements. If he was reminded of a job he had liked, he wrote of it eloquently.

Viscaya, a magnificent Italianate villa which Phillips admired very much, was given to Dade County by the heirs of John Deering, and the Dade County Parks offices moved onto the grounds. Phillips liked the ambiance and the minor jobs he did on the terraces. When he was in charge of running the annual Miami Flower Show held there in 1955, he recorded his impression of his own design and described for French his "Eyetalian garden," destined to be dismantled when the show closed:

> I worked five straight days on it, two of them at least 10 hours long. I had an allée running in along a grove of small trees (which might have been orange trees but were actually *Tabebuia pallida*), with an oleander hedge to the left backed by *Bucida* (which might have been live oaks), to a seeming terrace running off to the left, on the edge of a valley, beyond which there were rising fields and blue mountains, two of them snow-capped. A big terra cotta pot, with a purple bougainvillea in it, an urn, a green Chinese lantern, were placed around the terminus of the walk, silhouetted against the blue distance. The walk skirted, in back of the grove, to the right, backed by a rigid green hedge and denser growth behind that,

and returned to the public corridor with a bit of wall with two more pots, and two strange stone objects either side of a bench. It was a quiet, poetic and evocative scene. When the men had picked up the left-over stuff and swept up, I sat down and looked at it with a lot of satisfaction, quite transported by my own creation. It was as good a garden scene as I ever saw, perhaps better. It sticks in my mind strangely, although it only lasted three days.[6]

HE LOOKED BACK kindly on all of the key figures in his past and made his peace with Olmsted. "He was a great man," Phillips reminisced to his sister, "and I have always thought myself to have been fortunate in knowing him and in seeing so much of him." Thinking back to his student days at Harvard, he wrote that Olmsted "probably had much to do with instilling whatever good traits I may have had."[7]

His thoughts turned more often to Simone and their early years together. "I was thinking of Paris today," he wrote to French, "when Mary came and found me and asked what was this map I was looking at. It was the well worn map of Paris . . . used on my common route downtown when I lived on the Avenue d'Iena. I said here was the Boulevarde St. Michel. She said that meant nothing to her. Well—thinking to grab her by the literary ear— I said here was the Rue Cassette, on which stood the house of Aramis, where d'Artagnan found the mysterious hooded woman. . . . She looked at me as at one who had lost touch with realities."[8]

In March 1966, Phillips wrote to his daughter Juliette: "Mary loved Panama, was proud to view the work of her Dad in that far off day, over fifty years ago. It wasn't very important, I guess—my friend John Nolen, of Cambridge, a city planner of some repute, mentioned in an article, 'Mr. Phillips's fresh, original plan for Balboa . . .' Important or not, I like it the best of anything I ever did."[9]

In July, he wrote his last letter to Nixon Smiley, from the hospital, by hand, to say he would be going from there to a nursing home, and thanking Smiley for convincing Nell Jennings and the others that he did not want the rare plant house named for him; "I feel greatly relieved," he said. Instead, a plaque was installed at the entrance to the palm glade.[10]

Phillips's habitual correspondence had always helped him to stay in touch with faraway friends during his Florida years. Now he and Marquis, colleagues for sixty years, both ill and thoroughly aware of their situation, traded weekly jokes—Phillips's favorite was the "rabbit in Vermont."

Of all the many letters Phillips ever wrote, this one to Prentiss French, his closest friend of longest standing, best expressed his courage and philosophy:

> I've had good luck and bad luck in my life, so it is perhaps not to my credit that I have preserved some degree of equanimity. I read, however. . . . I see what happens to other people, and it is evident that strong emotions are very damaging. Feelings of envy, disappointment, inadequacy, insecurity, etc, are hard feelings to try to live with. The real villain is the sense of frustration, of being trapped, of being unable to solve one's problems. For God's sake, let us not give in to this sort of thing! I have seen [a friend] on the verge of nervous prostration. I refuse to have nervous prostration. I refuse to take the world more seriously than it deserves. I refuse to let my standards of accomplishment be measured by those of other people, dead or alive. This is a brief march we have to make. Let us take it in stride . . . stopping to look at this or that as fancy leads us.[11]

WILLIAM LYMAN PHILLIPS died on October 18, 1966.

"Today when I walk through the Garden," wrote Nixon Smiley, "I do so with the feeling I'm in one of the world's most beautiful man-made gardens. . . . His genius as a landscape architect created beauty spots which will lift the human spirit as long as his handiwork lasts."

List of Projects: Consultations, Design and Development,
Site Selection and House and Garden Placement, Supervision of
Construction and Planting Lists, Placement Property, Revision

As Architect

1908–1910

Col. Albert Hilton   1908   East Boothbay, Maine
Chester McFarland   1908   East Boothbay, Maine
Douglas Beaman, M.D.   1910   East Boothbay, Maine

1911–1912

Associate, Rickson Outhet, Quebec, small house development
Olmsted Brothers, Brookline, Mass. (1911–32): "Experience in large office
practice in design of estates, subdivisions, public grounds; increased use of
engineering skills; lectures in town planning" (Resumé file, Author's Collection)

1913–1914

Panama Canal Zone: Landscape architect and first assistant in municipal
department to lay out and build permanent town of Balboa, rebuild existing town of Pedro Miguel

1915

Built house for self, East Boothbay, Maine

1916–1918

For Ferruccio Vitale, New York: Large estates and work in the New York
City office
For Olmsted Brothers: Increased supervision

1918–1919

Construction Division, U.S. Army:
    San Juan, Puerto Rico
    Columbia, S.C., "Direct responsibility for layout of
Camp Jackson" (Resumé file, Author's Collection)
    Quartermaster Corps:
    Camp Bragg, S.C., planting plans, mapmaking
    San Antonio, Tex., planting plans, mosquito control studies, Camp
        Normoyle
    Camp Knox, Ky., record maps of cantonments

1920–1923

Olmsted Brothers
Engaged by Sun Yat-sen's commissioner to be city planner, Canton
Resident engineer and designer, Graves Registration Service of the Army,
    American Military Cemeteries in France

1923–1925

Olmsted Brothers, Palos Verdes, Calif., design, gardens, parks
Olmsted Brothers, Seattle, Wash., 100-acre subdivision
Olmsted Brothers, Boca Grande, Fla., subdivision plan of island for American Agricultural Company

1925–1931

Lake Wales, Fla., "Olmsted Representative in Complete Charge" at Mountain Lake Sanctuary and Mountain Lake Colony. Worked on all of the Colony homes, directly with and without F. L. Olmsted; new gardens for changing ownership:
    J. H. Ackerman, Charles H. Alvord, William L. Abbot, F. C. Ard, Roger W. Babson, Dr. Otho F. Ball, Percy Ballantine, Dr. A. J. Barrow, Irving J. Bush, S. R. Bush, William G. Bibb, C. A. Busch, M. P. Blomberg, H. E. Boyce, J. Kell Brandon, F. C. Buchanan, Charles A. Buck, Col. C. C. Carter, Alfred H. Chapin, E. Foster Clark, Dorothy Clemens, Mrs. C. G. Coakley, A. Cook, Horace T. Cook, S. Munson Corbett, Stewart W. Cramer, Mrs. R. W. Cox, Mrs. Arthur John Crowe, Kenneth Curtis, Mrs. F. K. Curtiss,

Clinton H. Crane, Manfon Davis, Herbert L. Dillon, Dr. A. R. L. Dohme, Mrs. J. H. Douglas, Roy W. Doolittle, Edmund C. Drago, Mrs. W. Drayton, James W. De Graff, Mrs. St. Clair Eastman, Mrs. H. E. Ellsworth, John S. Ellsworth, Mrs. Joseph R. Ensign, Helen Ferguson, George T. Fulford, Mrs. William Phelps Eng, F. Gallagher, Mrs. Alexander Glass, Grover C. Good, John B. Goss, Frederick Hale, James L. Hamill, F. Eberhart Haynes, Willis T. Hanson, Mrs. Charles A. Higgins, Clifford Hemphill, Omer F. Hershey, Mrs. T. Chittenden Hill, Charles B. Hinds, W. W. Holloway, Lawrence L. J. Howe, Edwin C. Jameson Jr., Clyde Jennings, R. F. Kilpatrick, S. E. and E. V. Kolb, F. Kingsbury, E. J. Kulas, O. A. F. La Frentz, Samuel Laird, Charles F. Lambert, Franklin Lunding, G. M. Laughlin Jr., Percival Manchester, I. D. Maguire, Mrs. I. T. Mann, H. W. Marsh, Mrs. W. H. Martin, Cassius Mallory, Mrs. James H. Mason, Thomas N. McCarter, Mrs. William McDonald, Mrs. Angus A. McDonell, Thomas H. McInnerney, Robert J. McKim, Dr. Robert Miller Jr., David M. Milton, Sidney Z. Mitchell, Louis deB. Moore, Dr. William I. Morse, W. H. Nichols Jr., Harold S. Norman, Jansen Noyes, C. Creps Peters, Joseph E. Pogue, Boyce C. Prevost, Joseph Owens, Capt. William Puleston, Mrs. C. L. Riker, E. W. Rice, Mabel Louise Riley, Frank W. Ritchie, Dr. Maxwell D. Ryan, Joseph B. Shelby, Mrs. E. Slater, Guy Snyder, Col. G. R. Solomon, W. Paul Starkey Jr., Paul Starrett, Q. M. Seitz, Samuel G. Stem, Wallace Templeton Jr., C. M. Thiele, A. M. Tilden, Allen Tobey, Charles H. Upson, William P. Viles, Milton J. Warner, Mrs. Whitney Warner, H. W. Wild, Mrs. Thomas Williams, Mrs. Richard Wood, Efrem Zimbalist

1931–1932

Plan for Palm Beach lakefront for Garden Club

Hillsborough road project, Tampa, and with P. French (both for Olmsted Brothers)

Independent design and planting: Mrs. George McClintock, Palm Beach; W. E. Cummer, Winter Haven; Leo Nash, Winter Haven; Joseph Vernor Reed, Hobe Sound; Enders M. Voorhees, Hobe Sound; Charles Austin Buck, Lake Wales

1932–1933

Opened independent office of landscape architecture, West Palm Beach

1933–1941

National Park Service CCC, project superintendent

1935

Florida State Road Works: plans, specifications, supervision of planting, improvements at Miami, Boynton, Stuart

1941–1956

Consultant, landscape architecture office, Dade County; parks designer

1942

Reynolds, Broynton, Smith, & Hills, Jacksonville, designing engineer; airport runways and aprons

1943–1966

Independent office, North Miami
Residences—private practice
Consultations, planting list supervision, design and development:
J. Y. Arnold   Palm Beach   1950s
Philip Augustine   N. Miami Beach   1959
W. L. Lyons Brown   Delray Beach   1955–66
Harry Burgin   Key Biscayne   1951
Dr. O Whitmore Burtner   Miami   1958–62
Frank Field Chase   Encinitas, CA   1944
E. H. Coal   Miami   1945
Elder Cornell Jr.   Coconut Grove   1955
Helen Cutten   Coconut Grove   1946
Mrs. Richard Cutts   Coconut Grove   1943
Addison Fay   Winter Haven   1938
Col. W. Garland Fay   Coconut Grove   1945
Douglas Felix   South Miami   1950
Dexter French   South Miami   1961
Mrs. Russell Firestone   Miami Beach   1952–56
Mrs. John Galbreath   Miami Beach   1963–64
R. H. Hemphill   South Miami   1955
Garret A. Hobart (with O.B.)   Belleair   1936–41

Melvin H. Jackson   South Miami   1956–57
W. Alton Jones   Miami   1963
Mrs. Gertrude Manigault   Palm Beach   1939
Hugh Matheson Jr.   South Miami   1950
George W. Mead   Miami Beach   1944
David J. Molloy   Miami Beach   1947
Clarence W. Nelson   Melbourne   1954–55
Dr. Emil Pellini   Coconut Grove   1947
Marshall Pollard   South Miami   1951
Robert H. Redden   Miami   1958
John W. Reish   Miami Beach   1956
William R. Robbins   Miami   1962, 1964
Mrs. Jessie C. Smith   South Miami   1960
William V. Swords   Palm Beach   1937–38
William Vanderbilt   Boca Raton and   1955–56
(with P. French)   Don Pedro Key   1955–56
Fred W. Vanderpool   South Miami   1953
Ralph K. Wadsworth   South Miami   1953
James N. Wallace   Delray   1940s
Payton Wilson   South Miami   1950

CEMETERIES

Woodlawn Park   Miami   1949–53
Inman Park   Tampa   1930s

CHURCHES

First Church Christ Scientist   Miami   1949   (in memory of Simone G.
    Phillips) (razed in the 1970s)
First Unitarian Church   South Miami   1954
All Souls Church   Miami Beach   1955

CLUBS AND HOTELS

Palm Beach Garden Club   1931
Indian River Garden Club   Vero Beach   1934
Indian Creek Club   Miami Beach   1940–45
Sebring Garden Club   Sebring   1952

College Arms Hotel and Golf Club   Deland   1946
Holland Inn   1940s
Biscayne Bay Yacht Club   Coconut Grove   1964
    (Ran and judged flower shows in Miami, Palm Beach, 1930, 1951,
    1955)

DEVELOPMENT, SUBDIVISION PROPERTIES

Southern Shore Estates   St. Lucy   1945
    (owner, Frank Stockton, Eau Gallie)
Matanzas Riverfront Promenade (for Olmsted Brothers)
    St. Augustine   1945
Kampong Division plan   Coconut Grove   1946–77
    (Mrs. David Fairchild)
Milton Mabry   Tampa   1953
Miami Waterfront Proposal   Miami   1955
Florida Development Commission   1956
St. Petersburg, Tampa Bay public waterfront area   1959
Jennings Subdivision   Coral Gables   1962

HOUSING, HOSPITALS

Veterans Hospital   Gainesville   1948–
Jackson Hospital Sewage Plant   1949–
University of Miami   Coral Gables   194?–49
G. A. Rogers Sr. (development plans) (G. A. Rogers Sr.)   Bradenton   1952
Newtowne Heights   Sarasota   1952–53
Central Park Village   Tampa   1952–58
Larchmont Gardens   Miami   n.d.

PARKS AND GARDENS

Mountain Lake Sanctuary   Lake Wales   1956–63 (now Bok Tower
    Gardens)
McKee Jungle Gardens   Vero Beach   1930–48

AS CCC SUPERINTENDENT

Royal Palm State Park   Paradise Key   1933–44
Greynolds Park (Nat'l. Hist. Reg.)   North Miami   1934–36
Sebring/Highland Hammock   Sebring   1934

As Dade County Consultant

Matheson Hammock (Nat'l. Hist. Reg.)   Coral Gables   1938–?
Fairchild Tropical Garden   Coral Gables   1938–60
Bayfront Park   Homestead   1938
Crandon Park   Key Biscayne   1941–47
Virginia Beach   Virginia Key   1941–?
More Park   North Miami   1942–?
Owaissa Bauer Hammock   Miami   1941
Redlands Fruit and Spice   Homestead   1943–44
Baker's Haulover   North Miami   1944
Seaquarium   Miami   1944
Crandon Park Zoo   Key Biscayne   1946–?

Independent Design

Camp Shelby (with P. French) Shelby, Miss.   1945–?
Girl Scout Camp   Miami   1944
Tony Jannus Park   Tampa   1946–47
Cincinnati Zoo   Cincinnati, Ohio   1952
Tropical Park   Hialeah   1953
Phipps Park   Orlando   1958–60
Memorial Park (Menninger)   Stuart   1930–60

Public Buildings

Post Office   Cocunut Grove
Alexander Graham Bell Museum   Baddeck, Nova Scotia   1940s
Cutler Power Station   Miami   1948
University of Miami Housing   Coral Gables   1946–49
University of Florida Housing   Gainesville   1949–50
Miami Herald   Miami   1945
Miami Sewage Plant   Virginia Key   1951
Miami Memorial Library   Miami   1951
Eleuthera Guided Missile Base (vegetational erosion control)   1953
Martin Marietta Co. of Orlando   Cape Canaveral   1956–?
Miami International Airport   Miami   1958
Interama (proposed PanAm City)   North Miami   1956–60

Roads, Highways, Causeways

Sanctuary Boulevard   Lake Wales
Bayshore Boulevard   Tampa   1927–31
Hillsborough River Parkway (with P. French)   Tampa   1932
Venetian Causeway   Miami Beach   1934–37

As State and County Project Superintendent

Project 102, Brickell Avenue   Miami   1933–34
Project 68-B   Boynton   1934–35
Project E-91   Stuart   1934–35
Red Road (Hist. Restoration, 1992)   South Miami   1935–36
LeJeune Road–NW River Drive   Miami   1935–36
Kendall Road   South Miami   1934–35
Rickenbacker Causeway   Miami to Crandon   1940–47
Florida Overseas Parkway to Key West   1937–40; 1958 (see Bibliography
    for reports)
Franklin Boulevard to State Capitol   Tallahassee   1956–57 (doubtful
    whether his plan was used)

NOTES

The following abbreviations appear in the notes section.

WLP   William Lyman Phillips
FLO   F. L. Olmsted, Jr.,
PF   Prentiss French
NS   Nixon Smiley
JP   Julia Phillips
SGP   Simone G. Phillips
MLC   Mountain Lake Colony
FTG   Fairchild Tropical Garden
BTG   Bok Tower Garden

Author's Collection   See bibliography

CHAPTER 1

1. Franklin Folsom Phillips, a book of poetry, *Idylls Beside the Strand* (Boston: Sherman, French, 1912), and *The White Isles*, a novel (C. M. Clark Publishing Co., 1911; Boston: Sherman, French, 1912), 263, 264.

2. Telephone interviews, correspondence, and visit to Stonington, Maine, July 1992, to talk with Nancy Kimball (Mrs. Chesley) Dunlap, Phillips's niece.

3. Telephone interviews and correspondence, November–December 1990, with Headmaster Anthony Fedele and Librarian James T. West, Somerville Latin High School.

4. Veda, *Avenues to Adulthood*, a study of the Latin schools of Massachusetts.

5. Phillips, *The Radiator*, 1904, a Somerville Latin school publication.

6. From one of many Phillips resumés, n.d. Over the years, when he applied for new positions, Phillips wrote another resumé more appropriate for the job. A dozen have been found and are collected in file "Resumés, WLP, Author's Collection." Most are undated.

7. WLP/Mrs. Henry Field, November 16, 1958 (Graduate Design Library, Harvard, copies in Author's Collection).

8. Olmsted to U.S. Civil Service Commission, April 28, 1915 (Manuscript Division, Madison Memorial Library).

9. Whiting and Phillips, "Frederick Law Olmsted, 1870–1957: An Appreciation of the Man and His Achievements."

10. Harvard School of Design catalog, 1908–10.

11. WLP signed his thesis "By Stadtebau [Town builder]," School of Landscape Architecture, Harvard University, 1910.

12. J. S. Pray to J. E. Edmonds, chairman, New Orleans Chamber of Commerce, May 4, 1915 (Manuscript Division, Madison Memorial Library).

13. Burton Tripp/WLP, September 15, 1945 (letters, Author's Collection).

14. Professor Jack Wister/WLP, March 16, 1946.

15. WLP/Wister, April 6, 1946.

16. WLP resumé, n.d.

17. FLO/WLP, June 7, 1911 (Olmsted National Historic Site and Author's Collection).

18. WLP resumé, n.d.

19. Theodore Kimball Hubbard, "John Charles Olmsted," 29–30.

20. Levee, "John Charles Olmsted."

21. Ibid.

22. Kalfus, *Frederick Law Olmsted*, 76–85; interview with Mary F. Daniels, librarian, Special Collections, Frances Loeb Library, Harvard University Graduate School of Design, December 14, 1993; Pray, "John Charles Olmsted"; Mische, "John Charles Olmsted: In Memoriam."

23. WLP/SGP, June 1932 (family letters file, Author's Collection).

24. WLP, "What Is a Garden?" (WLP writings file, Author's Collection).

25. WLP to his father, May 1913.

Chapter 2

1. WLP/PF, August 1965 (WLP/PF correspondence file, Author's Collection).

2. Abbot, *Panama and the Canal*, 266.

3. Ibid., 138–39, 144–45, 379.

4. McCullough, *The Path Between the Seas*, 510–11, 571, 603–4.

5. WLP, "The Town of Balboa, C.Z." (WLP writings file, Author's Collection).

6. FLO to Civil Service Commission, April 28, 1915 (Manuscript Division, Madison Memorial).

7. Directive by Colonel George Washington Goethals, July 1913; Abbot, *Panama*, 144.

8. "Balboa Town Site," Isthmian Canal Commission Report, 223.

9. Abbot, *Panama*.

10. WLP/FLO, February 1914.

11. *Canal Record*, December 17, 1913.

12. WLP, "Taboga" (WLP writings file, Author's Collection).

13. WLP/FLO, February 1914.

14. *Canal Record*, "Decorative Trees and Plants for Permanent Townsites," January 14, 1914.

15. Ambassador James, Lord Bryce, referring to the Panama Canal *(Path Between the Seas*, 543).

16. McCullough, *Path Between the Seas*, 554, 573.

17. WLP resumé.

18. Report of Engineer of Terminal Construction, Isthmian Canal Commission, 223; Abbot, *Panama*, 202–4.

19. WLP, "Balboa, Canal Town."

20. Goethals to Henri H. Rousseau, April 22, 1914.

21. WLP/FLO, March 22, 1914.

22. WLP/Colonel E. T. Wilson, July 3, 1913.

23. WLP/Rousseau, March 9, 1914.

24. McCullough, *Path Between the Seas*, 572.

25. WLP/FLO, October 16, 1914.

26. Austin Lord/WLP, December 10, 1914.

27. C. W. Powell, Balboa Dispensary/WLP, May 2, 1915.

28. *Miami Herald*, February 3, 1950.

CHAPTER 3

1. Pray to Captain George Gibbs, War Department Office of the Quartermaster General of the Army, December 13, 1917.

2. To WLP from ASLA Committee, Boston chapter (Raymond Aldrich, George Gibbs Jr., Thomas W. Sears, E. C. Whiting), November 18, 1914.

3. WLP, "You Ask What Is Wrong with the Panama Canal?" *Boston Herald*, November 27, 1915.

4. FLO/Civil Service Commission, April 28, 1915.

5. Interview with Juliette Phillips Coyle, Washington, D.C., January 16, 1989.

6. Ferruccio Vitale/WLP, January 26, 1916.

7. FLO/Vitale, January 22, 1916 (Manuscript Division, Madison Memorial, Library of Congress).

8. Olmsted/U.S. Civil Service Commission, "Confidential Statement," May 16, 1938.

9. Wister/WLP, March 16, 1946.

10. WLP/Wister, April 16, 1946.

11. WLP resumé.

12. Ibid.

13. Ibid.

14. WLP, "Planting and Mosquito Control," 166–70.

15. WLP resumé.

16. Mische, "John Charles Olmsted," 52–54.

17. Interview with Joseph Hudak, Westwood, Mass., June 1988.

18. Whiting and WLP, "F. L. Olmsted Appreciation."

19. Benjamin Forgey, "Rock Creek Park Turns 100," *Washington Post Magazine*, August 12, 1990.

20. Helphand, "Henry Vincent Hubbard."

21. Whiting and WLP, "F. L. Olmsted Appreciation." Copy of this section of the article, written by WLP, is in the Author's Collection.

22. Telephone interview with Joseph Hudak, November 18, 1993.

23. PF, foreword to letters from WLP to him, collected in 1967 for a possible book, never published.

24. Correspondence PF/WLP throughout 1945 (Author's Collection).

25. Gibbs/FLO, April 19, 1922.

26. Gibbs/WLP, April 22, 1922.

27. Whiting/Gibbs, May 8, 1922.

28. This information comes primarily from WLP's letters to his mother, Julia Phillips, September 25, 1922–August 1923 (Family Letters file, Author's Collection).

29. WLP/JP, October 18, 28, 1922.

30. WLP/JP, February 4, 1923.

31. WLP/JP, February 11, 1923.

32. WLP resumé (Resumé file, Author's Collection).

33. WLP/JP, December 8, 1922.

34. WLP/JP, December 26, 1922.

35. WLP/JP, January 7, 1923.

36. WLP/JP, n.d.

37. WLP/JP, March 31, 1923.

38. WLP/PF, August 13, 1944.

39. WLP/JP, April 25, 1923.

40. Gibbs/FLO, Paris, June 24, 1923.

41. Ibid.

42. WLP/JP, July 7, 1923.

43. Gibbs/FLO, August 5, 1923.

44. WLP/JP, August 20, 1923.

45. WLP resumé.

46. Dr. Beaman Douglas/WLP, June 16, 1925.

47. Interview with Frank Vanderlip Jr., St. Mary's City, Maryland, May 30, 1988; telephone interviews with Russell Benedict, son of Vanderlip Sr.'s partner, December 12, 1988.

48. Telephone interview with Russell Benedict, December 17, 1993.

49. WLP resumé.

50. Fink, *Time and the Terraced Land*.

51. For A. C. Frost; WLP resumé.

52. Ibid.

53. Douglas/WLP, June 16, 1925.

CHAPTER 4

1. WLP resumé.

2. Telephone interview with Joseph Hudak, March 1992; Smiley, *Yesterday's Florida*, 189; Amory, *The Last Resorts*, 369–71; Redford, "The Tents of Israel," in *Million Dollar Sand Bar*, 204–15.

3. Caldwell, *Mountain Lake: A History*.

4. Ibid.

5. WLP resumé.

CHAPTER 5

1. Bok, *America's Taj Mahal*.

2. FLO/Bok, July 4–7, 1922.

3. WLP resumé.

4. Interviews with Nixon Smiley throughout winter 1988, Robert Montgomery guest house, Miami, Florida.

5. WLP, "Mountain Lake Sanctuary: A Report."

6. "Mr. Phillips Progress Report for September 1927," BTG library.

7. FLO/Bok, September 19, 1927. A handwritten note (by a secretary?) on this letter in BTG library, dated September 21, 1927: "Mr. Bok said this was answered by telegram." Efforts to find it failed at The American Foundation, Inc., and the Frederick Law Olmsted Historic Site, Brookline.

8. "Mr. Phillips's Progress Report for December 1927," BTG Library.

9. FLO/Mrs. Bok, n.d., probably 1930–31.

10. "Mountain Lake Sanctuary: A Report."

CHAPTER 6

1. WLP resumé.

2. Amory, *The Last Resorts*, 37.

3. FLO, May 14, 1926, courtesy Frederick Law Olmsted Historic Site.

4. WLP/Whiting, January 23, 1927.

5. Whiting/WLP, February 7, 1927.

6. Amory, *The Last Resorts*, 372.

7. WLP resumé.

CHAPTER 7

1. Alice Martin/WLP, by hand, February 3, 1928.

2. WLP/David Fairchild, June 22, 1946.

3. WLP/William Vanderbilt, August 28, 1955.

4. Charles Wait to Thomas De C. Ruth, June 27, 1968.

5. Muir, *Miami, U.S.A.*, 147–48; Curl, *Mizner's Florida*; Amory, *The Last Resorts*.

6. WLP/Charles A. Buck, September 10, 1930.

7. WLP/Buck, September 30, 1930.

8. WLP/Buck, September 8, 1930.

9. Telephone interview with Rudy Favretti, May 1990; Jackson, "The Resurrection of Pinewood," 10–15; Schwarz, "Pinewood House and Garden."

10. Interviews with Jonathan Shaw, president, Bok Tower Garden Foundation, Lake Wales, Florida, March 1990.

11. WLP/sister Florence Kimball, May 4, 1952.

12. FLO/WLP, from Chesham, N.H., written by hand in pencil while convalescing, August 12, 1938.

CHAPTER 8

1. "What Is a Garden?" typescript, n.d., 2 pp., Author's Collection.

2. Ibid.

3. Ibid.

4. Phillips, "Character in the Garden," typescript, n.d., 3 pp., Author's Collection.

5. Ibid.

6. Ibid.

7. Ibid.

8. "Sounds in the Garden," typescript, n.d., 4 pp., Author's Collection.

CHAPTER 9

1. JP/WLP, February 15, 1931.

2. WLP/SGP, February 21, 23, 1931.

3. WLP/FLO, June 12, 1945.

4. FLO/WLP, April 6, 1932.

5. FLO/WLP, April 8, 1932.

6. FLO/WLP, April 10, 1932.

7. WLP/SGP, June 10, 1932.

8. WLP/SGP, June 12, 1932.

9. WLP/SGP, June 14, 1932.

10. FLO/WLP, October 21, 1932.

11. Phillips and French, "A Street-Planting Plan in Writing," 155–57.

12. Mrs. George McKinlock/WLP, "Saturday," n.d. (October/November 1932?).

13. WLP/FLO, January 20, 1933.

14. FLO/WLP, February 5, 1933.

CHAPTER 10

1. Douglas, *The Everglades: River of Grass*, 376.
2. Douglas, *Voice of the River*, 136.
3. SGP/WLP, "Saturday," November 1933.
4. Douglas, *The Everglades: River of Grass*, 6.
5. Carr, *The Everglades*, 44–45.
6. Smiley, "A Phillips Memoir," unpublished, n.d., possibly 1960s, possibly a draft for *William Lyman Phillips: A Remembrance*.
7. Phillips's CCC "Narrative Report for December/January, 1934." A plane table is a basic surveying instrument (drawing board on a tripod with ruler or transit), essential for use in the field, enabling a plan to be plotted and laid out on the ground.
8. May Mann Jennings/WLP, February 4, 1934.
9. Phillips's CCC "Narrative Report for April, 1934."
10. Phillips's CCC "Narrative Report for May, 1934."
11. WLP/May Mann Jennings, June 23, 1934.
12. Phillips, "Narrative Report for June, 1934."
13. Carr, *The Everglades*, 120.

CHAPTER 11

1. Simpson, *Out of Doors in Florida*.
2. FLO/WLP, May 4, 1934.
3. Telegram, FLO/Ray Vinten, May 3, 1934.
4. FLO/WLP, May 4, 1934.
5. WLP/FLO, June 30, 1934.
6. Telegram, WLP/Clara Thomas (at National Park Service), May 11, 1934.
7. WLP/Winton Reinsmith, June 30, 1934.
8. Ibid.
9. WLP/Ray Vinten, July 7, 1934. The "rough sketch" has disappeared.
10. WLP/H. L. "Harry" Baker, September 20, 1934.
11. WLP/H. L. Baker, October 25, 1934.
12. Vinten/WLP, October 31, 1934.

CHAPTER 12

1. FLO/WLP, January 1935.
2. "Metropolitan Dade County Preservation Board Designation Report, August 23, 1983," 172, Miami.
3. Barnes, "History of Dade County Park System," 174.
4. FLO/Brookline staff.
5. Barnes, "History of Dade County Park System," 176.

CHAPTER 13

1. Simpson, *Out of Doors in Florida*.

2. It is now on the National Historic Register, primarily because it was the home of William Lyman Phillips.

3. Barnes, "History of Dade County Park System," 174. See also "Matheson Hammock Park: Natural Acres Protection Plan," January 24, 1991.

4. Barnes, "History of Dade County Park System."

5. Phillips, *Fairchild Tropical Garden: A Memoir*, hereafter cited as *FTG Memoir*.

6. Other key vistas are the lake, boatyard, and bird sanctuary at Greynolds and Colonel R. P. Montgomery's sloping lawn to the lakes.

7. WLP, speech to Tampa Garden Club, Tampa, Fla., rough copy, n.d., Author's Collection.

8. Barnes, "History of Dade County Park System."

CHAPTER 14

1. Working notes for Crandon (on index cards), park planting, n.d., Author's Collection.

2. WLP/FLO and Wister, same day, November 16, 1947.

3. WLP/Julia Allen Field, July 30, 1954.

4. Barnes, "History of Dade County Park Systems," chapter on Crandon Park.

CHAPTER 15

1. Phillips, "Plan and General Scheme of Planting," typescript, n.d., Author's Collection, accompanying index cards mentioned in chap. 14, note 1. Attention paid to eventual size of trees and shrubs.

2. Zuckerman, *The Dream Lives On*.

3. Dr. Robert Merrill, director of Arnold Arboretum, dedication speech, March 23, 1938.

4. Zuckerman, *The Dream Lives On*.

5. William Robbins, quoted in *New York Times*, May 27, 1949.

6. Zuckerman, *The Dream Lives On*.

7. Douglas, "An Argument for a Botanical Garden to Be Called Fairchild Tropical Garden."

8. Zuckerman, *The Dream Lives On*.

9. Douglas, "Argument."

10. Barnes, "History of Dade Country Park System."

11. WLP/Charles Crandon, September 3, 1939.

12. WLP/Noel Chamberlin, March 28, 1938.

13. Smiley, *William Lyman Phillips: A Remembrance*, 1967.

14. Zuckerman, *The Dream Lives On*.

CHAPTER 16

1. Olmsted talking with Fairchild, reported by Smiley to Phillips, May 5, 1950.
2. WLP resumé.
3. WLP, *FTG Memoir*.
4. Ibid.
5. Ibid.
6. Wait, *Fairchild Tropical Garden: The First Ten Years*, 28.
7. WLP/PF, May 31, 1945.
8. WLP, *FTG Memoir*.
9. Interview with Stanley Kiem, 1990.
10. Wait, *Fairchild Tropical Garden*. In 1949 and 1950, William L. Phillips's catalogue of plants was published by Kells Press; a revised list by botanist Robert W. Read was published in 1960.
11. WLP/Fairchild, April 27, 1941.
12. WLP, *FTG Memoir*.
13. Wait, *Fairchild Tropical Garden*.
14. WLP/NS, June 1, 1962.
15. NS/WLP, June 6, 1962.
16. Wait, *Fairchild Tropical Garden*, 92.
17. WLP/Nell Montgomery, February 2, 1959.
18. WLP, *FTG Memoir*.
19. This anecdote appears in Barnes, "History of Dade Country Park System," and Smiley's correspondence.
20. WLP/Fairchild, April 27, 1942.
21. WLP/Karl Dahlberg, first superintendent, FTG, September 22, 1942: "Someone may have told you I'm in Jacksonville."
22. WLP/Montgomery, June 3, 1942.
23. Montgomery/WLP, June 5, 1942.
24. Montgomery/Crandon, February 8, 1943.

CHAPTER 17

1. PF/WLP, September 18, 1941, and telegram, September 22, 1941.
2. Zuckerman, *The Dream Lives On*.
3. Montgomery/WLP, May 7, 1945.
4. WLP/Montgomery, May 10, 1945.
5. FLO/WLP, March 8, 1940.
6. FLO/WLP, handwritten, January 13, 1946.
7. Interviews with Eleanor "Nell" Montgomery Jennings at her home, the Coconut Grove Palmetum, March 12, 1988, and several sessions thereafter until her death in 1991.

8. WLP/Fairchild, 1946.

9. Interviews with Juliette Phillips Coyle, 1988–93.

10. WLP/PF, December 19, 1948.

11. Interview with Nell Montgomery, possibly February 1992; interview with Nancy Dunlap, Phillips's niece, Stonington, Maine, July 1992.

12. WLP/Jack Corbin, n.d. (late 1953?).

13. FLO/WLP, January 5, 1950.

14. WLP/FLO, February 5, 1950.

CHAPTER 18

1. WLP/PF, February 19, 1956.

2. Arthur Parmelee/WLP, June 27, 1937.

3. WLP/NS, September 14, 1957.

4. Hans J. Koehler, "Mountain Lake Sanctuary in Florida," *Parks & Recreation* 23, no. 6 (February 1940): 221–31.

5. Koehler, "Mountain Lake Sanctuary in Florida," planting account.

6. PF/Mrs. Charles Ten Eyck, March 28, 1956.

7. Patterson, "Two New Homes In Mountain Lake, Florida"; French/Allied Arts Commission, February 5, 1932; Allied Arts Commission/*Town and Country*, February 8, 1932.

8. PF/WLP, March 4, 1956.

9. WLP/PF, February 19, 1956

10. WLP/Kenneth Morrison at MLS, April 11, 1958.

11. WLP/William Marquis, April 28, 1958.

12. Ibid.

13. WLP/Judge Curtis Bok, April 28, 1958.

14. Bok/WLP, May 27, 1958.

15. Telephone interviews with Joseph Hudak, February 8, 1992.

16. WLP/Bok, June 3, 1958.

17. Ibid.

18. Marquis/WLP, June 30, 1959.

19. WLP/Marquis, June 7, 1958.

20. Kenneth Morrison's *Mountain Lake Almanac*, published at Mountain Lake Sanctuary.

CHAPTER 19

1. Interviews with Stanley Kiem, Robbins Research Center, 1988–92.

2. WLP/Corbin, May 4, 1955.

3. Conversations with Bertram Zuckerman, Robbins Reseach Center, almost daily, 1988–93.

4. Interview with Stanley Kiem.

5. WLP/William K. Vanderbilt, Boca Raton, August 1958 (Author's Collection).

CHAPTER 20

1. Fairchild/WLP, June 16, 1948.

2. NS/WLP, May (1–3?) 1950; typed on yellow second sheets for a possible column.

3. WLP/NS, May 7, 1950.

4. NS/WLP, May 11, 1956.

5. WLP/NS, May 13, 1956.

6. WLP/NS, Smiley, n.d., summer 1957.

7. NS/WLP, April 28, 1958.

CHAPTER 21

1. WLP/NS, August 16, 1960.

2. WLP/NS, May 7, 1950. Long back, Phillips credited Dahlberg with doing more than anyone at the beginning of the Garden, "but he fell into disfavor with Fairchild and Montgomery [reason never stated] so they don't even like to hear him mentioned."

3. Phillips, *FTG Memoir*.

4. Ibid.

5. NS/WLP, September 9, 1958.

CHAPTER 22

1. Fairchild/WLP, June 16, 1948.

2. Interviews with Smiley at the Montgomery guest house and correspondence from 1988 until Smiley's death in 1990.

3. WLP/PF, August 28, 1960.

4. NS/WLP, August 3, 1960.

5. WLP/NS, August 7, 1960

6. WLP/PF, August, 1960.

7. Ibid.

EPILOGUE

1. Montaigne, *Essays*, chapter 11.

2. November, 1966, will read to me by Juliette Coyle.

3. WLP/Edward D. Stone, Jr., March 28, 1965.

4. WLP/Tom Ruth, Mountain Lake Colony, April 19, 1965.

5. Interview with Jonathan Seymour, FASLA, South Miami, 1990.

6. WLP/PF, July 26, 1964.

7. WLP/Florence P. Kimball, January 7, 1962.

8. WLP/PF, February, 1966.

9. WLP/Juliette Phillips Coyle, March 27, 1966.

10. WLP/NS, July 12, 1966.

11. WLP/PF, extract of a letter put in a collection by PF with 1949 only date given.

Abbott, Willis J. *Panama and the Canal.* New York, 1913.

Amory, Cleveland. *The Last Resorts.* New York: Harper Bros., 1948.

Author's collection. All material with Faith R. Jackson, Washington, D.C. Includes W. L. Phillips's papers, photographs, and memorabilia in informal files; his personal and professional correspondence, resumés, unpublished manuscripts, with separate files for his correspondence with F. L. Olmsted and Prentiss French, Parks material, and so on. Final disposition pending as of 1997.

Barbour, Thomas. *That Vanishing Eden.* Boston: Little, Brown, 1944.

Barnes, A. D. "History of Dade County Park System, 1929–69: The First Forty Years." Unpublished report, completed by Barnes in 1986. In files of the Metro-Dade Parks Service, Miami, Florida.

Bok, Edward W. *America's Taj Mahal: The Singing Tower of Florida.* Georgia Marble Co., 1929; The Bok Tower Gardens Foundation, Inc., 1989.

Caldwell, John W. *Mountain Lake: A History.* Lake Wales, Florida, 1984.

Carr, Archie. *The Everglades.* New York: Time-Life Books, 1973.

———. *A Naturalist in Florida: A Celebration of Eden.* New Haven: Yale University Press, 1994.

Church, Thomas D. *Gardens Are for People.* New York: McGraw-Hill, 1955.

Curl, Donald W. *Mizner's Florida: America's Resort Architecture.* American Architectural Series. Cambridge: MIT Press, 1944.

"Crandon Park: Natural Acres Protection Plan." Metro-Dade Parks and Recreation Department, The Nature Conservancy, and Fairchild Tropical Garden, March 5, 1991.

Douglas, Marjory Stoneman. "An Argument for a Botanical Garden to Be Called Fairchild Tropical Garden." Pamphlet. Fairchild Tropical Garden, Miami, 1937.

———. *The Everglades: River of Grass.* Rivers of America Series. New York: Rinehart, 1947.

———. *Florida: The Long Frontier.* Regions of America Series. New York: Harper & Row, 1967.

———. *Voice of the River* (an autobiography with John Rothschild). Englewood, Fla.: Pineapple Press, 1987.

Eckbo, Garrett. *The Landscape We See*. New York: McGraw-Hill, 1969.

Fairchild, David. *The World Grows Round My Door*. New York: Charles Scribner & Sons, 1947.

Fink, Augusta. *Time and the Terraced Land*. Palos Verdes, Calif.: Howell-North Books, 1966.

Forgey, Benjamin. "Rock Creek Park Turns 100." *Washington Post Magazine*, August 12, 1990.

French, Prentiss. "William Lyman Phillips, FASLA, 1885–1966." Typescript of WLP letters assembled for a memorial minute, 1967. Graduate Design Library, Harvard University.

Frères, Marie-Victorin, and Léon Frères. *Itinéraires Botaniques dans l'île de Cuba* (Botanical Travels in the Isle of Cuba). Montreal, 1942.

Graf, Albert Byrd. *Tropica: Color Cyclopedia of Exotic Plants and Trees from the Tropics and Subtropics*. East Rutherford, N.J.: Roehrs Co., 1978.

Graham, Stuart Thomas. *Great Gardens of Britain*. New York: Mayflower Books, 1979.

Griswold, Mac, with Eleanor Welles. *The Golden Age of American Gardens*. New York: Abrams, 1987.

Griswold, Oliver. *The Florida Keys and the Coral Reef*. Miami: Graywood Press, 1965.

Hall, Francis Wyly. *Be Careful in Florida: Know These Poisonous Snakes, Insects, Plants*. St. Petersburg: Great Outdoors Publishing Co., 1980.

———. *Palms and Flowers of Florida*. St. Petersburg: Great Outdoors Publishing Co., 1940.

Helphand, Kenneth I. "Henry Vincent Hubbard." In *American Landscape Architecture: Designers and Places*. Washington, D.C.: Preservation Press, 1989.

Hubbard, Theodora Kimball. "John Charles Olmsted." Vol. 7, *Dictionary of American Biography*, 1934.

Hudak, Joseph. "Nine Decades of Landscape Design." *Landscape Architecture* 45, no. 3 (1955): 121–33.

Isthmian Canal Commission and the Panama Canal Annual Report. "Balboa Town Site." Courtesy of Panama Canal Collection Technical Resources Center, Panama Canal Commission. Washington, D.C., and Balboa, C.Z., 1914.

Jackson, Faith. "The Resurrection of Pinewood." *American Horticulturist* (Alexandria, Va.) 69, no. 12 (December 1990): 10–15.

Jekyll, Gertrude. *Color Scheme for the Flower Garden*. 1908; reprint: Salem, N.H.: Ayer Co., 1983.

———. *Wall and Water Gardens*. 1901; reprint: Salem, N.H.: Ayer Co., 1983.

———. *Wood and Garden*. 1899; reprint: Salem, N.H.: Ayer Co., 1983.

Kalfus, Melvin. *Frederick Law Olmsted: The Passion of a Public Artist.* New York: NYU Press, 1990.

Kiem, Stanley. "Remembering William Phillips." Unpublished, 1991.

Koehler, Hans J. "Mountain Lake Sanctuary in Florida." *Parks and Recreation* 23, no. 6 (February 1940): 221–31, 247.

Lazzaro, Claudia. *The Italian Renaissance Garden.* New Haven: Yale University Press, 1990.

Levee, Arleyn A. "John Charles Olmsted." In *American Landscape Architecture: Designers and Places.* Washington, D.C.: Preservation Press, 1989.

Macmillan, H. F. *Tropical Planting and Gardening.* New York: Macmillan, 1935.

"Matheson Hammock Park: Natural Acres Plan." Metro–Dade Parks and Recreation Department, The Nature Conservancy, Fairchild Tropical Garden, January 24, 1991.

Maxwell, Lewis S., and Betty M. Maxwell. *Florida Trees and Palms.* Tampa: Maxwell, 1984.

McCullough, David. *The Path Between the Seas: The Creation of the Panama Canal, 1870–1914.* New York: Simon & Schuster, 1977.

McCurrak, Rev. James C. "Palms of the World." Pamphlet, May 1966.

Mische, Emmanuel Tillman. "John Charles Olmsted: In Memoriam." *Parks and Recreation* 3, no. 3 (April 1920): 52–54.

Muir, Helen. *Miami, U.S.A.* New York: Henry Holt, 1953.

Newton, Norman T. *Design on the Land: The Development of Landscape Architecture.* Cambridge: Harvard University Press, 1971.

Nolen, John. *City Planning.* New York: Appleton, 1916.

———. *New Ideals in the Planning of Cities, Towns, Villages.* New York: American City Bureau, 1919.

Patterson, Augusta Owen. "Two New Homes in Mountain Lake, Florida: Thomas N. McCarter and Allen Tobey." *Town and Country,* January 1, 1932, 26–32.

Phillips, William Lyman. "Character in the Garden." Manuscript, 3 pp., n.d. Author's Collection.

———. "Communication to the Montreal Parks Commission—Traffic Conditions and Facilities." Copy of speech, November 9, 1910. Author's Collection.

———. "Developing a Tropical Garden." *Landscape Architecture* 53, no. 2 (January 1963): 119–22; with photos, plan.

———. "Eleuthera Guided Missile Base: Erosion Control by Vegetation." Typescript, 3 pp., November 9, 1953. Author's Collection.

———. "Ernest Francis Coe, New Haven 1867–Miami 1951: A Biographical Minute." *Landscape Architecture* 41, no. 4 (July 1951): 174–75.

———. *Fairchild Tropical Garden—A Memoir.* With introduction by Nixon Smiley. Coral Gables, Fla.: Kells Press, 1958.

———. *The Fairchild Tropical Garden Catalog of Plants.* Coral Gables, Fla.: Kells Press, 1949, 1950. Fairchild Tropical Garden Library.

———. "The Florida Overseas Parkway: A Report on the Recreational Utility of the Florida Keys Region Showing the Need for Conservation Measures with Proposals as to the Content and Scope of a Master Plan." Made for Florida Forest and Park Service, National Park Service, 1939. Author's Collection.

———. "Florida Overseas Parkway to Key West: Master Plan by W. L. Phillips." 1950. Author's Collection.

———."An Immigrant Landscape: Florida's Unique Contribution to the American Scene." Typescript, 6 pp., n.d. Handwritten address, 24 Pilgrim St., Waban, Mass. Author's Collection.

———. Letter to the editor regarding Rickenbacker Causeway, Miami, Fla. *Landscape Architecture* 46, no. 4 (July 1956): 223–34.

———. Letter to the editor. *Landscape Architecture* 50, no. 2 (Winter 1959–60): 111. Includes essay by Ray Ward on park planning.

———. "Miami Conference." *Landscape Architecture* 41, no. 4 (July 1951): 175.

———. Mountain Lake Sanctuary Plant List. 1931. Bok Tower Gardens.

———. "The Mountain Lake Sanctuary, Mountain Lake, Florida: A Report Prepared [for Judge Curtis Bok] in Collaboration by Olmsted Brothers and William Lyman Phillips." July 2, 1956. 52 pp. Copies in Author's Collection; Bok Tower Gardens; Archives, F. L. Olmsted Historic Site, Brookline, Mass.

———. "Notes on Tropical Landscape . . . particular reference to Puerto Rico, Costa Rica, Isthmus of Panama." Handwritten address, 510 Belmont St., Watertown. Unpublished, 11 pp. with marginal notes, n.d. (probably 1919–20). Author's Collection.

———. "The Outside Plan." Lake Wales. (Other title "Mountain Lake: A Report on the General Appearance of the Community as Affected by Planting and the Management of Vegetation on Corporation Property and Private Grounds.") Written for the Mountain Lake Colony directors; signed "Olmsted Brothers, Landscape Architects, Brookline, Mass." Photos. 1930. Author's Collection.

———. "Places of Interest and Floral Displays." In *Traveler's Guide* by K. Taylor. Dover, Mass., 1949.

———. "Planting and Mosquito Control." *Landscape Architecture* 12 (April 1922): 166–70.

———. "A Review of the Extra Tropical Palms." Unpublished, 8 pp., 1944. Author's Collection.

———. "The Scenery of Porto Rico." Unpublished, 4 pp., n.d. (1918–19?). Author's Collection.

———. "Sounds in the Garden." Typescript, 4 pp., n.d. Author's Collection.

———. Review of *Los Jardines de Granada* by Francisco Prieto-Morano. *Landscape Architecture* 44, no. 1 (October 1953): 45–50.

———. "Taboga." Unpublished, 8 pp., n.d. (1915–16?). Author's Collection.

———. "The Town of Balboa, C.Z." Paper, Boston ASLA, in connection with his exhibit of photographs. Typescript, 21 pp., 1915. Author's Collection.

———. "What Is a Garden?" Unpublished, 2 pp., n.d. Author's Collection.

———. "Yesterday and Today in San Antonio, Texas." *House Beautiful* 47 (June 1920): 490.

———. "You Ask What Is Wrong with Balboa." *Boston Herald*, November 27, 1915.

Phillips, William Lyman, and Prentiss French. "A Street-Planting Plan in Writing." *Landscape Architecture* 24, no. 3 (April 1954): 155–57.

Pray, J. S. "John Charles Olmsted. A Minute on His Life and Service." Transactions of the American Society of Landscape Architects. 1921.

Redford, Polly. *Million Dollar Sand Bar: A Biography of Miami Beach*. New York: E. P. Dutton, 1970.

Schama, Simon. *Landscape and Memory*. New York: Alfred A. Knopf, 1995.

Schinz, Marina, and Susan Littlefield. *Visions of Paradise: Themes and Variations on the Garden*. New York: Stewart, Tabor & Chang, 1985.

Schwarz, Rebecca Spain. "Pinewood House and Garden: Historical Documentation Research." Prepared for Bok Tower Gardens, in collaboration with Arva Parks & Co., Miami, 1989.

Scully, Vincent. *Architecture: The Natural and the Man-made*. New York: St. Martin's Press, 1991.

Simpson, Charles Torrey. *Out of Doors in Florida*. Miami: E. B. Douglas Co., 1923.

———. *Florida Wild Life*. New York: Macmillan, 1932.

Smiley, Nixon. "All-Florida Design Rushed Through, but Garden Near Perfect." *Miami Herald*, February 12, 1956.

———. *Florida Gardening Month by Month*. Miami: University of Miami Press, 1957.

———. "Architect Whips Up a Design for Miami's Future." *Miami Herald*, October 23, 1955.

———. "Independence Was His Way of Life." *Miami Herald*, October 27, 1966.

———. "Meet a Man Whose Landscape Artistry Has Stood the Test of Time." *Miami Herald*, March 22, 1953.

———. *Subtropical Gardening in Florida*. Miami: University of Miami Press, 1951.

———. *William Lyman Phillips: A Remembrance*. Florida: Fairchild Tropical Garden, 1967.

———. *Yesterday's Florida*. Miami: Seaman Pub., 1974.

Stone, Doris M. *A Guide to the Great Public Gardens of the Eastern United States*. New York: Pantheon, 1982.

Tebeau, Charlton. *A History of Florida.* Miami: University of Miami Press, 1975.

Thacker, Christopher. *The History of Gardens.* Berkeley: University of California Press, 1979.

Van Zuylen, Gabrielle. *Gardens of France.* New York: Harmony Books, 1983.

Veda, Reed. *Avenues to Adulthood.* Cambridge: Cambridge University Press, 1987.

Wait, Lucita H. *Fairchild Tropical Garden: The First Ten Years.* New York: Ronald Press, 1948.

West, Erdman, and Lillian E. Arnold. *The Native Trees of Florida.* Gainesville: University of Florida Press, 1948.

Wharton, Edith. *Italian Villas and Their Gardens.* New York: Century, 1903.

Whiting, Edward Clark, and William Lyman Phillips. "Frederick Law Olmsted, 1870–1957: An Appreciation of the Man and His Achievements." *Landscape Architecture* 48, no. 5 (April 1958): 144–59.

"William L. Phillips Awarded Thomas Barbour Medal by Fairchild Tropical Garden." *Landscape Architecture* 40, no. 3 (April 1950): 134.

Zuckerman, Bertram. *The Dream Lives On: A History of the Fairchild Tropical Garden, 1938–1988.* Florida: Banyan Books, 1988.

———. *The Kampong.* Miami: National Tropical Botanical Garden and Fairchild Tropical Garden, 1993.

LIBRARIES AND ARCHIVES CONSULTED

American Battle Monuments, Washington, D.C.

American Graves Registration Service, Washington, D.C.

American Society of Landscape Architects, Washington, D.C.

Balboa Library, Panama Canal Zone

Bok Tower Garden Library, Lake Wales, Fla.

Dade County Historical Society, Miami, Fla. (Recent gift of some Phillips papers by Juliette P. Coyle)

Dade County Parks and Recreation, Planning and Research Division, Landscape Architectural Section, Kendall, Fla.

Fairchild Tropical Garden, Research Center, Miami, Fla.

Florida State Archives, Photographic Section, Tallahassee, Fla.

Frederick Law Olmsted Papers, American University, Washington, D.C.

Frederick Law Olmsted Papers, Madison Memorial Library, Washington, D.C.

Harvard University Graduate School of Design, Francis Loeb Library, Cambridge, Mass.

Historical Society of Palm Beach County

Library of Congress, Washington, D.C.

Madison Memorial Library, Manuscript Division, Washington, D.C.

Metro-Dade Parks and Recreation Department, Miami, Fla.

Miami-Dade Public Library, Romer Collection, Miami, Fla.

Miami Herald Archives (Nixon Smiley material)

Miami International Airport, Landscape Operations files

National Archives, Photographic Division, Washington, D.C.

National Park Service Archives, Frederick Law Olmsted National Historic Site, Brookline, Mass.

Panama Canal Commission, Washington, D.C., and Balboa, C.Z.

Phillips Collection. Papers temporarily in possession of author (Author's Collection) pending disposition to an archive, 1998–99, agreed upon by his heirs

University of Miami, Otto G. Richter Archives and Special Collections Library, Coral Gables. Contains some Phillips plans and materials left there by Henry Field in the 1980s (?)

INDEX